Photoshop® Type Effects

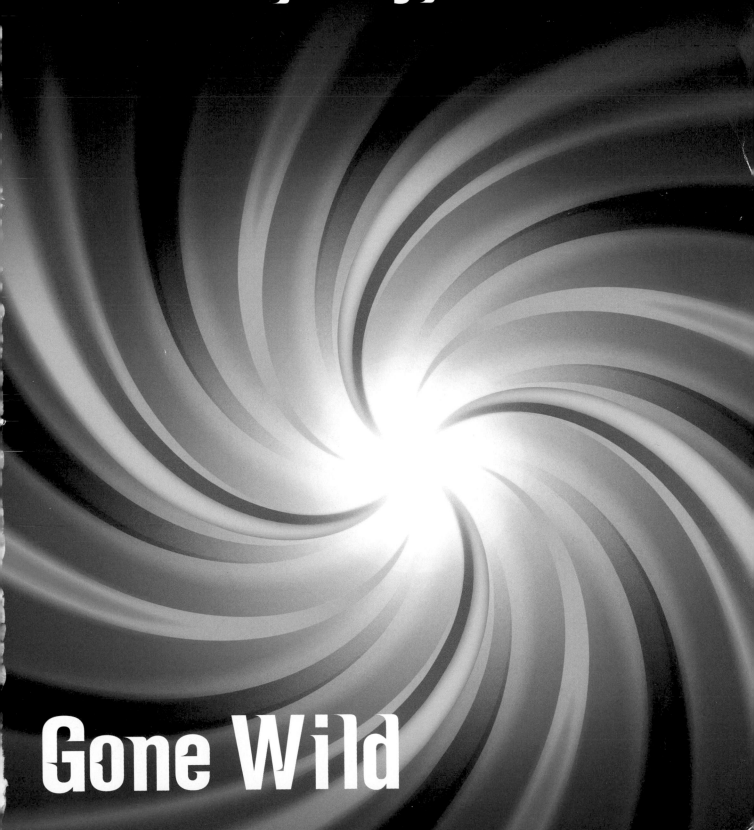

Gone Wild

Photoshop® Type Effects

Al Ward

1807
WILEY
2007

BICENTENNIAL
BICENTENNIAL

Wiley Publishing, Inc.

Gone Wild

Photoshop® Type Effects Gone Wild

Published by
Wiley Publishing, Inc.
111 River Street
Hoboken, N.J. 07030-5774
www.wiley.com

Copyright © 2007 by Wiley Publishing, Inc., Indianapolis, Indiana

Published simultaneously in Canada

ISBN: 978-0-470-04292-2

Manufactured in the United States of America

10 9 8 7 6 5 4 3 2 1

1K/TQ/QR/QX/IN

For general information on our other products and services or to obtain technical support, please contact our Customer Care Department within the U.S. at (800) 762-2974, outside the U.S. at (317) 572-3993 or fax (317) 572-4002.

Wiley also publishes its books in a variety of electronic formats. Some content that appears in print may not be available in electronic books.

Library of Congress Control Number: 2006939457

About the Author

Al Ward has been kicking around the Photoshop community for a number of years, writing and training on many subjects. His Website, `actionfx.com`, supplies custom-made Photoshop presets and information to users. At this writing, there are over 52,000 custom presets available for downloading. He has written and contributed to numerous Photoshop books, including *Photoshop for Right Brainers (1st and 2nd editions), Al Ward's Photoshop Productivity Toolkit, Photoshop Most Wanted, Photoshop Elements 2 Special Effects*, and *Photoshop 7 Effects Magic*.

Al is a regular writer for the official Website of the National Association of Photoshop Professionals (NAPP) and `www.photoshopuser.com`. He also writes for Planet Photoshop and is a contributor to several other Websites. He has been featured at the Photoshop Café, and has written for a number of print publications, such as *Photoshop User Magazine* and *Web Designer Magazine*.

Al is the official actions guru for the NAPP, a title given to him by Scott Kelby, and one that Al holds in very high esteem. In his free time, Al enjoys fishing the trout streams in Western Montana, spending time with his family, reading, enjoying a good movie, and searching the Web for graphics-related topics.

Credits

Acquisitions Editor
Courtney Allen

Project Editor
Timothy J. Borek

Technical Editor
Adam Pratt

Copy Editor
Marylouise Wiack

Editorial Manager
Robyn Siesky

Vice President & Group Executive Publisher
Richard Swadley

Vice President & Publisher
Barry Pruett

Business Manager
Amy Knies

Book Designer
LeAndra Hosier

Project Coordinator
Adrienne Martinez

Graphics and Production Specialists
LeAndra Hosier
Jennifer Mayberry
Shelley Norris
Rashell Smith
Amanda Spagnuolo

Quality Control Technicians
Cynthia Fields
Charles Spencer

Proofreading
Debbye Butler

Indexing
Estalita Silvoskey

Wiley Bicentennial Logo
Richard J. Pacifico

For Tonia, Ali, and Noah.
You are the three great loves of my life.

Preface

Photoshop Type Effects Gone Wild is a different kind of Photoshop book. It does not simply try to teach you Photoshop; instead, it shows you how to work with Photoshop on real projects that you can follow step-by-step. The benefit to this approach is that you learn Photoshop by default. The projects are designed not simply to create type effects as so many books have tried before, but to give you the tools to apply those effects in a design setting.

My approach to teaching Photoshop is to show the student a step-by-step project (rather than a process), from beginning to end. When the audience gets excited about what they see happening on their monitor, the lesson tends to sink in more quickly (in my humble opinion) and reduces the learning curve. Why do I think this is more effective than the 'this-is-a tool-and-this-is-its-function' approach? Quite simply because I myself learn better this way.

Readers of this book should have some experience with Photoshop. Layers, masks, tools, and palettes should already be a part of your vocabulary: If not, you may find some of the techniques a bit difficult to comprehend. If you get stuck, please refer to the Photoshop Help files for clarification. The Help files are probably the most overlooked feature in Photoshop CS2, but they are there at your fingertips for just these situations.

How to Use This Book

Photoshop Type Effects Gone Wild is not your typical type-effects book. As I mentioned earlier, one of the pitfalls into which other books in this genre fall has been to simply present an effect (steel, fire, what-have-you) and leave it at that, with little or no thought as to how you can use those effects in real-world design situations. Most of the projects in this book spend as much time, and more in some cases, focusing on where the type will be displayed as on the actual text itself. I hope that you find this approach useful and informative; I want to ensure that you have the necessary tools and knowledge to begin using this book in a practical, real-world setting from page one.

Using the CD-ROM

All of the images that you need to perform the various tasks are included on the CD-ROM that comes with this book. You get every photo, starting image, and supplementary file that you need. Just open the image from the CD-ROM and work on it in Photoshop. The supplementary files (patterns, styles, gradients, brushes, and shapes) can also be moved just as easily into Photoshop.

If you use a Mac, double-click on any PAT, ABR, CSH, or ASL document. The file automatically attaches itself to the correct location in Photoshop. In Windows, make sure that Photoshop is open. Then, drag the file from the CD-ROM and drop it into the open Photoshop application window. It becomes immediately available.

The images on the CD-ROM are divided into chapter folders. Most folders contain both an Additional Presets folder with Photoshop presets used in the chapter, and stock images provided by Photos.com and iStockphoto.com.

Customer Care

If you have trouble with the CD-ROM, please call the Wiley Product Technical Support phone number: (800) 762-2974. Outside the United States, call 1(317) 572-3994. You can also contact Wiley Product Technical Support through the Internet at: http://support.wiley.com. Wiley Publishing will provide technical support only for installation and other general quality control items. For technical support on the applications themselves, consult the program's vendor or author.

To place additional orders or to request information about other Wiley products, please call (877) 762-2974.

Acknowledgments

I say this time and again, but this page is undeniably the most difficult to write. Someone is inevitably left out who should have been mentioned, so let me offer this disclaimer up front: if you deserve to be here but do not see your name, consider yourself included.

First off, thanks to Tom Heine, Courtney Allen, and Tim Borek at Wiley. They were the navigators for this project, and had to crack the whip more often than this author cares to mention, but without them, you would not be reading this.

To my wife Tonia and my kids Noah and Ali. I love you all, and Daddy appreciates the time that you allowed him to be locked in the basement to get this project done.

To Colin Smith, my compatriot and occasional co-conspirator in this world of Photoshop design and debauchery (www.photoshopcafe.com). I have friends all over this big ol' world, but you have turned out to be one of the best, amigo.

To my good friend Richard Lynch (www.hiddenelements.com), a fine author in his own right. Although we have never met in person, you are one voice of reason in this business that I have come to appreciate and rely on. I think that it is about time you made a trip west for some trout fishing, don't you agree?

To all my friends at the Photoshop Café (see the Website address in Colin's paragraph) — Phil, Matt, Daz, Frank, and the rest. You give more of your time to helping this community for free than anyone I know, and the design world is a better place for it. Keep the coffee on and I will come and sit a spell.

To Scott Kelby and all my friends at the NAPP (www.photoshopuser.com). Scott gave me my first break in this business many years ago, and my family and I will never forget it.

To my parents Ken and Barb, my in-laws Ole and Linda, my brothers and sisters, and all my extended family: I love each and every one of you.

Special thanks to everyone in the MLMBC (you know who you are). We share the same road, and I am honored to be traveling it with you.

The greatest thanks and highest praise go to my God and Savior, without whom none of this would be possible or worthwhile. He saw fit to allow this Montana boy to realize his dream.

Again, if I forgot anyone who really needed to be here, please forgive me and consider yourselves included. To all my readers and friends far and wide, my deepest regards and a hearty thank-you from the bottom of my heart.

Contents

Contents

chapter

1

alphabet soup

Advertisers can be a diabolical bunch, inserting their logos directly into our homes so that often the first thing we read in the morning promotes a product of some sort. Advertising execs are paid to know how you think, and what will trigger you to purchase their product over another. This chapter gives you the keys to their kingdom. You will create a logo similar to that of a Seattle-based coffee company, lure parents and children to grab that 'must-have' breakfast cereal, promote a questionable adult beverage, and fill your cupboard with an off-brand soup that mimics another popular brand's labelling style. You will even take a logo and place it on a common household item that continues to advertise for the brand long after the initial product is purchased.

I Need Coffee...STAT!

My day doesn't begin until the first cup of coffee is seeping into my veins, and the same is true for millions of people around the world. Discovered in Arabia centuries ago by a man who would definitely be my best friend were he alive today, it has become so ingrained in our culture that it is the second-most traded commodity behind oil. Ask.com says that the United States of America is the biggest consumer, with over 119 million people drinking coffee in one form or another in 1999. The technique that I demonstrate here shows how to use Photoshop to mimic a popular coffee seller's logo that appears on nearly every street corner in the big ol' U.S.A.

THE PLAN

- Convert a portrait to an artist's rendering
- Type a corporate phrase on a path around the logo's central image

(1) Open the image blonde.jpg. The stock photography in this book is provided courtesy of Photos.com. The model in this photo serves perfectly for this effect.

TIP

If you have trouble judging a Transform resize manually or you simply want to change the dimensions exactly, the Transform settings in the Options bar allow you to enter precise amounts of change, both vertically and horizontally. You can also specify the amount of rotation for the layer that you are transforming.

(2) Duplicate the background layer. The first step in the process is to create an artistic rendering of the photo, and a few items on the Filter menu allow you to do that quickly and easily. With the duplicate layer selected, choose Filter⇨Artistic⇨Cutout. Due to an image resolution that is fairly high (300 ppi), the following settings work well in separating the colors and maintaining the integrity of the lines between them:

* **Number of Levels:** 6
* **Edge Simplicity:** 8
* **Edge Fidelity:** 3

(3) Select the Magic Wand tool and click in the black area surrounding the model in the duplicate layer (Layer 1). Delete the selected area and choose Select⇨ Deselect. Choose Filter⇨Artistic⇨Poster Edges, and set the Edge Thickness to 0, Edge Intensity to 2, and Posterization to 4. Click OK to apply the filter. This adds lines along the edges of color, enhancing the illusion that the photo is drawn rather than shot in a studio.

Return to the first document and drag Layer 1 into the new image. Choose Edit➪Transform➪Scale and adjust the size of the model's layer to fit comfortably in the center of the new document, leaving room for the type that you will insert in the next few steps.

(4) Create a new document (File➪New) with the following dimensions:

* **Name:** Coffee Logo
* **Preset:** Custom
* **Width:** 5 inches
* **Height:** 5 inches
* **Resolution:** 300 pixels/inch
* **Color Mode:** RGB, 8 bit
* **Background Contents:** White

Click OK.

Change the foreground color to a semi-dark green using the values R = 10, G = 100, and B = 1.

(5) Choose Image➪Adjustments➪Threshold. Set the Threshold level to 175 and click OK. You may alter the Threshold setting, depending on the amount of white-and-black separation you want in the image. Open the Select menu and choose Color Range. Set Fuzziness to 40, click on the woman, and hit OK. Fill the selection with the foreground color (Shift+F5), turning the drawing a nice deep green. Choose Select➪Inverse and then choose Select➪Modify➪Expand. Increase the size of the selection by 1 pixel and click OK. Press Delete. This cleans up quite a bit of unnecessary color from the two-color image that the logo will comprise.

6 Open the Select menu and choose Inverse once again. Open the Paths palette and click on the 'Make Work Path from Selection' icon on the bottom of the palette. Photoshop generates a circular path that the type will follow. Select the Horizontal Type tool and set up the font to use in the logo.

For this example, use:

* **Font:** Arial Black
* **Style:** Regular
* **Font Size:** 28 pt
* **Anti-aliasing method:** Smooth
* Center justified

Click on the path at the top, and enter the text for the logo. In this case, my message to the world advertises "Shakespeare Classic Roast Coffee." Use the Transform tools (Edit⇨Transform Path⇨Rotate) to rotate the text as you want it to appear. The Direct Selection tool also allows you to manipulate the center point for the type on the path.

Time to round this image out a bit. Select the Elliptical Marquee tool and create a selection around the woman. Select most of the head and hair, but leave some outside the circle. For a perfectly round selection, hold down the Shift key. Invert the selection and press Delete.

Once your logo is ready, save the master PSD file to a folder. Make the background layer invisible, and save another copy of the logo as a PNG file. This allows you to both retain the transparency of the background and easily move the logo layer between images. Try displaying your logo on various products, such as in the following example. How did I do that, you ask? Stay tuned... I demonstrate affixing logos to cups later in this chapter.

A short recap

Granted, you probably do not own a massive coffee conglomerate, nor will you in the foreseeable future. You may, however, decide to sell a product one day through a service such as CafePress, or you may be asked to design a mock-up ad similar to this for a client. This technique was fairly basic, but this simple style has served at least one company extremely well. When you practice this technique, I encourage you to use images that you have taken of friends or family members. Affix their faces to a mug in a 'pretend' logo, and I guarantee that it will be a gift that they will not soon forget or part with!

A Balanced Breakfast

As a father of two grade school-aged children and having been a child once long ago, I'm well versed in the tactics used by companies to lure children to their products. Sit down for some quality time with any children's television program, and prepare yourself to be pummeled by colorful, zany commercials with the newest, coolest, or tastiest "new thing" firing at your eye sockets at lightning speed. This technique is comparatively subdued, but it uses quirky type with fanciful, innocent images to generate a cereal box cover. Yes, even the packaging in the store is designed to appeal to our youngsters, while giving special messages to the parents, thus prompting a second look and perhaps inspiring a purchase.

THE PLAN

- Create three-layered, cartoonish type
- Warp the type into a stylized shape
- Create a fanciful cereal box cover
- Affix the type to the box
- Add additional text messages to the box to complete the image

(1) Create a new image (File⇨New) with the following specifications:

- ✱ **Name:** Cereal Box Type
- ✱ **Width:** 9 inches
- ✱ **Height:** 6 inches
- ✱ **Resolution:** 300 pixels/inch
- ✱ **Color Mode:** RGB, 16 bit
- ✱ **Background Contents:** White

Click OK.

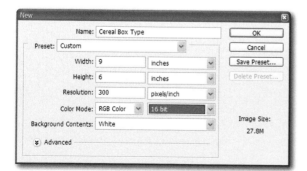

(2) Press the D key to reset the foreground and background colors to their default settings (black in the foreground, and white in the background). Cereal boxes and other product packaging that are intended to appeal to children often use whimsical font styles for the name. Select the Horizontal Type tool from the toolbar. In the Type Options bar, choose a bloated, script-style font such as Forte with the following initial specifications:

- ✱ **Font Size:** 160 pt
- ✱ **Anti-aliasing Method:** Smooth
- ✱ **Center Justified**

You now need to further adjust the text. On the right side of the Options bar, click the icon that opens the Character and Paragraph palettes. In the Character palette, tweak the settings as follows:

- ✱ **Leading:** 90 pt
- ✱ **Tracking:** -50
- ✱ **Vertical Scale:** 80%
- ✱ **Horizontal Scale:** 103-105%

Type the name of your new cereal.

TIP

Have you ever wished that you could return to a type setting that you used somewhere in the past, including the exact font? Now you can. Once you have set up the font and characteristics for the type that you would like to save, open the Tool Presets palette. With the Type tool selected, click on the 'Create new tool preset' icon on the bottom of the palette. The font and its exact settings are added to the Tool Presets and you may use them again and again. To ensure that they are not lost due to a computer crash or an improper closing of the software, open the Tool Preset menu and select Save Presets from the list. Once you save the presets, you can return to these settings at anytime in the future.

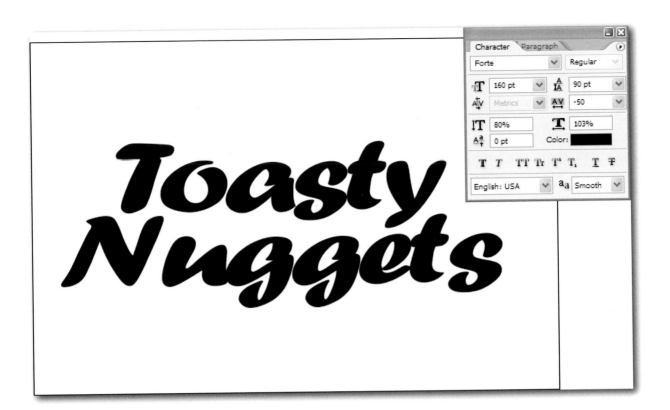

(3) You are not quite finished with the type yet. Use the Warp tools to add to the cartoonish design. In the Options bar, open the Warp Tools dialog box. Select Flag as the warp type, and distort the text layer with the following settings:

* **Horizontal:** checked
* **Bend:** 16%
* **Horizontal Distortion:** -20%
* **Vertical Distortion:** 0%

With the cartooning done (at least as far as the shape of the type is concerned), the text layer no longer needs to be editable, providing the spelling is correct. Right-click the text layer and select Rasterize, or choose Layer⇨ Rasterize⇨Type. Again, you can no longer edit the text with the Type tool, so ensure that it is correct! If you prefer to retain a type layer just in case, you can duplicate the type layer that you want to rasterize and then simply turn this one off in the Layers palette.

At this point, you are ready to work with stylized coloring and shading. This logo has three levels of color: a bright reflection, a main color, and a background edge. All three colors need to be in roughly the same family, as well as to reflect the product itself. Because the product in this case

is cereal and a photo of the product is to be included in the cover design, three shades of earthy hues will serve nicely.

The reflection is the foreground color, and so we can tackle it first. Click on the foreground color to open the Color Picker dialog box, and change it to a bright, creamy yellow (R = 226, G = 220, and B = 169).

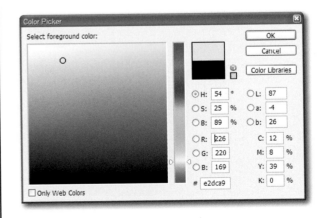

(4) Duplicate the background layer, and then Command/ Ctrl+click the newly copied layer to generate a

selection around the logo. Create a new layer and select the Move tool. With the arrow keys, nudge the selection to the right ten clicks so that the selection is offset from the original text. Fill the selection in the new blank layer with the Foreground color. Using the move arrow keys, move the selection another ten clicks to the right. Delete the contents of the selection.

In the Layers palette, select the Toasty Nuggets copy layer directly below the reflections layer with which you have been working. Command/Ctrl-click the Toasty Nuggets copy layer to generate a selection around the type. Change the foreground color to something darker and richer to serve as the main text color. In this instance, use the settings R = 255, G = 157, and B = 3.

Fill the selection with the foreground color. You can see how the reflection plays on the typeface, giving the illusion of dimension in a cartoonish style.

5 Now you will work with the third layer of dimension in the text: the backdrop. Choose Select⇨Modify⇨Expand and increase the size of the selection by 20 pixels. Change the foreground color one more time using the settings R = 109, G = 67, and B = 2.

Select the original type layer (the one that you rasterized initially), and fill the selection with the foreground color. This serves to outline the logo from the background, making it stand out so that the name of the product can be clearly seen. Once you place the logo on the box, you will see what I mean. The final image will be a bit busy, with a lot of color and different things combined to spark the attention of the buyer, and so the product name needs to stand out.

6 Once upon a time not so many years ago, a designer who wanted to save a flattened image with a transparent background had to do so as a transparent GIF, which often resulted in less-than-stunning results. Not so anymore with the PNG format. PNG allows for high-quality, single-layer images with the transparency intact, and in this author's humble opinion, it is by far superior to GIF, especially for this type of work.

To save the logo as a flattened image with transparency, turn the Background layer off in the Layers palette. Choose File⇨Save As and navigate to a folder where you would like to store the new logo, or create a new one that you can easily remember. Name the image and select PNG as the file format. Click OK.

Open the new file in Photoshop and set it aside for a moment. Open the file Box-NoType.jpg, located on the CD. I created this image from a few different photos to represent the product and to appeal to younger consumers. Whether I succeeded or not we'll never know, but it serves our purposes here.

7 It's time to merge the logo with the box. Have both images (the logo file and the box art) open side-by-side. Select the PNG file and drag the type logo layer over to the box art photo. Resize the logo with the Transform tools (Edit⇨Transform⇨Scale works well), and position it in the light area at the top. If the text overlaps the girl's head somewhat, create a mask on the logo layer and paint with black in the area where the text overlaps the hair. This gives the illusion that the type is behind the girl, adding yet another dimension to the overall effect.

8 For the final image, simply add some additional type as you would see on an actual cereal box. In the image shown here, I've used a custom shape of a turtle to give my product a "mascot," if you will. I've also added the weight of the contents and a special message indicating this product's superiority over competitors to entice parents to give it a try.

A short recap

I can hear what some of you are thinking already. Why didn't I generate the type with Layer Styles? Why go through the process of creating three separate layers just for one line of text? Granted, Layer Styles would allow for the creation of reflections, a stroked outline, and so forth. They are not an end-all, however, and in this instance to get the cartoonish layering, it seemed best to approach this without resorting to Layer Styles. This is especially true for the foreground reflection. Rest assured that there is a lot of Layer Styles work coming. Sometimes, it is nice to do things 'Old School'.

Alphabet Soup

Some products instill a feeling of comfort simply because they have been around for so long and have been a part of our lives since we were young. The colors used in the labelling and design of the logo remind us of simpler times. I recall when I was a child my grandmother fixing me a can of my favorite soup to calm me down and take my mind off a serious scalding I'd received. All of these years later, I still recollect the injury received from the burn, but what I remember most vividly is that bowl of soup, my grandmother's love, and the comfort that both gave me.

When a company or product captures the hearts of its consumers so that its brand instantly comes to mind when one mentions soup, soda, or what have you, other companies try to capitalize on that recognition and mimic that style in order to promote their products. Underhanded, to be sure, but if it works...

This effect mimics the label of a popular brand (my personal favorite for the reason described above). This technique doesn't simply deal with text, but demonstrates how to create an entire label and then affix it to a cylindrical object. Modern advertising usually incorporates a bit of Photoshop sleight of hand.

chapter 1 ◆ alphabet soup

THE PLAN

- Create a label for a can of soup
- Stylize the logo to mimic another, more popular brand
- Add an image of the product to entice the consumer's taste buds
- Add additional product information
- Affix the label to a can for advertising purposes

① Create a new image (File⇨New) and name it **Soup Label**. This image serves two purposes, only one of which is demonstrated here: First, it must be large enough to create a final label, complete with nutritional information, a recipe, and so forth. This is not demonstrated here, but I wanted to explain why the image must be so wide. The second purpose, and also the one demonstrated in this technique, is to generate an advertisement and have it be as photo-realistic as possible.

Set the dimensions of the new image as follows:

- **Preset:** Custom
- **Width:** 16 inches
- **Height:** 6 inches
- **Resolution:** 300 pixels/inch or greater
- **Color Mode:** RGB, 16 bit
- **Background Contents:** White

Click OK.

② The two main colors are white and red for the label. The white is taken care of with the background color, and so the red comes next. Change the foreground color to R = 177, G = 22, and B = 1.

It's time to add the secondary color to the label. Select the Rectangular Marquee tool in the toolbar. Create a new layer. Ensure that you select the "Add to selection" option in the Options bar and set the feather to zero. Make a selection of the upper 40% of the document, covering the entire width of the image. Make a second selection that covers a very narrow portion on the bottom of the image and that also spans the entire width. Fill the selection with the foreground color.

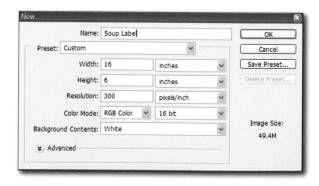

I mentioned there being two main colors in this label style, but there is one other color (besides black) that I am using to dress things up a bit. I use this extra color to provide edging and highlights, thus giving a subtle boost to the other hues.

Set the foreground color to R = 176, G = 156, and B = 124.

Command/Ctrl-click Layer 1 in the Layers palette to generate a selection around the red fill color. Create a new layer beneath Layer 1 and move the selection down ten clicks using the arrow keys. With the new layer selected, choose Edit➪Fill and fill the selection with the foreground color.

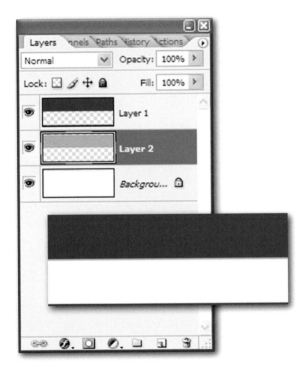

3 There isn't anything too difficult with the type effect on this label style, but the thought here is that it resembles a well-recognized design. As such, some careful attention to the original design is needed, and knowing how to mimic that style as closely as possible without getting into legal trouble is a must.

Press the D key to select black as the foreground color. Select the Horizontal Type tool and choose a Script-Style font.

Open the Character palette. Change the Character settings as follows:

* **Font:** Freestyle Script
* **Style:** Bold
* **Font Size:** 72 pt
* **Leading:** 60 pt
* **Tracking:** 125 pt
* **Vertical Scale:** 110%
* **Horizontal Scale:** 100%
* **Baseline Shift:** 0 pt
* **Color:** Black
* **Anti-aliasing method:** Smooth
* Center Justified

If the rulers are not visible, choose View➪Rulers. Right-click on the ruler and select Percent from the menu that appears. Use this as a guide to start typing in the horizontal center of the image. Enter the name of your product. The name that I've chosen is Carmicheal's.

On the competitor's label, the name is underscored by a small trademark symbol. The trademark symbol needs to be quite a bit smaller than the name brand, so create a new type layer and change the font size to 12 points. Change the font to Arial or some standard, non-scripted style TTF.

To create this symbol, hold down the Alt/Command key and type the numbers **0174**. This adds the ASCII copyright symbol in Photoshop, Word, or whatever program you are using, which can be a good thing to know! Mac users can simply use the Option+R shortcut for the same result.

To make the type stand out a bit more, it needs a drop shadow. Command/Ctrl-click the type layer with the product name to generate a selection. Create a new layer beneath the type layer, and select the Move tool. Using the arrow keys, offset the selection ten clicks to the right and ten clicks down. Fill the selection with black.

④ Creating a border around the logo in this design is very straightforward. Create a new layer at the top of the layer stack, and select the Rectangular Marquee tool. Ensure that the feather is set to zero and the selection type to Normal. Draw a rectangular selection around the type area, leaving some room on the top, bottom, and sides.

Set the foreground color to black. Choose Edit⇨Stroke, and set the location to Outside. Enter a stroke setting of 10 pixels and click OK.

Change the foreground color to the tan/gold hue that is used to edge the background (R = 176, G = 156, and B = 124).

Choose Edit⇨Stroke, select Inside for the location, and set the size to 8 pixels. Click OK.

There is one final stroke to perform. Set the foreground color to white, choose Edit⇨Stroke, and select Center for the location. Enter 10 pixels for the size and click OK. You now have a subtle rectangular outline around the logo using all of the main colors except red.

The final step in the product brand design is to enter a line of stylized text that tells what product family the label represents, in this case, soup. Select the Horizontal Type tool again and open the Character palette. Give the type the following characteristics:

* **Font:** Arial
* **Style:** Regular
* **Font Size:** 14 pt
* **Leading:** 60 pt
* **Tracking:** -25 pt
* **Vertical Scale:** 160%
* **Horizontal Scale:** 100%
* **Baseline Shift:** 0 pt
* **Color:** Tan/Gold (same settings as above)

Using all capital letters, type **CONDENSED SOUP** below the logo's border. Position it with the Move tool or the arrow keys so that it rests just beneath the border and is centered, using the logo as a reference.

⑤ Open the image soup.jpg. This photo serves as the actual product in the can, although it has been doctored to appeal to one's appetite. The bowl needs to be removed from the background, resized, and placed on the label. Choose Filter⇨Extract. In the Extract dialog box, select the Magic Marker tool on the top left. Set up the marker's characteristics on the right side of the dialog box as follows:

* **Brush Size:** 50 (ensure Smart Highlighting is on)
* **Highlight:** Green
* **Fill Color:** Blue

* **Extraction:** blank or 0
* **Show Highlight/Show Fill:** checked

Choose a starting point on the edge of the bowl, and trace around the diameter of the object. Keep the brush size narrow and ensure that just the edge of the bowl is under the highlighter, with the majority of the green on the outside of the bowl's edge. This helps to prevent too much cleanup after the extraction is made, and keeping the brush as narrow as possible also helps in this regard.

Once you have traced around the entire bowl, select the Paint Bucket tool and click inside the highlighted area. This tells Photoshop what to keep, and the non-filled areas are discarded. Click on Preview and check the edges around the bowl's exterior. Do any cleanup that you need to perform with the Cleanup tool and Edge Touchup tool, and then click OK.

6 Drag the extracted soup bowl to the label document. It is quite a bit larger than the label, and so it needs to be resized and placed in position on the label. Select the bowl layer and choose Edit⇨Transform⇨Scale. You may need to zoom out in order to see the bounding boxes around the bowl due to its size. To reduce the view, press Command/Ctrl+minus sign (-).

Resize the bowl so that it fits within the white area below the logo. Leave room above the bowl so that you can add the name of the soup in the next step.

(7) Select the Horizontal Type tool. Select a plain font such as Arial or Verdana. In this example, I'm using Berling Antiqua, but if this is not installed on your system, then another non-scripted font will suffice. Open the Character palette and set your font up as follows:

* **Font:** Berling Antiqua
* **Style:** Regular
* **Font Size:** 14–18 pt
* **Leading:** 60 pt
* **Tracking:** -10 pt
* **Vertical Scale:** 140%

* **Horizontal Scale:** 100%
* **Baseline Shift:** 0 pt
* **Color:** Black

In either the Options bar or the Paragraph palette, ensure that the text is center justified. Just above the bowl in the white space below the logo, type the name of your soup. Mine is called Stir Fry Beef.

The final points of text for this tutorial are the product weight information and a line of text that says, "SERVING SUGGESTION." You place these on the lower-left and lower-right sides of the soup bowl, respectively. The font specifications for these two product messages are:

* **Font:** Arial
* **Style:** Regular
* **Size:** 12 pt (weight information); 10 pt * (serving suggestion)
* **Leading:** 14 pt
* **Tracking:** -10 pt
* **Vertical Scale:** 140%
* **Horizontal Scale:** 80%
* **Baseline Shift:** 0 pt
* **Color:** Black

Each message requires its own type layer. Instead of just clicking and typing, with the Type tool selected, click with the mouse and draw a bounding box for the text while holding the mouse button down.

Align the weight information to the left, and the "SERV-ING SUGGESTION" text to the right.

With these two final messages in place, the label is effectively done for our purposes; we can now move on to placing this label on an actual can in a product shot. If this were to be an actual label design, you would see nutritional information, what the contents of this delicious soup actually are, and perhaps a recipe or other tidbit of information to expand your knowledge of and interest in the product.

8 The final step in the process involves conforming this label to an actual photograph of a can. In earlier versions of Photoshop, you could do this with the 3D Transform filter and some help from the Spherize filter. In Photoshop CS2, there is a new tool at your disposal to tackle the process. Photoshop CS2 gives you the ability to warp a layer much like a type layer, but with more control.

Duplicate the label image (Image⇨Duplicate) and check the box "Duplicate Merged Layers Only." Click OK. Leave this image open.

Open the file soup.jpg. This serves as the foundation for the soup can advertisement.

Return to the label image that you just duplicated as a merged document. Press Command/Ctrl+A to select the entire document, and then Command/Ctrl+C to copy the label. Return to the can image and press Command/Ctrl+V to paste the label into a new layer. The label is much larger than the can, but resizing it down is no problem.

With the label's layer selected, choose Edit⇨Transform⇨ Scale. Using the corners of the Transform bounding box, resize the label so that the logo and text are positioned over the front portion of the can. Don't worry that the can opener is in the way, because that will be dealt with shortly. Position the label so that the upper and lower edges fit between the metal lips that connect the two lids to the can.

Select the Rectangular Marquee tool. In the Options bar, set the feather to 0 and the selection type to Normal. Reduce the opacity of the label layer so that you can see the can through the label, and make a selection that extends just beyond the edges of the can by a few pixels on either side. Choose Select⇨Inverse and delete the selected area. You may have to move the layer around to ensure no additional layer information is still present beyond the boundaries of the image. All this must be deleted before proceeding to the next step.

9 Choose Select⇨Inverse again. With the label layer still selected, choose Edit⇨Transform⇨Warp. This cool tool allows you to easily conform the label to the curve of the can. If you are familiar with working with paths, then this tool is a piece of proverbial cake!

Each corner and grid point on the edges has a direction line that works similar to those found when using paths. Manipulating the direction lines for the corners bends the layer so that the label conforms to the curve of the can. Move the direction lines down for the top corners until the top portion of the label follows the curve of the can just under the lip. Repeat the process for the bottom corner direction lines so that the lower edge of the label resides just above the lip of the base. Once you are done, accept the transformation and increase the opacity of the label layer to 100%.

10 Some carefully manipulated shading and highlights can make this label appear as though it belongs in the real world. This is done with careful manipulation of the Dodge and Burn tools. Select the Burn tool. In the Options bar, set the following parameters:

* **Brush:** Round, Feathered
* **Brush Size:** 170-180
* **Range:** Midtones
* **Exposure:** 32%

Paint over the label's left- and right-side edges with the Burn tool by holding down the Shift key and clicking at a point at the top of the label. Move the brush to the bottom of the label vertically, and click again. This slightly darkens the area where you applied the brush stroke and keeps the stroke in a straight line. Repeat the process on both sides of the can. Freehand the Burn tool over the area where the can opener resides, going beyond the can opener just a bit. This simulates the shadow caused by the can opener being over the label and blocking the light, although in reality the label layer resides above the can opener. If you need to reduce the opacity of the label layer to help you, by all means do so.

Select the Dodge tool. You can use the same settings as the Burn tool, although you may want to reduce the width of the brush to 100-120 pixels. Create a few lines of high-lights on the label by clicking, holding down the Shift key, repositioning the mouse vertically, and clicking again.

Set the opacity of the label layer to 95%. Create a mask for the layer and set the foreground color to black. Paint over the can opener in the mask so that the can opener becomes visible. You may want to create a selection around that portion of the label with the Polygonal Lasso tool for more precise edges. Fill the selection with black at 100% opacity.

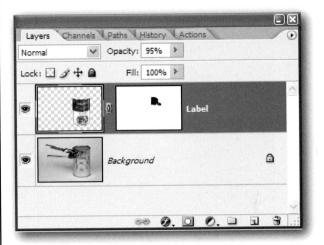

(11) By setting the opacity of the label layer to 95%, the grooves in the can are slightly visible. This adds to the realism, because the labels on the cans are often pressed into the contours as a result of shipping or rubbing up against other cans. Rather than paint the lines or try to manipulate the Dodge and Burn tools along the curve of the can, a simple opacity trick works well and much more quickly.

When all is said and done, the image below is the result.

A short recap

The trick for creating Photo-realistic objects and images really doesn't depend so much on color, but on how light plays on the surface of the object. A decent photo-realistic artist plays with light and shadows to generate basic faux 3D, but a stellar artist of this nature includes light and shadow in odd angles, reflections on the surface of the object, and even how light plays inside a transparent object such as a marble. Different materials reflect light in a myriad of ways, and perspectives come into play for each of these materials, as well. This tutorial dealt with reflections on paper and how a few simple areas of light and shadow aid in photo-realism. More advanced techniques of this sort are forthcoming in the following chapters.

A Spot o' Tea

Let's take a quick head count. Thus far, you have created logos from images, generated text with a hand-drawn artistic flair, and conformed a label to a curved surface. Some distortion of type using a curve also came into play. You have also manipulated Layer Styles, and dealt with differing opacities and a variety of other Photoshop tricks. All of this, and you are still in the first chapter!

This tutorial is an offshoot of both the first technique and the previous one, with a twist. This time you create another logo from scratch using a custom shape and type, and then conform it to a curved surface. Only this time around, you warp the type using a different method, and the surface is curved horizontally and vertically. Oh, did I mention the surface is transparent? I'll throw that in for good measure.

THE PLAN

- Create a logo by manipulating custom shapes
- Add text to the logo
- Affix the logo to a cup
- Blend the logo into the photo for a realistic effect

1 Create a new image with the following characteristics:

* **Name:** Tea Logo
* **Preset:** Custom
* **Width:** 9 inches
* **Height:** 9 inches
* **Resolution:** 300 pixels/inch
* **Color Mode:** RGB, 16 bit
* **Background Contents:** White

Select the Custom Shape tool. Open the Shapes menu and select All from the list. This loads all of the default shapes that shipped with Photoshop CS2. Scroll down the Shapes palette until you reach flower 5. The name pops up when you hold the mouse over the shape for a second or two. Press the D key to change the foreground color to black.

2 Create a new layer and ensure that the Paths button is depressed in the Options bar. Hold down the Shift key and draw the shape so that it covers about half of the image in the center. Using the Shift key ensures that the shape is symmetrical both horizontally and vertically. You may move it as needed once you create the shape.

3 Duplicate the shape layer by dragging and dropping the layer to the Add a New Layer icon on the bottom of the Layers palette. The thought here is to create another series of petals or leaves that are offset from the originals that you made with the first shape layer. With the top shape layer active, choose Edit⇨Transform Path⇨Rotate. For this particular shape, the layer need only be rotated 15 degrees, so enter **15 degrees** in the Angle of Rotation field in the Options bar. This offsets the petals perfectly if the shape is symmetrical.

The hue is a creamy tan/peach. The only other style setting to add is a stroke to better define the edges. Choose Stroke settings and set the color to black. Set the size to 8 pixels and save the Layer Style. Click OK.

5 Select the second shape layer just beneath the top layer. Apply the Layer Style that you just created and open the style settings again. Select Color Overlay and change the color to R = 123, G = 147, and B = 93.

The resulting hue is a muted green, almost a dark pastel. Because the style that you applied included the stroke settings from the first layer, there is no need to change these. Select the topmost layer again and reduce the opacity to 75%. The result is a layered flower in two tonal ranges.

TIP

Although you can move an object to the approximate center of a document by visually estimating, you can use Photoshop to ensure that an object in a layer is perfectly centered both horizontally and vertically. Select the layer that you want to center and click on the Move tool in the toolbar. Press Command/Ctrl+A to make a selection around the entire layer. In the Options bar, you see a series of icons that allow you to justify the contents of a layer similar to the way that you justify type. Click the Align Vertical Centers icon to center the object vertically. Click the Align Horizontal Centers icon to center it horizontally. Now the center point of the object is also the center point of the document.

4 You now add color to the leaves and petals, and Layer Style settings perform this function nicely. Ensure the top layer is selected, and open the Layer Styles dialog box. Choose Color Overlay. Enter the color settings R = 231, G = 187, and B = 130.

6 Now that you have created and modified the general shape of the logo, it is time to apply some type. To keep with the same theme, the type should match one of the colors that you used in the floral design. Set the foreground color in the toolbar to the same green that you used on the shape layer in the last step (R = 123, G = 147, and B = 93).

7 Select the Horizontal Type tool. Open the Character palette and set up the font as follows:

* **Font:** Verdana
* **Style:** Regular
* **Font Size:** 60 pt
* **Leading:** 90 pt
* **Tracking:** 200 pt
* **Vertical Scale:** 60%
* **Horizontal Scale:** 100%
* **Baseline Shift:** 0 pt
* **Color:** Green (the foreground color)

8 In the Options bar, set the justification to Centered. Begin typing just above the center of the topmost petal. Type the name **GREENSTREET** in all capital letters as the name for the tea. (You can certainly use another name if you want.) If you are unsure whether the text is centered, use the method in the last tip to center the text horizontally.

The second line of text goes beneath the floral logo. In the first technique, a round path was used as the guide, and the text followed the path when you typed it. This time, the Warp tools create the arc so that the text follows the curve of the design.

9 Center the Type tool below the design and type **HERBAL TEAS** in capital letters. Use the same character settings as before. Again, use the centering trick to ensure that the type is centered horizontally.

In the Type Options bar, click the icon that opens the Warp tools. Choose Arch from the Style menu. Enter the following settings for the arch:

* **Horizontal**
* **Bend:** -50%
* **Horizontal Distortion:** 0%
* **Vertical Distortion:** +5%

10 Click OK. The result is text that follows the curve of the pattern, arched but still legible in common left-to-right format. The vertical distortion that you apply bends the text somewhat so that it appears to radiate from the center, and the tops of all of the letters almost point to the center of the imaginary circle.

11 The logo itself is done at this point, providing that you are happy with the white background. It is interesting to test your designs against other background colors, and advertisers frequently use their designs against backdrops of varying hues and textures. By dropping a black layer behind the logo, you get the following (which would serve perfectly well on a T-shirt or other advertising medium).

12 Okay, now to place this logo on a curved, transparent surface. Turn off any background layers in the Layers palette, and save a copy of the logo to your hard drive as a PNG file. Open the new file and also open the image teacup.jpg. Drag the logo from the logo document to the teacup photo. Select the logo layer and choose Edit⇨Transform⇨Scale. Reduce the size of the logo until it fits within the constraints of the glass, leaving some space on the glass above and below so that the logo is basically centered with space around it on the cup face. Accept the transformation.

13 Choose Edit⇨Transform⇨Warp. Manipulate the corner direction lines so that the logo curves around the face of the cup. Keep in mind that the left portion of the logo now appears narrower. Also, because the cup is now curved vertically, it also pinches closer together on the left side. Perspective is key! Once you complete the warp, accept the transformation.

14 The next step deals with light playing on the logo. Duplicate the logo layer and set the Blend mode to Multiply. Change the opacity of the new layer to 45%. This makes the color appear deeper, and actually enhances the effect that this is affixed to the cup.

15 Select the Burn tool. In the Options bar, set up the tool's characteristics as follows:

* **Brush:** Round, Feathered
* **Brush Size:** 100
* **Range:** Midtones
* **Exposure:** 32%

16 Select the original logo layer. Apply the Burn tool to the left and right portions of the text and logo, leaving the center portion untouched and therefore lighter.

The end result is a realistic rendering of the new logo affixed to a transparent cup, complete with lighting that indicates that it belongs in a real-world setting.

A short recap

As discovered in the last technique, realism depends heavily on lighting. I might add that perspective plays an equal role in generating realism in your digital art. Although this technique was similar to others in this chapter, it stands on its own due to the variations that you applied. I've said it before, and I'll say it again: once you have reached a point working with the software where the processes become intuitive, you are limited only by your creativity.

Time for a Cocktail

This technique takes a rather mundane object (a bottle of colored water) and turns it into an ultra-cool product advertisement. In reality, the advertisement is cooler than the product being represented, but from an ad exec's point of view, that is a good thing. Using some relatively easy type applications and a few coloring alterations and Photoshop CS2 tricks, you'll turn a plain bottle into a fantastic, mouth-watering ad in a snap.

THE PLAN

- Remove the color in the primary image
- Add text to the surface of the bottle
- Extract the bottle from its background
- Create a new background from scratch

1. Open the image bottle.jpg. From this foundation image, you will create an entire advertisement, including a background and reflective surface.

The pink color needs to be removed from the bottle and turned a pristine white for the illusion of transparency to take effect. Double-click the background layer and turn it into an editable layer. Name the layer **Bottle**. Create a new layer and place it beneath the bottle layer. Fill the new layer with white.

To remove the color from the bottle, create a new layer and place it above the bottle. Fill the new layer with black and change the Blend mode to Hue. This removes all color, and leaves a grayscale rendering of the bottle. You want to keep the color of the cork, so grab the Eraser tool and erase the black from the cork area.

② Select the Dodge tool. In the Options bar, set the following characteristics for the tool:

* **Brush:** Round, Feathered
* **Brush Size:** 200
* **Range:** Midtones
* **Exposure:** 50%

Click on the layer named Bottle. Paint with the Dodge tool over the face of the bottle to brighten the gray tones, but leave the sides of the bottle, the cork area, and the bottom edge untouched. Continue lightening the central area until the bottle appears completely white, as though the glass were completely transparent and allowing the white background to shine through.

③ I'll bet that you can guess what company's ad this tutorial seeks to imitate, even without looking forward a few pages. The main text color for the logo (in this case the logo is the name of the product) is a deep, yet subdued blue. Set the foreground color to R = 65, G = 87, and B = 137.

4 Select the Horizontal Type tool. Open the Character palette and set the following parameters for the font:

* **Font:** Arial Black
* **Style:** Regular
* **Font Size:** 36 pt
* **Leading:** 14 pt
* **Tracking:** -10 pt
* **Vertical Scale:** 140%
* **Horizontal Scale:** 80%
* **Baseline Shift:** 0 pt
* **Color:** Blue (the foreground color)

5 At the top of the bottle's face, type the word **DEFINIT** in all capital letters. Reduce the font size for the Type tool to 30 points, add a new type layer above the previous, and type **CORN MASH**. Add a third type layer, this time with the font size set to 14 points, for the trademark symbol. Hold down the Alt/Command key and type **0174** to type the trademark symbol ® (Option+R on a Mac). Position the type layers so that there is a space about the height of the second line of text between "DEFINIT" and "CORN MASH." Move the trademark symbol to the upper right of the product name.

6 Create a new type layer and return to the Character palette. Set up the font for the scripted message that you will place on the face of the bottle, as follows:

* **Font:** BixAntiqueScript (if this is not installed on your system, select a script font as a substitute)
* **Style:** Regular
* **Font Size:** 24 pt
* **Leading:** 14 pt
* **Tracking:** -10 pt
* **Vertical Scale:** 140%
* **Horizontal Scale:** 80%
* **Baseline Shift:** 0 pt
* **Color:** Black

7 Type a new line of text between the two blue lines. On the original logo, the company states the country where the product is manufactured. With tongue firmly set in cheek, mimic this style, but instead, type **County of Hazzard**.

8 Open the Character palette again, and enter the following settings:

* **Font:** BixAntiqueScript (if this is not installed on your system, select a script font as a substitute)
* **Style:** Regular
* **Font Size:** 14 pt
* **Leading:** 24 pt
* **Tracking:** -5 pt
* **Vertical Scale:** 120%
* **Horizontal Scale:** 10%
* **Baseline Shift:** 0 pt
* **Color:** Black

9 Draw a paragraph box over the face of the bottle beneath the logo type area. Enter a paragraph describing the product. If you prefer, you can read from my example and enter your text accordingly.

Established in 1929, this quality hooch is refined from the finest corn blends found south of the Mason-Dixon line. This fine tonic is produced at the famous Duke Family Distilleries, with nearly 80 years of expertise in each bottle. Definit prides itself on being more than just Bootleg Whisky; it serves as a great alternative fuel as well.

10 On the bottom of the bottle face, enter two more lines of text. The first should be set up with the same font and color as the logo, although the font size will be somewhat smaller. This line of text includes information about the product's alcohol volume and amount.

You can also enter the next text message via a paragraph box. Use a standard font such as Verdana or Arial, and enter production and company information.

great alternative fuel as well

40% VOL.   **700 ML.**

PRODUCED AND BOTTLED IN HAZZARD COUNTY, USA
BY THE DEFINIT COMPANY
A DIVISION OF THE DUKE FAMILY DISTILLERIES

11 Select the Bottle layer and choose Filter⇨Extract. Use a narrow brush size (24–30 pixels) and make an outline around the bottle with the Highlighter tool. Fill the selection with the Paintbucket tool once the line has made the circuit around the entire bottle, and press Preview. Do any necessary edge cleanup, and click OK to accept the extraction. The white area around the bottle is wiped away and prepares the image for work on the background.

12 Press the D key and then the X key to place white in the foreground and black in the background. Select the Gradient tool. Open the Gradient Editor and select the White-to-Black gradient that resides in the first spot. Move the positions of the color stops to 40% (White) and 80% (Black). This narrows the transition area between the two colors.

13 In the Options bar, select Radial as the gradient type. Click on Layer 1 (in this case the background layer) and draw the mouse from the center of the image toward one of the corners. Don't draw it all the way to the corner; about half-way will suffice. The result is a white glow on a black background, positioned directly behind the bottle.

(14) Almost there! Okay, duplicate Layer 1. Choose Edit⇨ Transform⇨Scale and reduce the height of the layer to about one-quarter of its original size. This gives the image a reflective tabletop effect.

(15) Click on the topmost layer and hold down Command/Ctrl. Select each layer that is NOT part of the background: the bottle, the black-filled layer, and all text layers. Choose Layers⇨Group Layers (Command/Ctrl+G). Now you can reposition the group on the background with the Move tool to where you would like. You need not move it at all — it is up to you.

(16) Lastly, duplicate the Layer group that you just created. Choose Edit⇨Transform⇨Flip Vertical. Select the Move tool and position the group so that the two bottle bases match up. Ensure that the Blend mode for the Group 1 copy is set to Pass Through, and decrease the opacity of the group to 35%. Select Group 1 and decrease the opacity to 95% so that the corner in the background begins to show through the bottle.

TIP

You may find that the edges of the bottle are not as defined as you would like. If this is the case, open Group 1 and use the Burn tool on the edges of the bottle in the bottle layer. Use it sparingly! It need not be too dark to fulfill the illusion.

A short recap

A glance at the final image gives the impression that this effect is incredibly involved, when in reality it is one of the easier processes thus far. Many companies have been bypassing actual product photography for computer-generated renderings for some time (a certain MP3 player's ads instantly spring to mind). It gives the designer control over how clean the image appears, and as you see in this case, a few digital tricks render a polished ad that could make a company proud and a consumer thirsty.

chapter

2

home sweet home

Text effects and type treatments are so much a part of our lives that you may not realize how common they are in the world around you. As I glance around my office, I see literally thousands of variations. Whether it be calligraphic script on my Honorable Discharge from the Navy hanging on my wall, or the book covers lining my shelves, there are enough variations here to fill dozens of books that just demonstrate techniques on how to achieve them. This chapter is devoted in part to books, or rather book-cover type treatments, and you'll create a novel cover and comic book cover. You'll also generate a logo for a shampoo bottle as well as the bottle itself, help a band out by generating a logo and CD cover that fits in a jewel case, and even etch type into your own brand of soap. I'll round out the chapter by demonstrating the fabrication of liquid metal text, and create a message written in oil and water.

In a Lather

Labels are often designed with the product container in mind. This technique approaches the labeling process a bit differently. In this instance, you generate the label first, and then create the bottle photo-realistically from scratch. To tie it all together, you adjust a photo to match the overall tone of the product and create an advertisement out of it. A bit backward, perhaps, but where Photoshop is concerned, the road from concept to end result is often relative to the designer.

THE PLAN

- Create a label for a shampoo bottle
- Generate a photo-realistic bottle from scratch
- Affix the label to the bottle
- Fabricate an advertisement using the bottle and a photo

① Open the image lilac.jpg. The image used here provides not only a background for the logo text, but also a fill for the type.

Once you open the image, press Command/Ctrl to select the entire document. Choose Edit➪Define Custom Pattern. Name the new pattern and click OK.

② Create a new image with the following characteristics:

- **Name:** Shampoo_Label
- **Width:** 8 inches
- **Height:** 8 inches
- **Resolution:** 300 pixels/inch
- **Color Mode:** RGB
- **Background Color:** White

Click OK.

③ Select the Custom Shape tool. Much of this technique entails generating aspects of the final image from scratch, and the logo is no different. You can use existing custom shapes to create something entirely different — in this case, the shape of a flower with many wide petals.

Open the Custom Shapes in the Options bar and expand the Custom Shapes menu. Select 'All' from the list to load all of the shapes that installed with Photoshop. About a quarter of the way through the icons is a shape called Flower 6. Select this shape. Press the D key to place black in the foreground. Click the Fill Pixels button in the Options bar and create a new layer in the Layers palette. Draw the shape so that it fills 80% of the blank image.

Select Pattern Overlay again. Move the pattern so that a good mix of the overlay image is visible. Ensure that the edges of the photo never overlap into the image — that will ruin the effect! Once you position the photo, save the Layer Style and click OK.

(4) Open the Layer Styles dialog box for the new shape layer. Select Pattern Overlay from the list. Open the loaded patterns and select the image that you defined in Step 1. Change the Scale to 150%. Click Snap to Origin.

Layer Styles serve perfectly for adding a border to the label. Select Stoke from the left side of the Layer Styles dialog box. Open the Color Picker and set the color to R = 1, G = 22, and B = 101.

This is a deep blue/purple that serves well for this effect and the overall tone of the image. Don't ask me why, but some shampoo manufacturers try to give their products almost an edible quality in their advertising. There has to be some psychology to this, but I digress...

(5) Set the following attributes for the stroke:

* **Size:** 20 px
* **Location:** Outside
* **Opacity:** 100%
* **Fill Color:** Same as above

(6) With the foundation of the label in place, it is time to work on the type treatment. Select the Type tool and open the Character palettes. Set up the font as follows:

* **Font:** Cooper Black (if not installed on your system, a large, thick font with rounded edges is fine)
* **Style:** Regular
* **Font Size:** 140 pt
* **Leading:** 60 pt
* **Tracking:** -50
* **Vertical Scale:** 70%
* **Horizontal Scale:** 100-105%
* **Color:** Black

TIP

You are not restricted to leaving a pattern fill in a Layer Style in the same position. You can move the pattern around as you need to by selecting the Pattern Overlay in the Layer Styles dialog box and then simply clicking and dragging the pattern where you want it in the image. You can visually place where the pattern looks best.

(7) Type **Lilac Dreams** in two lines across the label face. The text extends beyond the edges of the shape, but that's OK. The main thing to look for is that the text is centered horizontally and resides above the centerline of the label.

(8) Ensure that the type layer is selected, and open the Layer Styles palette. Apply the style that you created and applied to the custom shape. If you forgot to save the style, simply go through the process of creating the shape style as outlined above and affix it to the type.

The image that is embedded in the style has a lot of varying elements, including fruit, flowers, and a wooden box. For the text, the focus should be on the flowers, so open the Layer Styles for the type layer and select Pattern Overlay. Increase the size to 300% and move the overlay so that the floral portion of the photo fills the type.

The type also needs to stand out from the logo, and the Satin setting in Layer Styles helps in this regard. Select Satin and enter the following settings:

* **Blend Mode:** Hard Light
* **Color:** Pink/Light Purple
* **Opacity:** 100%
* **Angle:** 19 degrees
* **Distance:** 11 px
* **Size:** 14 px
* **Contour:** Default Contour
  * **Anti-aliased:** checked
  * **Invert:** checked

Again, save the style so that you can use it later, and click OK.

(9) The logo text is almost done, but it can use a little flourish. Open the Type Warp dialog box and select the Wave style. Use the following settings:

* **Horizontal:** checked
* **Bend:** +50%
* **Horizontal Distortion:** -15%
* **Vertical Distortion:** 0%

Click OK. Check your progress against the following image, and reposition the text as needed.

10 The background image in these types of ads usually contains elements of the actual product. In this instance, the oranges don't really fit unless they represent something dealing with the shampoo being advertised. Let's imagine that for this product, some qualities of oranges have been found beneficial to hair care, and the manufacturer has added these elements. Of course they want the consumer to know that their product contains this special ingredient, and so they place this information on the label.

Create a new layer. Select the Shape tool and select Rounded Rectangle as the shape type. In the Options bar, enter the following attributes for the shape:

* **Radius:** 10 px
* **Mode:** Normal
* **Opacity:** 100%
* **Anti-aliased:** checked

Set the foreground color to a bright orange and the background color to black. Draw the shape just above the *ila* in the logo text, spanning the width of those three letters and roughly the height of the *a*. Position the shape so that it resides within the main area of the label shape but along the top edge. Rasterize the shape (Layer⇨Rasterize⇨Shape).

Choose Edit⇨Stroke and give the shape a black stroke of 10 pixels. Set white as the foreground color. I'm going to leave you to your own devices in regard to font and size for the text that appears in the orange shape. In this example, I am using 14-point Verdana, Faux Italic. Place the type layer just above the orange shape layer.

11 Add additional information to the label, experimenting with shapes and text for hair-type banners and so forth. Include the bottle's volume for added realism. You may use the image here as a guide, or select one from your own bathroom.

12 Save the label as a PSD file so that you may edit it later. Create a duplicate of the label image (Image⇨Duplicate) and merge all layers together, with the exception of the background. Turn off the background layer and save the duplicate image as a transparent PNG file. Have this version ready for affixing to the bottle that you are about to create.

Let's make a plastic bottle to house the product. Create a new image with the following specifications:

* **Name:** Bottle-MockUp
* **Width:** 12 inches
* **Height:** 16 inches
* **Resolution:** 300 pixels/inch
* **Color Mode:** RGB
* **Background Contents:** White

Click OK.

Create a new layer. Select the Shape tool and select Rounded Rectangle as the shape type. In the Options bar, enter the following attributes for the shape:

* **Radius:** 100 px
* **Mode:** Normal
* **Opacity:** 100%
* **Anti-aliased:** checked

Set black as the foreground color and draw a vertical shape in the new layer. Think of the shampoo bottles that you have in your own home or have seen on shelves in the local store. The shape should cover 80% or so of the layer vertically, and be roughly half as wide as it is high.

(13) Command/Ctrl-click on the shape layer to generate a selection. Select the Gradient tool and open the Gradient Editor. Create a gradient that begins with pink on the left side and moves gradually to deep purple on the right. Save the gradient just in case you would like to use it later.

In the Options bar, select Reflected as the gradient type. Beginning at the center of the shape, draw the gradient to the left or right side, holding down the Shift key to ensure

that the gradient is straight across the face of the shape. This creates the foundation of the bottle.

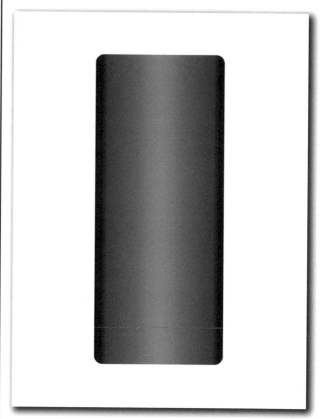

(14) To simulate the cap, create a new layer and again draw a rounded rectangle shape. This time, create the shape about one-quarter of the way down from the top of the first shape, and extend it beyond the edge of the first shape on both sides so that the curve on the corners just begins where the two shapes intersect. Command/ Ctrl-click the new shape layer to generate a selection.

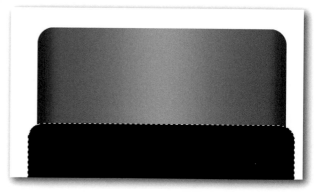

15 Create two new layers. Name the top layer **BlackStroke** and the one beneath **WhiteStroke**. Set the Blend Mode for each to Soft Light, 100% opacity.

Set white as the foreground color and ensure that the WhiteStroke layer is active. Choose Edit➪Stroke and create a 16-pixel stroke on the selection.

Select the BlackStroke layer. Set the foreground color to black and apply a stroke to the selection (Edit➪Stroke). Select the Move tool and use the arrow keys to move the BlackStroke layer up 2 clicks.

Select the Eraser tool. Select the original colored bottle-shape layer. Using a round brush with the Hardness set to 80-90% and a brush size of 6-10 pixels, erase small divots where the white and black stroke lines meet the edge of the bottle.

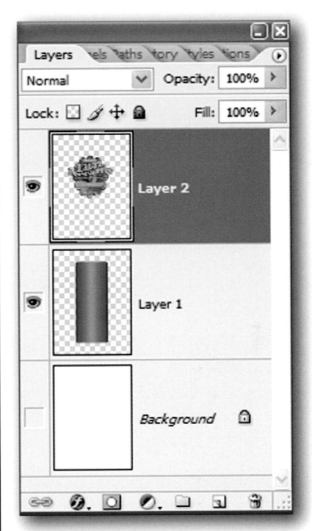

16 The excess stroke lines need to be removed, so Command/Ctrl-click the original shape layer and choose Select➪Inverse. Click on both stroke layers one at a time, and press Delete.

Go to the PNG version of the label and drag it into a new layer in the bottle image. The label should be a bit bigger than the bottle; select the label layer and choose Edit➪Transform➪Scale. Adjust the label size and position it so that it covers the central face of the bottle below the cap.

17 Open the image bath.jpg. This step places the bottle in an advertisement, and this image serves perfectly.

Okay, almost perfectly. One thing that you can change is the overall tone of the photo. The bath photo's color scheme resides more in earth tones than purples and oranges. In this case, the Match Color feature comes to the rescue.

Duplicate the bottle image. Merge all layers together except the background. Return to the bath photo and choose Image⇨Adjustments⇨Match Color. Use the following settings in the Match Color dialog box:

* **Luminance:** 115
* **Color Intensity:** 57
* **Fade:** 41
* **Neutralize:** checked
* **Source:** Bottle-MockUp copy
* **Layer:** Layer 1

Click OK. The tone of the bath photo has faintly taken on the hues from the bottle image.

18 Drag the bottle from the Bottle-MockUp copy document into bath.jpg. Choose Edit⇨Transform⇨Scale. In the Options bar, change the size both horizontally and vertically to 30%. Position the bottle so that it resides on the right side of the bath photo, with the bottom edge extending outside the photo. Use the faucet as a guide and position the bottle just beneath it.

19 With the bottle layer selected, choose Edit⇨Transform⇨Warp and use the top bars to round the bottle top a bit. Bend it so that it looks as though you are peering up at the bottle slightly.

Select the Burn tool. Although you will need to change the brush size to complete this step, use the following settings in the Options bar as an initial guide:

* **Brush:** Round, Feathered
* **Brush Size:** 100 px
* **Range:** Midtones
* **Exposure:** 20%

Darken the edges of the bottle and cap, being careful not to cover one area too often with this tool. The idea is to create realistic shadows on a curved surface. Burn the area lightly where the cap joins the bottle. Use the following image as a guide for the shading, as well as for the highlights.

Select the Dodge tool to add the highlights and reflections to the bottle. Set up the Dodge tool in the Options bar as follows:

* **Brush:** Round, Feathered
* **Brush Size:** 65 px
* **Range:** Shadows
* **Exposure:** 50%

Dodge the bottle vertically along the left edge until it is almost white. Create a vertical line somewhere to the left of center and running the height of the bottle. You may also want to dodge the left side of the label a bit. Again, use this image as a guide while dodging and burning.

20 Because the bottle is supposed to exist in the real world, you can use a real-world element in the image to add to the overall effect. Open the image bubbles01.jpg. You can take the bubbles from this photo and place them on the face of the bottle.

21 Select the entire image (Command/Ctrl+A), copy it (Command/Ctrl+C), and paste it into a new layer in the ad document (Command/Ctrl+V). Resize the image with the Transform⇨Scale settings to fit over the bottle face, leaving most of the logo untouched by the bubbles. With the Magnetic Lasso tool, select the bubble edges close to the sides of the bottle, and delete those bubbles that extend beyond the sides. You can make the selection rough. You also need to remove the gray area above the bubbles.

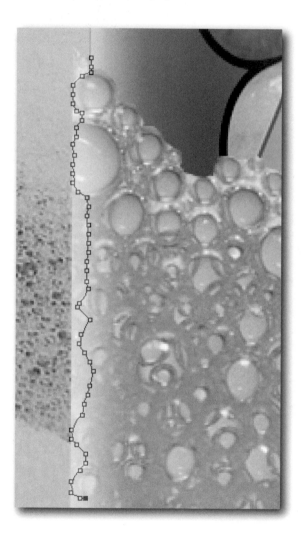

22 Open the Layer Styles for the bubbles. In Blending Options, choose the Blend If section at the bottom of the dialog box. Hold down the Command/Alt key and move the inside This Layer black slider from 0 to 198. This removes much of the darker gray portions of the bubbles layer, and leaves the reflective bubbles on the bottle's face. Click OK and exit the Layer Style settings.

In the example below, I am adding two additional lines of type to the ad: one uses a purple Verdana font, and the other uses the same font, style, and Wave setting as the type on the bottle. Do you remember saving all of those settings earlier? Here's where the Layer Style comes into play. You can do this on your own, but the image here shows how everything fits neatly together in theme and form.

23 A last step to put everything in place and make the final image appear more ad-like is to apply Lighting Effects to the bath layer.

Give your hair a

Vacation

Now with CITRUS OIL

Lilac Dreams

FORTIFYING SHAMPOO

SLEEK & SOFT

FL. OZ. (750 ml)

A short recap

Whew! There is quite a bit involved in this technique, but the end result justifies the process. In the real world, a company would have already designed its logo and product packaging, making the creation of the advertisement a somewhat easier process. This just goes to show you that, with Photoshop, you can create more than just the ad — you can generate an entire product around an idea.

Something Smells Funny

This tutorial carries over the hygiene theme, but the process is less involved. This time, you stamp a logo on your own bar of soap, so that even while consumers are bathing, you are sending a message to them. Is no place sacred anymore?

THE PLAN

- Conform Type to a bar of soap
- Add a shape for the logo
- Etch the type and shape into the bar
- Adjust the highlights and shadows for better realism

(1) Open the image soap02.jpg.

(2) Select the Eyedropper tool and sample the deep orange on the side of the soap. This places that color in the foreground.

Select the Type tool and open the Character palette. Set up the font with the following characteristics:

- ✳ **Font:** University Roman (Times, Times New Roman, or a similar font also works well)
- ✳ **Style:** Faux Bold, Faux Italic
- ✳ **Font Size:** 72 pt
- ✳ **Leading:** 90 pt
- ✳ **Tracking:** 100
- ✳ **Vertical Scale:** 90%
- ✳ **Horizontal Scale:** 120%

Enter the name of the soap in a new type layer using the foreground color. Position the text above the soap bar with

the Move tool, choose Edit⇨Transform⇨Rotate, and turn the layer so that the type matches the angle of the bar.

(3) Select the Custom Shape tool. In the Options bar, click the Fill Pixels button. Open the Shapes menu and select All. In this example, I've named my soap Quail. The menu contains a shape of a flying bird that suits this name, so select the bird shape and draw it just below the text in a new layer. Rotate the shape as you did the type layer. Merge the bird shape layer with the type layer. Photoshop asks if you want to rasterize the type layer. Click OK.

4 Duplicate the new logo layer (which should now contain both the type and the bird shape). With the top layer selected, open the Layer Styles and select Inner Shadow. Set the following attributes for the Inner Shadow:

* **Blend Mode:** Multiply
* **Color:** Median Brown (R = 142, G = 88, and B = 60)
* **Opacity:** 75%
* **Use Global Light:** unchecked
* **Angle:** 145 degrees
* **Distance:** 7 px
* **Choke:** 0%
* **Size:** 2 px
* **Quality:**
  * **Contour:** Half Round (one of the default contours)
  * **Anti-aliased:** checked
  * **Noise:** 0%

Save the style just in case you want to use it later, and click OK.

5 Duplicate the logo layer again and set the opacity for both copies to 90%. Select the bottom copy and click on the Move tool. With the arrow keys, move the layer to the right four clicks and down two clicks.

Open the Layer Styles for the bottom copy and select Stroke. Enter the following stroke attributes:

* **Size:** 2
* **Position:** Outside
* **Blend Mode:** Multiply
* **Opacity:** 20%
* **Fill Type:** Color
* **Color:** median gray (#666666 works well)

You need to alter the Inner Shadow a bit for this layer. Set the following attributes for the Inner Shadow:

* **Blend Mode:** Multiply
* **Color:** Median Brown (R = 142, G = 88, and B = 60)
* **Opacity:** 60%
* **Use Global Light:** unchecked
* **Angle:** 50 degrees
* **Distance:** 5 px

* **Choke:** 0%
* **Size:** 2 px
* **Quality:**
  * **Contour:** Half Round (one of the default contours)
  * **Anti-aliased:** checked
  * **Noise:** 0%

Save the style and click OK.

6 You have now completed the embedding. All that you need to do now is to darken and lighten the logo to bring it into the realm of the real world. You can use our old friend the Burn tool to do this.

Select the Burn tool and adjust the Options bar settings as follows:

* **Brush:** Feathered, Round
* **Brush Size:** 60 px
* **Range:** Midtones
* **Exposure:** 20–32%

7 Command/Ctrl-click one of the logo layers to generate a selection. Starting on the bottom-most layer, apply some darkening around the inside edges of the logo, and lightly apply the Burn tool to each of the three layers in these areas.

If the result seems a bit too dark, try reducing the opacity of the logo layers until you get a blend that you find acceptable. The end result should leave a casual observer with the impression that this is a real bar of soap with the logo stamped in it at the factory.

A short recap

This technique was very straightforward and rarely left the realm of Layer Styles. Sometimes less is more, and still renders realistic results. We will revisit etching text later when you test your skill at chiseling things in stone, and so this tutorial provides good practice for that exercise.

Heaving Hearts and Pulsing Pecs

Ah... to be young, in love, and to look like Fabio! This technique pays homage to my wife's favorite book genre, the romance novel. Although not a fan myself (I'm more a sword-and-sorcery guy), I can appreciate the work that goes into dressing up these covers. Intended to stimulate the consumer's carnal side (I doubt romance has anything to do with these designs), they catch the eye with impossibly beautiful models either sketched or photographed, and place them in risqué poses in ridiculous situations. This technique beefs up a male model, gives information on the author's other work in the book series, and dresses up the title with embossed, reflective type that is designed to grab browsers' attention and draw them to the cover art.

THE PLAN

- Buff up a male model with the Liquify feature
- Add information on the author, previous books in the series, and the title of the book
- Emboss the type with eye-catching, semi-reflective type

1 Open the image romance05.jpg and duplicate the background layer.

2 Choose Filter⇨Liquify, and select the Bloat tool from the left-side controls.

3 On the right side, enter the following settings:

- ∗ **Brush Size:** 285
- ∗ **Brush Density:** 87
- ∗ **Brush Pressure:** 77
- ∗ **Brush Rate:** 90

4 Increase the size of the man's chest, shoulder, neck, and upper back muscles. Some stretching of pixels may occur, but you can correct that shortly. Use the image on the next page as a guide, and then click OK when you are happy with his extra time in the gym.

Tool Options

Brush Size: 285

Brush Density: 87

Brush Pressure: 77

Brush Rate: 90

Turbulent Jitter: 50

Reconstruct Mode: Revert

☐ Stylus Pressure

5 The sand on the man's shoulder as well as some of the goose bumps may have stretched to strange proportions. To correct this, select the Clone Stamp tool from the toolbar. Turn off the liquefied layer and Command/Alt+click the smaller grains or unstretched skin texture to be corrected on the original background layer. Turn on the liquefied layer again and stamp over the trouble spots in the *same area* from which the sample was taken.

6 Set white as the foreground color and select the Type tool. Open the Character palettes and set up the font as follows:

* **Font:** Times New Roman
* **Style:** Regular
* **Font Size:** 14 pt
* **Leading:** 90 pt
* **Tracking:** 25
* **Vertical Scale:** 90%
* **Horizontal Scale:** 80%

At the top of the page, type the phrase **Author of** *Pearl for a Pirate*. Ensure that you reselect the title and italicize it to stand out. This tells the readers that the author wrote another book that they may have already enjoyed, or that this is another book in a continuing series. Center the text at the very top of the page.

Author of *Pearl for a Pirate*

7 Below the first line of text, click with the Type tool again, creating a new type layer. You will place the author's name, Alice Hatch, in this location. If such a person exists, I apologize... trust me, the name came from my imagination. Please don't take offense, Alice!

Set up the Character palettes as follows:

* **Font:** Times New Roman
* **Style:** Regular
* **Font Size:** 90 pt
* **Leading:** 90 pt
* **Tracking:** 25
* **Vertical Scale:** 90%
* **Horizontal Scale:** 60%

Ensure that the text is centered horizontally, but resides above the heads of the two lovebirds. As the text is white, a portion is washed out by the background, but you will correct that soon.

8 Create another type layer for the title. The name of this book is *The Pirate's Booty*. Type the entire text on three lines, using the settings that you used for the author's name for *The* and *Booty*. Italicize these two words. For the *Pirate's* text sandwiched in the middle, set up the Character palettes as follows:

* **Font:** FrancineHMK (or substitute with another flowing script in the Times family)
* **Font Size:** 140 pt
* **Leading:** 90 pt
* **Tracking:** 25
* **Vertical Scale:** 90%
* **Horizontal Scale:** 60%

9 Bring a guide out from the left side of the document window and use this to align the right side of all three words.

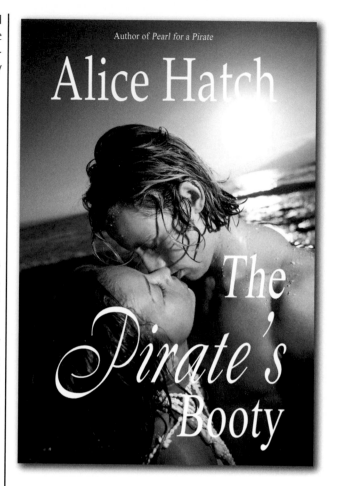

10 Okay, now to make that text reach out and grab you. Select the layer with the author's name, and open the Layer Styles, selecting Bevel/Emboss first. Use the following settings:

* **Style:** Emboss
* **Technique:** Smooth
* **Depth:** 90-95%
* **Direction:** Up
* **Size:** 33 px
* **Soften:** 0 px
* **Angle:** 120 degrees
* **Use Global Light:** unchecked
* **Altitude:** 30 degrees
* **Gloss Contour:** Special - See the figure in Step 11.
* **Highlight Mode:** Normal
* **Highlight Color:** R = 65, G = 10, and B = 100
* **Highlight Opacity:** 100%

- * **Shadow Mode:** Multiply
- * **Shadow Color:** Black
- * **Shadow Opacity:** 100%

11 For the gloss contour, double-click inside the contour window and open the Contour Editor. Create a contour that resembles the following dialog box.

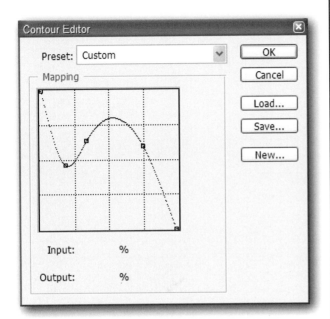

12 Select Inner Glow and enter the following settings:

- * **Blend Mode:** Screen
- * **Opacity:** 100%
- * **Noise:** 0%
- * **Color:** R = 181, G = 252, and B = 98
- * **Technique:** Softer
- * **Source:** Edge
- * **Choke:** 0%
- * **Size:** 20 px
- * **Contour:** Ring Double
- * **Anti-aliased:** checked
- * **Range:** 50%
- * **Jitter:** 0%

13 Save the Layer Style for future use — you will need it in a moment. Once you save it, click OK.

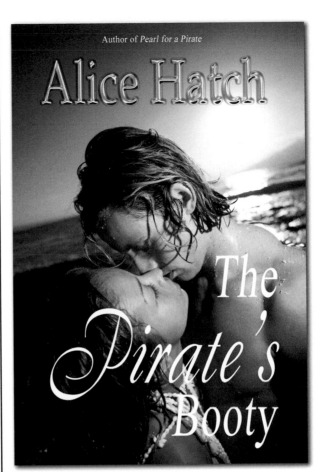

14 The title text is similar to the author's name effect, but not exactly the same. Publishers often vary these styles slightly to distinguish between them.

15 Select the title layer. Apply the Layer Style that you just saved. It is easier to alter an existing style than to start from scratch. Open the Bevel/Emboss settings and enter the following:

- * **Style:** Emboss
- * **Technique:** Smooth
- * **Depth:** 90-95%
- * **Direction:** Up
- * **Size:** 33 px
- * **Soften:** 0 px
- * **Angle:** 120 degrees
- * **Use Global Light:** unchecked

* **Altitude:** 30 degrees
* **Gloss Contour:** Special - See example
* **Highlight Mode:** Normal
* **Highlight Color:** R = 54, G = 6, and B = 144
* **Highlight Opacity:** 100%
* **Shadow Mode:** Multiply
* **Shadow Color:** Black
* **Shadow Opacity:** 100%

 Select Inner Glow and enter the following settings:

* **Blend Mode:** Screen
* **Opacity:** 100%
* **Noise:** 0%
* **Color:** R = 245, G = 160, and B = 38
* **Technique:** Softer
* **Source:** Edge
* **Choke:** 0%
* **Size:** 21 px
* **Contour:** Ring Double

* **Anti-aliased:** checked
* **Range:** 50%
* **Jitter:** 0%

 Choose Color Overlay and enter the following:

* **Blend Mode:** Normal
* **Color:** R = 136, G = 206, and B = 247
* **Opacity:** 100%

⟨18⟩ Choose the Stroke settings and set them up as follows:

* **Size:** 6 px
* **Position:** Outside
* **Blend Mode:** Normal
* **Opacity:** 100%
* **Fill Type:** Color
* **Color: Color:** R = 136, G = 206, and B = 247

⟨19⟩ Save the Layer Style and click OK.

chapter 2 ● home sweet home

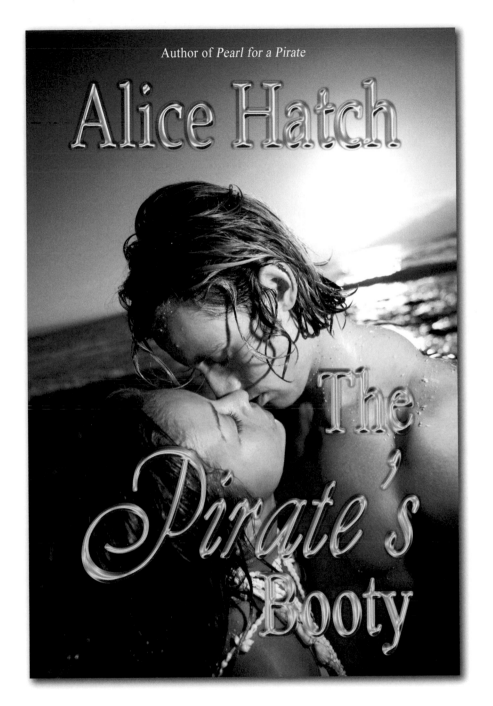

A short recap

Granted, the process for embossing an actual book cover is quite a bit more involved, but you get the drift. For the Photoshop version, Layer Styles once again come to the rescue and do a great job mimicking what you may see in the non-digital reality.

We Gotcha Covered

Because we have been talking about books, let's move to the genre that this title would fall under: that of the Photoshop design category. These books try to catch the eye like other types of publications, but they try to do so with the target audience and the corporate blueprint in mind. Rarely are authors allowed to design their own covers. Of the more than ten books that I've written or contributed to, I've helped on the cover of two titles.

The idea for this project is to design a book cover for a title on Photoshop, model photography, and collaging effects. The cover reflects these elements by the images that you choose and how you display them. This isn't a long tutorial, but there is quite a bit of pixel manipulation involved.

THE PLAN

- Create a new model's face using elements of three separate women
- Add a photographer to the mix
- Lay out the book's title
- Include information on the contents

(1) Open the images cameraman.jpg and yellowflowers.jpg.

(2) Bring cameraman.jpg to the front and click on the Magic Wand tool. Select all of the areas of white in the background by holding down the Shift key to add to the selection while clicking.

(3) Once you select all of the white, choose Select⇨Invert and then Select⇨Modify⇨Contract. Contract the selection by 1. Press Command/Ctrl+C to copy the man, and then switch to yellowflowers.jpg. Press Command/Ctrl+V to paste the man into his own layer. You may need to use the Transform tools to scale his size down a bit. Create a Layer Mask for the new camerman layer by clicking the Add a Layer Mask button on the bottom of the Layers palette.

(4) Command/Ctrl-click the cameraman layer to select him and the layer mask. Press the D key to reset the foreground and background colors. With the default Foreground to Background gradient, fill the selection in the mask from the bottom of his feet to the top of his head, rendering his lower half invisible and leaving his head, shoulders, and camera.

(5) Open the images woman02.jpg, woman03.jpg, and woman04.jpg. Beginning with woman04.jpg, select the woman's eyes with the Rectangular Marquee tool. Copy the selection and paste it into the cover document. Bring a guide down from the top ruler to help line up the eyes horizontally. Choose Edit⇨Transform⇨Rotate and turn the layer so that the eyes are on the same horizontal plane.

6 Select woman02.jpg and repeat the process used on the first model photo, only this time select from the bridge of her nose to just below her nostrils. As this photo is very tilted, you may want to use the Polygonal Lasso tool to make the selection. Paste the selection into the cover document, and position it a few pixels below the eyes layer. Leave a gap between the two. Rotate the layer and scale the image as needed.

7 Select woman03.jpg. Repeat the process outlined above, this time selecting the mouth and chin. Paste it into the new cover document and place it a few pixels below the nose layer.

8 Select any one of the face layers and open the Layer Styles dialog box. Select Stroke and enter the following settings:

* **Size:** 40 px
* **Position:** Inside
* **Blend Mode:** Normal
* **Opacity:** 100%
* **Fill Type:** Color
* **Color:** White

Save the style and apply it to all three face layers.

9 Select the mouth layer and choose Edit⟹Transform⟹Rotate. Rotate the layer so that the mouth aligns with the rest of the face. This results in the layer being rotated at an angle, but that's fine — it is part of the effect. Accept the transformation.

Reduce the opacity of all three face layers to 85-90%. This allows the flower in the background to faintly show through.

10 Create a new layer at the top of the Layers palette. With the Rectangular Marquee tool, create a selection roughly 1½ inches wide, and running the length of the page vertically along the left-hand side. Fill this selection with black.

⑪ Create another layer and create a selection roughly 1½ inches high, and running the width of the cover at the top of the page. Leave some space between the selection and the top edge. Fill the selection with the color R = 190, G = 152, and B = 1.

⑫ Select the Vertical Type tool. Set white as the color in the Options bar, and enter the following settings in the Character palettes:

* **Font:** Verdana
* **Font Size:** 90 pt
* **Leading:** 72 pt
* **Tracking:** -100
* **Vertical Scale:** 110%
* **Horizontal Scale:** 100%

⑬ Justify the type to the top. Beginning from about a half-inch from the top over the black strip, type the word **Photoshop**. Select the Horizontal Type tool. Create a new type layer with the same font characteristics. Just right of where the two bars meet, type **hantasies**. The thought is to use the first *P* as the beginning letter of both title words.

⑭ The final touch for this cover is to add a descriptive paragraph about the contents. Select the Type tool again and set up the font in the Character palette as follows:

* **Font:** Verdana
* **Font Size:** 18 pt
* **Leading:** 18 pt
* **Vertical Scale:** 80%
* **Horizontal Scale:** 100%

⑮ Draw a paragraph box in the upper-right corner, roughly three inches wide and two inches high, and below the banner. Enter a descriptive paragraph describing the contents. You may use the image shown here as a guide.

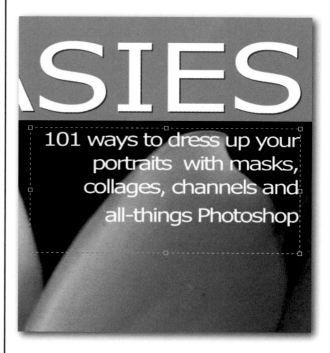

⑯ As a final touch, add your name as the author in the lower-right corner.

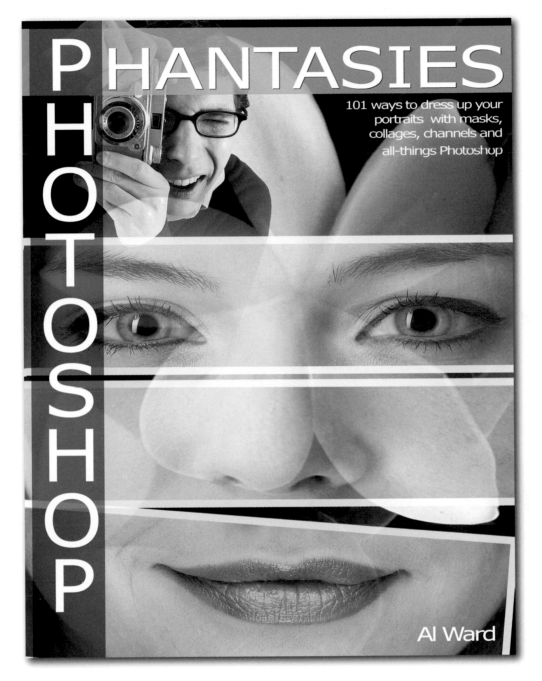

A short recap

Masking, blending modes, opacity changes, and positioning are major components of book-cover development. Mix this Photoshop know-how with the designer's imagination, and you can quickly generate art that can dress up the bookshelves or simply give the illusion that they belong there.

Bif! Pow!

I can't do a series of book-style tutorials without paying homage to one of my favorite genres, the comic book. These days I believe the term has morphed into "graphic novel"; no matter, I still think that they rock, and I'm halfway to 80 years old. Some kids never age, I suppose.

This technique demonstrates type treatments for this kind of book. Styles again come into play, although with an interesting twist: the style settings for one layer are going to create the desired effect on another. We experiment with different font types and variations of layout settings, and you also create a mock UPC barcode. I wish I had space to show how the main art is done, but that will have to come another day.

THE PLAN

- Create a flame-style logo for a comic book cover
- Add additional type treatments
- Create a faux UPC barcode

1 Open the image hero.jpg. I'm not an artist, and so I had to create this compilation from a series of images, but you get the drift. Our heroine's main power is the manipulation of flame, and so the logo reflects that power.

2 Select the Type tool and open the Character palettes. Font choice is pretty important: I'm looking for something with irregular edges that have sort of a melting or chaotic quality. The font that I use here is called 'An ode to noone'; you may choose another font if this is not installed on your system. One thing to keep in mind is the thickness of the font; the heavier the font, the better the result.

3 Type **Fire Sprite**, with the *F* and *S* at 200+ points, and the rest at 150 points.

Set up the font as follows:

- **Font:** An ode to noone
- **Font Size:** 150-200 pt
- **Leading:** 100 pt
- **Tracking:** -100
- **Vertical Scale:** 80%
- **Horizontal Scale:** 100%

4 Open the Type Warp dialog box and select Rise. Enter the following settings:

- **Horizontal:** checked
- **Bend:** +25
- **Horizontal Distortion:** -40%
- **Vertical Distortion:** +1%

⑤ Time to get down, and get funky! The following process involves a few filter applications, but it helps to generate the fire for the text. Duplicate the type layer and select the bottom type layer. Rasterize the layer. Choose Image⇨Rotate⇨90 degrees CCW.

Open the Filter menu and select Blur⇨Motion Blur. Set the Angle to 3 and the Distance to 134 pixels. Click OK.

Open the Filter menu again, and choose Stylize⇨Wind. Set the following options:

* **Method:** Blast
* **Direction:** From the Right

⑥ Run this filter with the same settings a second time. Rotate the canvas back 90 degrees CW, and then choose Filter⇨Stylize⇨Diffuse. Set the Mode to Normal and click OK.

⑦ Choose Filter⇨Blur⇨Gaussian Blur. Set the Radius to 4 pixels and click OK.

⑧ Choose Filter⇨Distort⇨Ripple. Set the amount to 150 and the size to Medium. Click OK. The text should look bright, white, and fuzzy. Now it's time to bring in some color.

⑨ Select the top type layer and open the Layer Styles dialog box. Select Stroke from the list and enter the following attributes:

* **Size:** 105 px
* **Position:** Outside

* **Blend Mode:** Overlay
* **Opacity:** 100%
* **Fill Type:** Gradient
* **Gradient:** create a gradient that transitions from dark red on the left to bright yellow on the right
* **Reverse:** unchecked
* **Style:** Shape Burst
* **Align with Layer:** checked
* **Angle:** 90 degrees
* **Scale:** 100%

When you have created the gradient, be sure to save it. Then save the style for later use (always save your styles — you never know when you may need them again!), and click OK. As a progress check, your text should look like the example here. The gradient stroke on the top layer adds the flame hues to the layer beneath it.

⑩ Open the image flame01.jpg. This gives the text in the foreground a flame-like appearance.

⑪ Press Command/Ctrl+A to select the entire image. Choose Edit⇨Define Pattern. Name the new pattern flame and click OK. It is now loaded and ready to use.

⑫ Open the Layer Styles for the top layer again and select Pattern Overlay. Set up the overlay as follows:

* **Blend Mode:** Normal
* **Opacity:** 100%
* **Pattern:** Flame
* **Scale:** 250%
* **Link with Layer:** checked

13 Move the Layer Styles dialog box to the side for a moment. Position the cursor over the canvas and hold down the left mouse button. Position the pattern so that the flames appear within the text.

14 Proceed to Gradient Overlay and enter the following settings:

* **Blend Mode:** Screen
* **Opacity:** 66%
* **Gradient:** same as the stroke outlined above
* **Reverse:** unchecked
* **Style:** Linear
* **Align with Layer:** checked
* **Angle:** 90 degrees
* **Scale:** 33%

15 For the next style setting, select Satin. Enter the following:

* **Blend Mode:** Screen
* **Blend Color:** Bright Yellow
* **Opacity:** 20%
* **Angle:** 20 degrees
* **Distance:** 10 px
* **Size:** 14 px
* **Contour:** Gaussian
* **Anti-aliased:** checked
* **Invert:** checked

16 Select the Bevel/Emboss settings. Enter the following:

* **Style:** Inner Bevel
* **Technique:** Smooth
* **Depth:** 300%
* **Direction:** Up
* **Size:** 18 px
* **Soften:** 0 px
* **Angle:** 120 degrees
* **Use Global Light:** unchecked

* **Altitude:** 70 degrees
* **Gloss Contour:** Linear
* **Highlight Mode:** Screen
* **Highlight Color:** R = 251, G = 252, and B = 171
* **Highlight Opacity:** 100%
* **Shadow Mode:** Multiply
* **Shadow Color:** R = 245, G = 116, and B = 116
* **Shadow Opacity:** 100%

17 Select the Inner Glow settings. Enter the following:

* **Blend Mode:** Multiply
* **Opacity:** 75%
* **Color:** #333333
* **Technique:** Softer
* **Source:** Edge
* **Choke:** 0%
* **Size:** 25 px
* **Contour:** Linear
* **Anti-aliased:** checked
* **Range:** 50%
* **Jitter:** 0%

18 One last style setting: select Inner Shadow and enter the following:

* **Blend Mode:** Multiply
* **Color:** R = 142, G = 2, and B = 2
* **Opacity:** 75%
* **Angle:** 120 degrees
* **Use Global Light:** checked
* **Distance:** 26 px
* **Choke:** 0%
* **Size:** 38 px
* **Contour:** Linear
* **Anti-aliased:** unchecked
* **Noise:** 0%

Save the style and click OK.

19 The next step is to add any additional type elements such as subtitle, issue number, and publisher's logo and name. The majority of this is left to your ingenuity, but for the example created here, the type treatments are variations on the following font and font characteristics:

* **Font:** Arial
* **Style:** Regular, Italic, and Bold as needed
* **Size:** 24 pt
* **Tracking:** 100 pt
* **Leading:** -100
* **Vertical Scale:** 80%
* **Horizontal Scale:** 100%

Place these around the page as dressing. For the TM symbol behind the subtitle, the same font characteristics are used, except that the Superscript button is depressed on the bottom of the Character palette.

20 Create a new layer below the type layers. Select the Rectangular Marquee tool and create a selection along the left side of the document, roughly one inch wide and running the height of the page. Fill with a light-gray to lighter-gray linear gradient, from left to right.

21 Create a new layer. In the lower-right corner of the document, make a rectangular selection roughly 2½ inches wide by 1 inch high, and fill the selection with white. Set the foreground color to black and make another smaller rectangular selection inside the white box. Select the Pencil tool and draw several 1-pixel-wide vertical lines (hold down the Shift key to draw them completely straight) across the width of the selection. Stagger the distance so that the distribution of the lines is irregular. Increase the size of the pencil to 3 pixels and draw a few more lines in the same manner. Increase to 5 pixels and draw a few more lines until you have a group of vertical lines at various distances apart.

22 Delete a section of the lines on the bottom edge, leaving a few lines streaming down on either side. Add a price, a rating code, and a make-believe, 12-digit UPC code for added authenticity.

23 Further dress up the border by adding additional text such as "Premier Edition" over the gray gradient area that spans the height of the page. Another touch is to generate a pattern using the same font as the logo and lightly fill the border with the pattern.

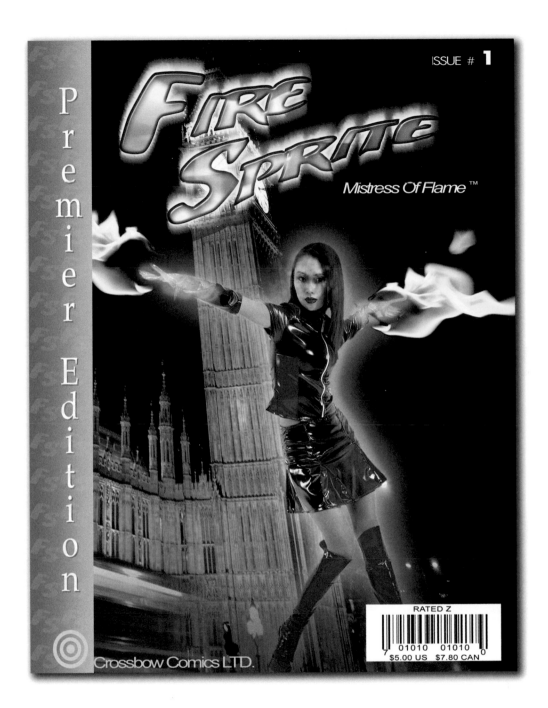

A short recap

Fortunately for me, this book isn't about using Photoshop to generate professional, hand-drawn artwork: I'll leave it to someone who is addicted to his or her drawing tablet to write that title. Here you have seen how layout and themed-type effects can make your characters more interesting. The hero's power is flame, which prominently displays in the photo. The text that I used in the logo reflects that power to a degree. You may not have a desire to create comic books, but you can certainly make your friends or family members appear as though they star in one. You'll be their hero.

Rockin' Out

A good friend of mine who is a fine Photoshop author in his own right pointed out to me a few months ago that skulls show up in almost every book that I've written. I scoffed, but later found that he was actually right: I do work with skull photos quite often.

This tutorial uses a skull, and not simply because I'm fond of them. The idea is to create a rock band CD cover — something that fits in a 5-inch by 5-inch jewel case cover. Because the band doesn't exist, let's say it's a big hair metal band (how I miss the '80s) that hopes that the cover of their CD inspires sales where their music may not. Nothing says rock like rusty metal, embedded steel type, and a skull, right?

THE PLAN

- Manipulate a texture for a CD cover
- Add a skull to blend with the background
- Create metallic text for the band logo
- Add lighting effects for the final image

1 Open the image metal01.jpg. This serves as the backdrop for the CD cover. On the bottom of the Layers palette, click the "Add an adjustment layer" icon and select Brightness/Contrast from the list. Set Brightness to -25 and Contrast to +15.

2 Choose Image➪Image Size. Resize the image to the following dimensions:

* **Width:** 5 inches
* **Height:** 5 inches
* **Resolution:** 300 pixels/inch
* **Constrain Proportions:** unchecked
* **Resample Image:** Bicubic Sharper

Click OK.

3 Select the Type tool. Open the Character palette and set up the font as follows:

* **Font:** Old English Text
* **Style:** Regular
* **Font Size:** 150 pt
* **Leading:** 36 pt
* **Tracking:** 0
* **Vertical Scale:** 80%
* **Horizontal Scale:** 100%
* **Baseline Shift:** 0 pt
* **Color:** Black

This is going to be tricky to explain, and so if you get confused, take a look at the example image to help clear things up. The text for the band's name, Mac Deth, is done in three type layers. The first type layer contains *Mac*, with the *M* set to a font size of 250 points normal and the *ac* at 150 points italic. The second type layer contains only the *D* set to 250 points normal. The third layer contains *eth* set to 150 points italic. Now position the third layer just beneath the *ac*. All of the type should be positioned above the midline of the image, and centered horizontally.

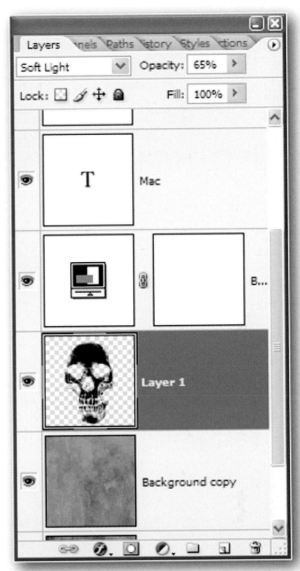

4 Open the image skull.jpg. This image won't appear in its true form on the cover, but will rather appear faded into the background. You can do this in a couple of ways. For this technique, you turn it into a paintbrush and apply it to the image. Choose Image⇨Adjustments⇨Invert. Next, choose Image⇨Adjustments⇨Threshold. This creates a bitmap-style version of the skull in black and white. Set the Threshold level to 100 and click OK.

5 Choose Edit⇨Define Brush Preset. Name the brush **Skull** in the Brush Name dialog box and click OK. It now resides in the Brushes palette and is ready to use.

6 Set the foreground color to black and click on the Paintbrush tool. Create a new layer just below the adjustment layer, open the brushes, and select the Skull brush from the bottom of the menu. Set the Master Diameter of the brush to 1400 pixels so that it covers the majority of the photo. Without moving the brush around, click to apply the paint to the new layer in one spot, centered in the document. Change the Blend Mode for the paint layer to Soft Light and reduce the opacity to 65%. The skull now appears stained into the rusty background.

TIP

Another option for applying the skull is to create the brush as described, but use the Burn tool with the skull on the desaturated layer. I've chosen the method outlined here because it gives you more control over the skull's appearance, thus allowing you to manipulate the paint layer separately from the background.

8 Turn off all of the non-type layers and choose Layer⇨Merge Visible. Name the layer Logo-Merged. Command/Ctrl-click the Logo-Merged layer to generate a selection, and create a new layer beneath the logo.

9 Choose Select⇨Modify⇨Expand. Increase the size of the selection by 20 pixels.

10 Select the Gradient tool. Click inside the gradient to open the Gradient Editor, and create a gradient of alternating gray tones similar to the one shown here.

11 Fill the selection with the gradient from top to bottom.

12 Open the Layer Styles for the gradient layer and select Bevel/Emboss. Enter the following settings:

* **Style:** Pillow Emboss
* **Technique:** Chisel Hard
* **Depth:** 371%
* **Direction:** Up
* **Size:** 1 px
* **Soften:** 0 px
* **Angle:** 120 degrees
* **Use Global Light:** unchecked
* **Altitude:** 25 degrees
* **Gloss Contour:** Linear
* **Anti-aliased:** checked
* **Highlight Mode:** Screen
* **Highlight Color:** R = 219, G = 192, and B = 156
* **Highlight Opacity:** 75%
* **Shadow Mode:** Multiply
* **Shadow Color:** Black
* **Shadow Opacity:** 89%

Save the style and click OK. Set the Blend Mode for the gradient layer to Difference.

7 Included on this book's CD-ROM is a folder containing Layer Styles for Chapter 2. In this folder, I include a Style set called MacDethLogo. Go to the Layer Styles palette and load this style set. Select each type layer and apply this style to the text.

* **Horizontal**: checked
* **Bend**: -50%
* **Horizontal Distortion**: +2%
* **Vertical Distortion**: +8%

(15) Reposition the title so that it bends around the bottom of the logo. Change the Blend Mode of the title layer to Soft Light and the opacity to 85%.

(16) The final touches involve lighting the background. Duplicate the Background and choose Image⇨Adjustments⇨Desaturate. Reduce the opacity for the new layer to 75%. Select the desaturated version of the background and choose Filter⇨Render⇨Lighting Effects. Enter the following settings:

* **Style:** Default
* **Light Type:** Spotlight (positioned to shine down from above)
* **On:** checked
* **Intensity:** 25-35
* **Color:** White
* **Focus:** 69
* **Material:** 69
* **Ambience:** 8
* **Texture Channel:** None

Click OK to apply the filter.

(13) Now it's time to give the album a title. Select the Type tool and open the Character palette. Enter the following font settings:

* **Font:** Trajan
* **Style:** Bold
* **Font Size:** 36 pt
* **Leading:** 36 pt
* **Tracking:** 0
* **Vertical Scale:** 80%
* **Horizontal Scale:** 100%
* **Baseline Shift:** 0 pt
* **Color:** White

(14) Type **CIRCLE O' DETH** and center it just below the logo. Open the Warp tools for the text and select Arch as the Warp Style. Enter the following settings:

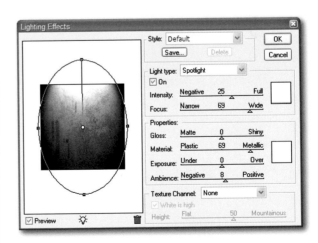

(17) Double-click the background layer to convert it to a standard layer. Choose Filter⇨Render⇨Lighting Effects again and use the same settings as before, only this time position the light so that it shines up from below.

A short recap

When you have a tough image to uphold, you need a tough CD cover. Let me add a disclaimer to this technique as I close: this was in no way intended to offend either burger lovers or those who use that other computer platform. Don't take this as an apology, however: rock and roll is all about bucking the system, anarchy, and conforming with the non-conformists. Oh yeah, it's also about generating wads o' cash for the rebels in the band. At least now you can capitalize along with them by designing their CDs. Rock on!

Look, Mom! The Thermometer Broke!

Most of the effects in this book have a practical application attached, but sometimes it is cool just to sit down and create effects for the sake of creating them. There are many varied ways to create metal effects, from the extremely simple brushed metal tutorials that dominate the Web to advanced chrome techniques. The process all depends on what you are trying to achieve and your knowledge of the software.

This technique shows that some effects, even as seemingly simple as metal text, can become quite involved before you get to a final result. You take plain old black text, liquify it, and turn it into something that could be mercury, dripped solder, or whatever your imagination decides that it is. You throw an actual photo in at the end, but this is simply for a background — everything else is from scratch.

THE PLAN

- Create spotty text on a white background
- Turn the text to liquid metal
- Add perspective to the type
- Place the text on a new background

(1) Create a new image and name it 'Liquid Metal Text.' Use the following settings for creating the new document:

- **Width:** 11 inches
- **Height:** 11 inches
- **Resolution:** 300 pixels/inch
- **Color Mode:** RGB, 8 bit
- **Background Contents:** White

Set the foreground color to R = 134, G = 133, and B = 133.

(2) Select the Type tool. Open the Character palette and use the following font settings. If you do not have this font installed, use one of your own choosing; something that appears drawn with a crayon will work fine.

- **Font:** WallowHmkBold (any drawn/crayon style font will work)
- **Style:** Regular
- **Font Size:** 250 pt
- **Leading:** 36 pt
- **Tracking:** 0
- **Vertical Scale:** 80%
- **Horizontal Scale:** 100%

- **Baseline Shift:** 0 pt
- **Color:** Gray (the foreground color)

(3) Type **LIQUID** in the center of the document. Rasterize the type. Select the Paintbrush tool and choose a round brush with the hardness set to 100. Paint a few additional dots around the text.

(4) Rather than jump straight to styles, the foundation of this effect resides in Channels. Choose the Channels palette and duplicate one of the channels — any one will do. Choose Image⇨Adjustments⇨Invert.

⑤ Choose Filter➪Blur➪Gaussian Blur. Blur the new channel with a Radius of 40 pixels. Blur it again, this time with a Radius of 20 pixels. Blur it one last time, this time with a Radius of 10 pixels.

Turn off the new channel. Don't delete it — you will need it shortly.

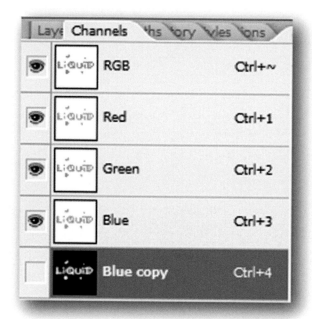

⑥ Duplicate the type layer. Choose Filter➪Render➪Lighting Effects. A dialog box tells you that the layer needs to be rasterized, and asks if you would like to do so. Click OK. Enter the following settings when the Lighting Effects dialog box appears:

* **Style:** Crossing — position the two lights so that their center points are angled from the right and left, overlapping in the middle
* **Light Type:** Spotlight
* **Intensity:** 28
* **Focus:** 69
* **Material:** 100 Metallic
* **Ambience:** 25
* **Texture Channel:** Blue copy (or the channel that you created and blurred)
* **White is High:** unchecked
* **Height:** 85

Click OK.

⑦ Choose Filter➪Sketch➪Chrome. Set the Detail to 1 and Smoothness to 10. Click OK.

Set the Blend Mode of the top layer to Overlay and opacity to 75%.

Command/Ctrl-click the top layer to generate a selection, and then create a Curves adjustment layer. Use the image below as a guide when creating the curve.

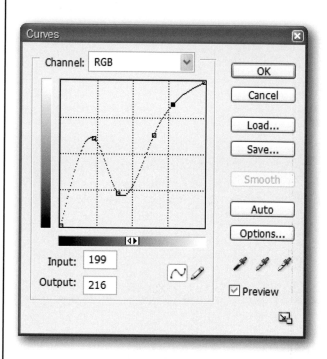

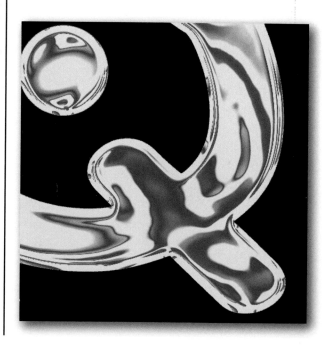

Create a Gradient Overlay adjustment layer. Create a gradient similar to the one used in the previous tutorial. If you saved it, then all the better — simply apply the varied-gray gradient here.

8 Create a new layer above the background and fill it with black. Turn the two background layers (black and white) off, and then choose Layer⇨Merge Visible.

9 Choose Filter⇨Artistic⇨Plastic Wrap. Use the following settings:

* **Highlight Strength:** 20
* **Detail:** 3
* **Smoothness:** 15

Click OK.

10 Duplicate the type layer and select the top version. Change the Blend Mode to Overlay. The detail is a bit sharp, so create another copy. Select the middle type layer, set the Blend Mode to Normal, and choose Filter⇨Blur⇨Gaussian Blur. Set the Radius of the blur to 10 pixels and click OK.

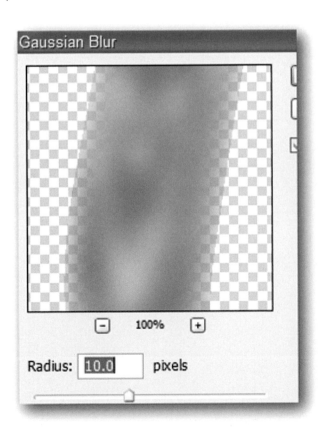

11 I mentioned that this was going to be an involved process, and I wasn't kidding! Now we get to Layer Styles once again. Open the Layer Styles dialog box and select Bevel/Emboss. Enter the following settings:

* **Style:** Inner Bevel
* **Technique:** Smooth
* **Depth:** 321%
* **Direction:** Up
* **Size:** 43 px
* **Soften:** 0 px
* **Angle:** 120 degrees
* **Use Global Light:** unchecked
* **Altitude:** 65 degrees
* **Gloss Contour:** Linear
* **Anti-aliased:** checked
* **Highlight Mode:** Screen
* **Highlight Color:** White
* **Highlight Opacity:** 75%
* **Shadow Mode:** Multiply
* **Shadow Color:** R = 163, G = 163, and B = 163
* **Shadow Opacity:** 75%

12 Open the Satin settings. Enter the following:

* **Blend Mode:** Soft Light
* **Opacity:** 50%
* **Angle:** 19 degrees
* **Distance:** 11 px
* **Size:** 14 px
* **Contour:** Default
* **Anti-aliased:** checked
* **Invert:** checked

13 Open the Color Overlay settings. Enter the following:

* **Blend Mode:** Multiply
* **Color:** R = 70, G = 70, and B = 70
* **Opacity:** 85%

Save the style and click OK.

14 Create a new Curves adjustment layer above the styled type layer. Generate a curve like the one shown in the example here. The resulting type should resemble the example — use this image to check your progress.

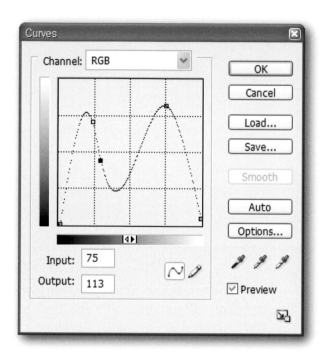

15 It's coming together now! However, it needs to be liquefied a bit. Create the selection again. Select the bottom type layer and choose Filter⇨Blur⇨Gaussian Blur. Enter a Blur Radius of 10 pixels and click OK.

16 Select the top type layer and apply a Gaussian Blur setting of 1 pixel to soften the reflections a bit. Click OK.

17 Merge all of the type layers together. Choose Filter⇨Liquify and select the Bloat tool, as shown on next page. Use a variety of brush sizes in the 200 to 300 range to bloat portions of the text, enhancing the liquid feel of the type. Once you are happy with the distortions, click OK.

18 Open the image steel-blue.jpg. Drag and drop the metal text into the steel-blue image. Duplicate the background layer. Choose Filter⇨Blur⇨Gaussian Blur and enter a Blur Radius of 20. Click OK.

19 Duplicate the blurred layer. Choose Filter⇨Distort⇨ Polar Coordinates. Select Polar to Rectangular and click OK. Set the Blend Mode to Overlay, and the opacity to 50%. This adds colored reflections to the face of the type.

20 Move the type layer beneath the distorted layer, and then choose Image⇨Adjustments⇨Brightness/ Contrast. Increase the contrast to +25 and click OK.

21 Generate a selection around the type, and create a Levels adjustment layer just above the text. Move the sliders closer together in the Histograms, lightening and darkening to obtain the result you want. Keep an eye on the text! When you like what you see (a liquid chrome is the idea), click OK.

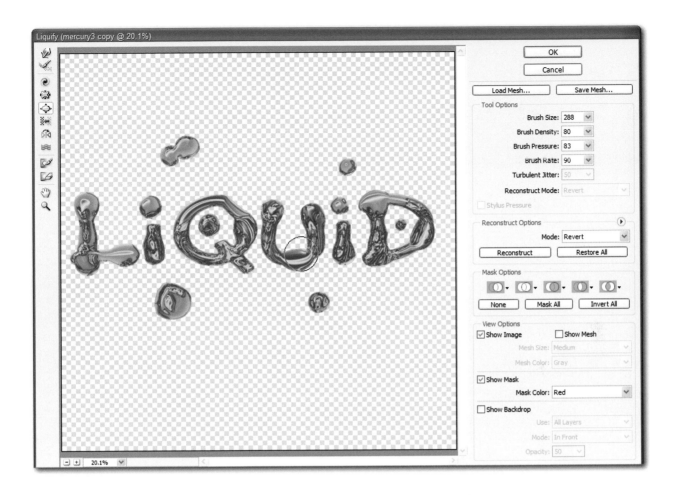

A short recap

That was quite a process, but well worth it. Working in Photoshop is in many ways like cooking: once you know what to expect from your spices, you can experiment with those that you think will work well together. Generating effects such as this is very similar. Although it is true that metal can be easy to replicate, it is when you want to assign specific characteristics to the metal (such as ultra-reflective liquid metal) that the process becomes more involved and intense. Ask a patron of any high-end restaurant and he or she will tell you that the time the chef spends on the dish is well worth it in the end.

Mess on the Driveway

I'll close this chapter with a variation on the liquid-chrome lettering that we created in the previous project. This time, however, the type takes on an entirely different quality. You still work with liquid text, but instead of metal, the word is written in oily water, or watery oil if you prefer.

THE PLAN

- Create text on a photo of pavement
- Distort the type
- Manipulate the text for a liquid effect

① Open the image pavement.jpg. Select the Type tool. Open the Character palettes and use the following font settings. If you do not have this font installed, then use one of your own choosing.

- * **Font:** WallowHmkBold (any thick, hand-drawn font will work)
- * **Style:** Regular
- * **Font Size:** 250 pt
- * **Leading:** 36 pt
- * **Tracking:** 0
- * **Vertical Scale:** 80%
- * **Horizontal Scale:** 100%
- * **Baseline Shift:** 0 pt
- * **Color:** Gray (the foreground color)

② Enter some text; any word will do. Open the Warp tools to the text and set the Style to Arc. Enter the following settings:

- * **Horizontal:** checked
- * **Bend:** -23%
- * **Horizontal Distortion:** 0
- * **Vertical Distortion:** +16

Click OK. Position the text around the bottom of the photo.

③ Open the Layer Styles for the text layer. Begin with the Drop Shadow settings:

- * **Blend Mode:** Color Burn
- * **Color:** Black
- * **Opacity:** 70%
- * **Angle:** 120 degrees
- * **Use Global Light:** unchecked
- * **Distance:** 5 px
- * **Spread:** 0%
- * **Size:** 95 px
- * **Contour:** Linear (default)
- * **Anti-aliased:** checked

④ Move on to the Inner Shadow settings:

- * **Blend Mode:** Multiply
- * **Color:** Black
- * **Opacity:** 75%
- * **Angle:** 30 degrees
- * **Use Global Light:** unchecked
- * **Distance:** 25 px
- * **Choke:** 0%
- * **Size:** 30 px
- * **Contour:** Linear
- * **Anti-aliased:** checked
- * **Noise:** 0%

5 Select the Inner Glow settings. Enter the following:

* **Blend Mode:** Color Burn
* **Opacity:** 50%
* **Color:** #333333
* **Technique:** Softer
* **Source:** Edge
* **Choke:** 0%
* **Size:** 29 px
* **Contour:** Linear
* **Anti-aliased:** checked
* **Range:** 50%
* **Jitter:** 0%

6 Select the Bevel/Emboss settings. Enter the following:

* **Style:** Inner Bevel
* **Technique:** Smooth
* **Depth:** 230%
* **Direction:** Up
* **Size:** 24 px
* **Soften:** 0 px
* **Angle:** 120 degrees
* **Use Global Light:** unchecked
* **Altitude:** 70 degrees
* **Gloss Contour:** Linear
* **Anti-aliased:** checked
* **Highlight Mode:** Screen
* **Highlight Color:** White
* **Highlight Opacity:** 100%
* **Shadow Mode:** Screen
* **Shadow Color:** R = 186, G = 124, and B = 43
* **Shadow Opacity:** 75%

7 Choose Color Overlay. Enter the following:

* **Blend Mode:** Overlay
* **Color:** Gray (#999999)
* **Opacity:** 100%

8 Choose Gradient Overlay. Create a gradient that goes from dark gray to lighter gray and back to dark gray.

Set the Gradient Overlay options as follows:

* **Blend Mode:** Normal
* **Opacity:** 80%
* **Reverse:** checked
* **Style:** Linear
* **Angle:** 90 degrees
* **Scale:** 100%

9 Save the Layer Style and click OK. Duplicate the type layer. Create a new layer beneath the top layer and select the top layer. Choose Layer⇨Merge Down to collapse the style and retain the effect. Set the Opacity and Fill for both type layers to 80% each. Reselect the top layer.

10 Let's make some liquid. Choose Filter⇨Sketch⇨ Chrome. Set the Detail to 4 and the Smoothness to 2, and click OK.

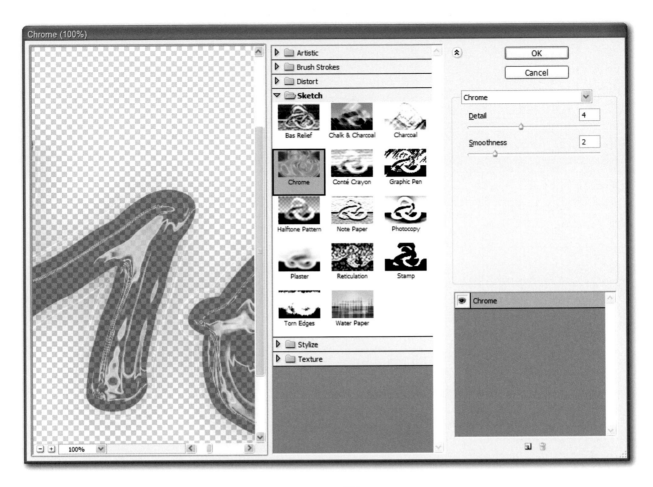

11 Open the image sunset.jpg. Copy and paste the sunset photo into a new layer above the type, and move it so that the bright horizon rests over the letters. Command/Ctrl-click the type layer, choose Select➪Inverse, and delete the extra portions of the sunset layer that are not immediately over the type. Set the Blend Mode of the sunset layer to Overlay. Change the opacity of the type layer below the sunset layer to 75%.

12 With the type layer selected, choose Filter➪Liquify. As with the previous tutorial, use the Bloat tool to expand areas of text, bloating these areas and giving the text a "spreading liquid" look. Save the mesh on the right side before accepting, and then click OK.

13 Select the top layer and again choose Filter⇨Liquify. This time, simply load the mesh that you saved; the type expands to match the previous layer. Click OK.

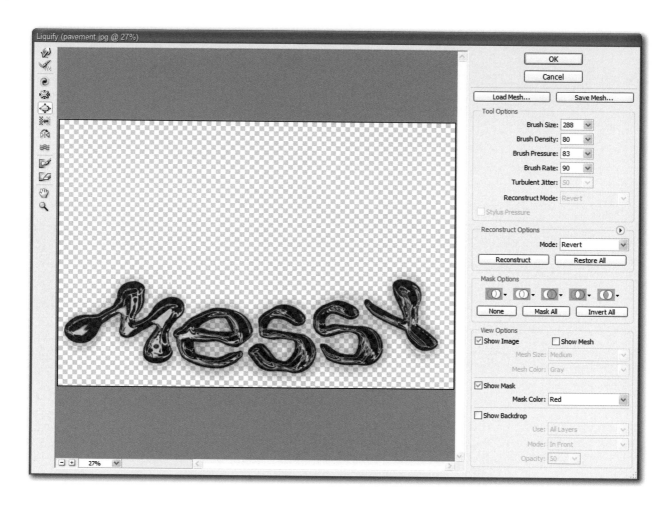

A short recap

You can often generate entirely different type effects by manipulating a few settings. Although they may look starkly different, the processes to achieve them are strikingly similar. This effect was fairly simple when compared to that of liquid metal, and as to whether it looks like watery oil, oily water, or neither, I'll let you be the judge. This is one of the few effects in the book that is a direct offshoot of another effect, but you can apply the same principle to almost, if not all, the techniques that you see here. Experiment and see what variations you can come up with — you may surprise yourself!

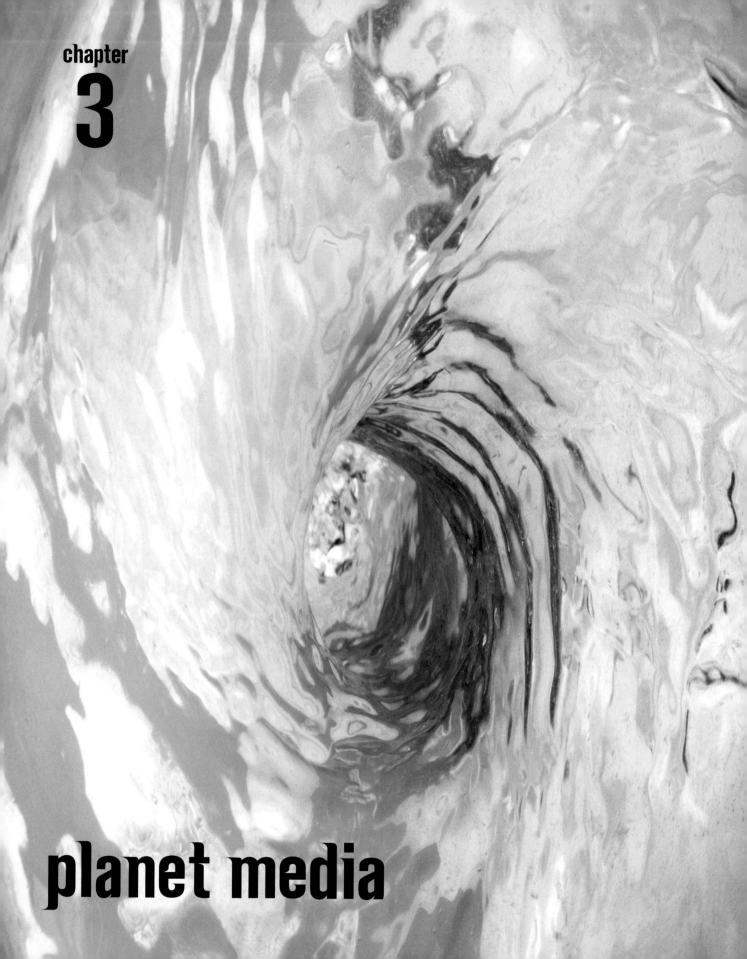

planet media

Photoshop has done wonders for the various forms of media around us. From standard newspapers dressing up their advertisements with 3D font effects to splashy Web-style designer screens on news stations, Photoshop is everywhere. When you combine it with programs such as Adobe After Effects, Photoshop typography can really shine via animation. This chapter demonstrates a few techniques that show various ways in which you can use Photoshop to reflect the media genre. You can create a newspaper from scratch, bring the news of the day to the masses with your own cable channel, design a logo for a new broadcast giant, and bring some not-so-good weather news to a nervous public. You can even deliver bad news with flair when Photoshop is at the helm.

Create the Headlines

A popular effect among digital scrapbookers is to make digital photo albums appear as though they have been printed as a newspaper, complete with photos, date, and so forth. What can be tricky is finding a photo of a newspaper to which they can apply their images and text. This technique eliminates that frustration by creating the newspaper itself, and then applying the images and text.

THE PLAN

- Create a textured newspaper background
- Add photos, headlines, and text
- Blend the type and photos to appear realistically printed on the paper

1 Create a new image using the dimensions of a standard newspaper. Our local paper is cut 12 inches wide by 22.5 inches high, and so I am using these dimensions as the model when setting up this document. Choose File⇨New and create the following document:

- ✳ **Width:** 12 inches
- ✳ **Height:** 22.5 inches
- ✳ **Resolution:** 300 pixels/inch
- ✳ **Color Mode:** RGB, 8 bit
- ✳ **Background Contents:** White

2 Create a new layer. Set the foreground color to R = 207, G = 204, and B = 194. Fill the new layer with the foreground color.

3 Select the Dodge tool. In the Options bar, enter the following characteristics for the tool:

- ✳ **Brush:** Feathered, Round
- ✳ **Brush Size:** 1500
- ✳ **Range:** Highlights
- ✳ **Exposure:** 24%

4 Lighten two areas on either side of the page vertically. Begin on the left side at the top. Hold down the Shift key and click at the top of the page. Move the brush to the bottom of the page and click again. This lightens a strip the length of the page. Move to the top right and repeat the process, but angle this lightened area slightly.

5 Press the D key to ensure that white is the background color, and choose Image⇨Canvas Size. The canvas needs to be larger in order to work on the edges of the paper and give them that real-world feel. Increase the canvas size 120% both in width and height.

6 Create a new layer above the background and fill it with black. This helps to distinguish the edges of the paper for this step. Click on the paper layer and select the Polygonal Lasso tool. Using very short strokes, create a jagged selection along the top of the paper. These need to be very small to replicate the perforation along the edges of an actual newspaper. You may opt to select a short area, delete the selection, and then move the selection farther along the edge until you have cut the width of the paper.

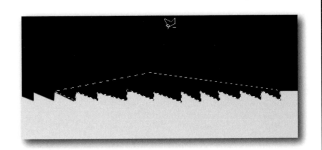

10 To help emphasize the header, create a new layer and select the Rectangular Marquee tool. Set the foreground color to dark red, dark blue, dark green — your choice. Create a thin bar selection running across the page, a quarter inch from either side and roughly two inches from the top. Fill the selection with the foreground color. You may now use the Move tool on the type layer to position the text slightly above the bar.

7 Command/Ctrl-click the paper layer. The Add Noise filter adds that grainy, textured feel to the image. Choose Filter⇨Noise⇨Add Noise. Use the following settings in the Add Noise dialog box:

* **Amount:** 15%
* **Distribution:** Uniform
* **Monochromatic:** checked

Click OK.

8 Duplicate the paper layer and choose Image⇨Adjustments⇨Hue/Saturation. Reduce the saturation in the layer to -50% and click OK. This adds a touch of gray to the cream tone of the paper, but still retains the overall cream cast.

9 With the basic structure of the paper created and textured, the layout, photo, and text application process can begin. Think of this as being an actual newspaper in all of these regards. The effect must mimic not only the layout, but also how the ink plays on the texture. The headline is a good place to start. Select the Type tool. Open the Character palette and set up the font as follows:

* **Font:** Times New Roman
* **Font Size:** 120 pt
* **Leading:** 36 pt
* **Tracking:** 0
* **Vertical Scaling:** 140%
* **Horizontal Scaling:** 80%
* **Color:** Black

Beginning about an inch from the top and left side, type the name of your paper. For this example, the paper is titled *CITY EXAMINER*, a good, generic name with that hometown feel.

11 Select the Type tool again and click on the title layer. Select 'Examiner' and change it to italics in the Character palette. Select 'ity' and reduce the size of the font to 100 pts, then select 'xaminer' and do the same. The idea is for the beginning letter of each title word to be larger than the rest, thus adding further character to the title.

12 Open the image graph.jpg. This photo can serve to alert the reader to additional content inside the pseudo paper. Select the photo, copy it, and paste it into the newspaper document. Choose Edit⇨Transform⇨Scale and reduce the size of the image so that it appears about two inches wide in relation to the paper.

13 Move the image above the bar to the upper-left corner. Change the Blend mode of the layer to Multiply, and reduce the opacity to 80% to allow the grain of the paper to show through. You may have to select the title layer and move it to the right to accommodate the photo.

14 Create a new type layer, again using Times New Roman. Reduce the font size to 14 pt and, using all capital letters, add an article title and page location to accompany the photo. Use italics for the page location. Place the text just above the photo.

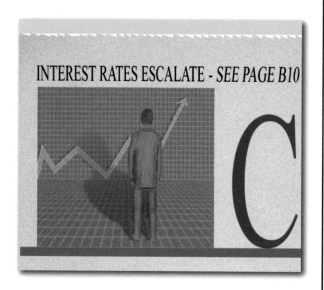

15 Ensure that the rulers are turned on, and bring a guide down from the top. Line it up just beneath the text on the left side of the page. Create a new type layer and enter a date on the right side of the page.

16 The layout of the paper is very important. Everything should be scaled into single columns, or multiples of columns. Drag three guides from the left ruler, and divide the paper into four vertical columns to help in laying out the page.

TIP

For headlines, switch to Arial Bold or other dynamic font, and connect the headline to a photo.

17 Now all you need are articles, either fake or real. For this example, I am simply adding text from an article that I wrote years ago, and using it to fill out the page in a four-column format. Stick with the Times New Roman font (or other font in the Roman family) when creating your smaller articles. Typically the title of the article is in capital letters, the name of the reporter in slightly smaller italics, and the article itself in standard paragraph format. Use text boxes to keep the articles within the column boundaries and away from the edge of the page.

18 Once you have all of your images, tiles, and text in place, be sure to set ALL type and photo layers to Multiply and reduce the opacity of each to 80%. Add a drop shadow via Layer Styles to the paper layer, fill the background with a light color and your newspaper is complete!

A short recap

This tutorial focuses primarily on the foundation of the paper, type, and photo layouts, rather than telling you what to enter for your article. Use your imagination! Articles from history, funny stories that you copy and paste from the Web, or even recipes can work. If you have the time and imagination, you may even want to write your own articles.

No News Is Bad News

If you watch any of the cable news channels these days, you have to ask who is influencing whom – does television take its graphics cue from the Web or is it the other way around? For years, television graphics were pretty stale, but specialty news channels took a turn in their packaging about ten years ago, giving their look a decidedly Web-like overhaul.

This technique creates a still shot of a fake news program. You have a host, an interviewee, technical backdrop, channel logo, and splashy header to get the attention of passing channel surfers. If you can't attract a bee with pure vinegar, try adding a little visual honey.

THE PLAN

- Create a collage of photos to reflect a news-channel debate show
- Add newsticker information
- Make a dynamic header to grab the attention of channel surfers

① Create a new image and name it **News Logo**. This design is actually incorporated into the next two techniques, and so you need to save it in three ways: as a brush, as a custom shape, and as a pattern. But first you need to design it. Set up the new image with the following settings:

- **Name:** News Logo
- **Width:** 10 inches
- **Height:** 10 inches
- **Resolution:** 300 pixels/inch
- **Color Mode:** RGB, 8 bit
- **Background Contents:** White

Click OK.

② Select the Custom Shape tool. From the Shapes menu, load the set Animals. Select the shape Dog Print from the group. Create a new layer and press the D key. In the Options bar, click on the Fill Pixels icon (third from the left) and draw the paw shape across most of the layer, leaving some room on all four sides. Holding down the Shift key will help constrain the proportions of the shape as it is being drawn.

③ Select the Type tool and open the Character palette. Set up the font for the logo as follows:

- **Font:** Broadway BT
- **Font Size:** 150 pt

- * **Leading:** 18 pt
- * **Tracking:** 0
- * **Vertical Scaling:** 100%
- * **Horizontal Scaling:** 80%
- * **Color:** Black

④ Create a type layer and type **DAWG** below the paw print. Choose Layer⇨Rasterize⇨Type, and then choose Layer⇨Merge Down to merge the shape layer and type layer together.

TIP

Before you can define the logo as a brush, it needs to fall under the brush size rule: the longest side can be no greater than 2500 pixels. Any larger and the Define Brush option won't be available.

(5) Because you don't need the extra white space, choose Image⇨Trim. Check Top Left Pixel Color and trim away the white from all four sides. Click OK.

(6) Choose Image⇨Image Size and select Constrain Proportions. Change the wider dimension (more likely the height) to 2500 pixels and click OK.

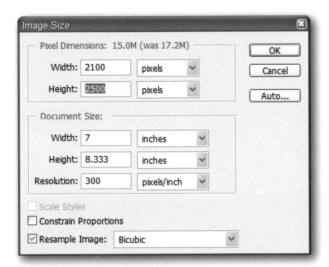

(7) Choose Edit⇨Define Brush Preset. Name the brush, click OK, and then save the brush set. You may opt to delete the other brushes in the set first, as outlined earlier in this book.

(8) Next choose Edit⇨Define Pattern. Name the pattern and save it. Again, you may want to delete the other patterns in the presets before saving the new pattern to its own set.

(9) To save the logo as a shape, Command/Ctrl-click the layer to generate a selection. Go to the Paths palette. On the bottom of the palette, click the "Make work path from selection" icon. Then choose Edit⇨Define Custom Shape. Again, save the shape to its own set for future use.

(10) For the creation of the actual video display, start by opening the images techsquares.jpg and newsman.jpg.

11 Copy and paste the newsman image into a new layer in the techsquares photo. Choose Edit⇨Transform⇨ Scale and reduce the size of the layer so that you can place the newsman on the right side of the screen with some room above, below, and to the right, with a large open area to the left.

12 Create a mask for the newsman layer. Press the D key to reset the foreground and background colors, and select the Gradient tool. Mask the bottom edge of the layer with a white-to-black gradient to allow the background to bleed through the lowest regions, but leaving the majority of the layer fully visible.

13 Make a new layer and select the Custom Shape tool. Set black as the foreground color and select the logo shape. Click on the Fill Pixels button in the Options bar, then draw the shape in the new layer in the lower-right corner. Change the Blend mode of the logo layer to Screen and the opacity to 50%. Open the Layer Styles and select Color Overlay. Change the color to white and click OK.

14 Open the images doctor.jpg and xray.jpg. Copy and paste each into the techsquares.jpg document. Resize each and place them on the left side of the image, with the doctor above the x-ray. The doctor serves as the man being interviewed (in mid-denial, it appears), and the x-ray simply adds a bit of drama to the image. Create a mask on the x-ray layer, and paint with black along the top and bottom edges of the image so that they fade into the background.

15 If you want to blend the x-ray further, either paint with gray in the mask over the image, or simply change the Blend mode or opacity until you get a mix with which you are happy.

16 Create a new layer and name it **Scroll Text Bar**. At the bottom of the image, use the Rectangular Marquee tool to make a rectangular selection that leaves some space along the bottom but runs the width of the image. Fill the selection with black. Set the opacity of the new layer to 40%.

17 Select the Type tool and set the following attributes in the Character palette:

* **Font:** Verdana
* **Font Size:** 24 pt
* **Leading:** 18 pt
* **Tracking:** 0
* **Vertical Scaling:** 100%
* **Horizontal Scaling:** 80%
* **Color:** White
* **Style:** Italic

18 Type a message over the black area that you want to scroll across the screen. I'm using "SPECIAL REPORT---Top Doc Disputes Smoking Dangers."

19 Return to the Character palette and set up a new font as follows:

* **Font:** Arial Black
* **Font Size:** 60 pt
* **Leading:** 18 pt
* **Tracking:** 0
* **Vertical Scaling:** 100%
* **Horizontal Scaling:** 80%
* **Color:** White
* **Style:** Italic

20 At the top of the screen, type **BREAKING NEWS** and center it above the photos. Reposition the image layers as needed so that they do not extend all the way to the top of the screen.

21 It's time to add some shine to the big, bold letters at the top of the screen, but let's go about it a bit differently. Instead of building the effect from scratch, select the Actions palette and open the palette menu. Select Load Actions from the list, and navigate to the Chapter 3 Presets folder on the CD. Load the Action set called CS2-MetalTypeFX-070906-01.atn. Open the set and select AFX-ReflectMetal-01. Click Play and follow the directions given in the action. When asked to enter your text, type **BREAKING NEWS**, using the same font as the image.

22 Once the action runs to completion, turn off the background layer in the new text document. Choose Layer⇨Merge Visible, and then move the merged layer to the TV screen image. Use the transform tools (Edit⇨Transform⇨Scale gives the best result) and resize the metal type so that it is the same size as the white text. Position the metal type over the white text, leaving the white exposed slightly on the top and left.

(23) At the top of the Layers palette, create a Levels adjustment layer and move the center slider to the right, darkening the image a bit. Click OK. Select the mask for the adjustment layer and choose Filter⇨Sketch⇨ Halftone Pattern. Use the following settings:

* **Size:** 2
* **Contrast:** 50
* **Pattern Type:** Line

Click OK. The result of running the filter on the adjustment layer gives a scan-lines effect that is many times easier than creating it from scratch in older versions of Photoshop.

A short recap

Okay, so not many modern televisions suffer from scan lines. However, their addition does add to the illusion, and so I included them in this tutorial. Even television isn't safe from the Photoshop-savvy designer. Dynamic color, stark images, and bold, shiny text all contribute to the drama, even when the content of the show is questionable in entertainment value.

What's on the Tube?

It seems that every network now has multiple divisions and stations: broadcast stations that are usually locally based and free to the public, news-specific stations with their corporate stamp, and movie channels that require basic cable at a minimum. Continuing with the theme that we created with the logo in the previous tutorial, let's expand on that idea and give the network a flashy logo to appear in their advertising or at the end of their standard programming. Think of a certain peacock...

THE PLAN

- Design a metallic border for the channel's logo
- Add colorful, glossy elements and text

① Create a new image with the following attributes:

- ✳ **Name:** Bold Logo
- ✳ **Width:** 10 inches
- ✳ **Height:** 10 inches
- ✳ **Resolution:** 300 pixels/inch
- ✳ **Color Mode:** RGB, 8 bit
- ✳ **Background Contents:** White

② Select the Custom Shape tool. From the Shapes menu, load the set that you created in the last tutorial if it isn't loaded already. Select the logo shape that you created in the last tutorial. Create a new layer and press the D key. In the Options bar, click on the Fill Pixels icon and draw the logo shape across most of the layer, leaving some room on all four sides.

③ Command/Ctrl-click the shape layer to generate a selection. Choose Select⇨Modify⇨Contract. Reduce the size of the selection by 16 pixels. Choose Layer⇨New⇨ Layer via Copy. Turn the new layer off for a minute by clicking the small eye to the left of the layer. Turning this off renders the layer invisible. Select the original shape layer. Reselect it and click on the Gradient tool. Open the Gradient Editor by clicking on the gradient window in the Options bar. Create a gradient of alternating light-and-dark grays. Use the image here as a guide. Click OK once you create the gradient.

④ In the Options bar, click the Linear Gradient icon (first on the left). Set the Blend mode to Difference. Draw the gradient over the selected area several times from different angles and varied starting points. This creates a rippled metal pattern over the shape.

⑤ Increase the contrast of the metal by choosing Image⇨Adjustments⇨Curves. Create a curve roughly the shape of a sine wave, as shown in the example here. Click OK.

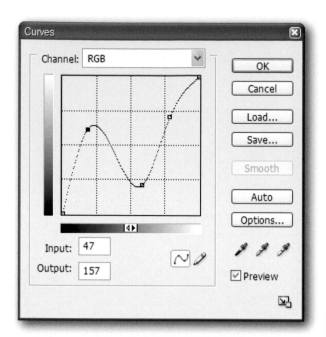

7 Now choose Filter⇨Render⇨Lighting Effects. Use a single spotlight and center it above the middle. You may use the default settings for the most part, but move the Material slider to 100 Metallic and set the Texture channel to Layer 1 Transparency or any of the channels that make the paw stand out from the background in the viewer window. Use the image here as a guide while setting up the effect. Once you are done, click OK.

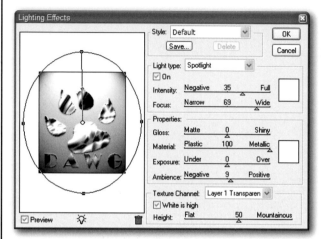

6 A final touch for the metal layer is to bring it out from the background just a bit, and you can do this in a couple of ways. This step combines these methods to add extra shine to what will be the border around the pads of the paw. Starting with Layer Styles, open the Bevel and Emboss settings. Set the following attributes for the style:

* **Style:** Inner Bevel
* **Technique:** Smooth
* **Depth:** 680%
* **Direction:** Up
* **Size:** 1 px
* **Soften:** 1 px
* **Angle:** 120 degrees
* **Use Global Light:** unchecked
* **Altitude:** 25 degrees
* **Gloss Contour:** Linear (default)
* **Anti-aliased:** checked
* **Highlight Mode:** Screen, White
* **Opacity:** 84%
* **Shadow Mode:** Multiply, Black
* **Opacity:** 75%

Save the style or simply click OK.

8 To add color and depth to the pads on the paw, you need to isolate each of the toes and the palm (if it can be called that) from one another on separate layers. If all were to be the same color, depth, and so on, this would not be the case, but as each will have its own distinctive color coupled with beveling and reflections, separating them is the way to go.

9 Go to the Layer Styles palette and delete all of the styles except for the Blank style (if it resides in the palette). Turn the topmost paw layer back on in the Layers palette. Using one of the selection tools (the Polygonal Lasso tool works well here), select the pad on the top left. Choose Layer➪New➪Layer via Cut, placing that toe in its own layer. Fill the background layer with black.

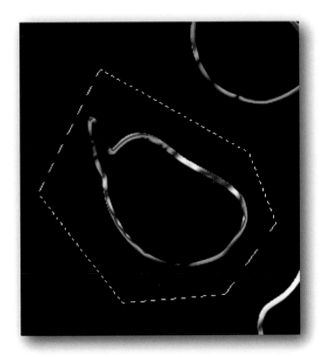

10 Repeat this process for each element in that layer, including the individual letters. Name each layer so that you can keep track of where each one falls in the layer stack.

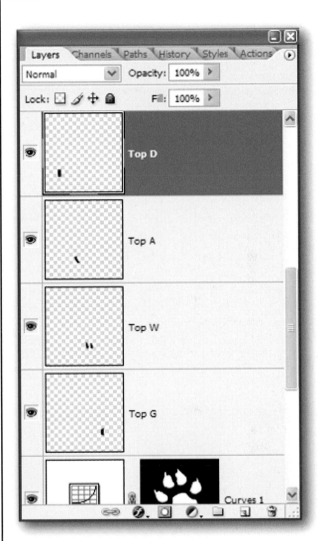

11 To create the glossy colored effects for each of the foreground logo elements, Layer Styles again serves the purpose. The foundational style settings (bevel and basic structure settings) are the same for each layer for continuity purposes. You must change the color for each, and so you need to save each variation as its own style for later use and application.

(12) Select the first toe layer (upper left). Open the Layer Styles for this layer and select the Bevel and Emboss settings. Enter the following attributes:

* **Style:** Inner Bevel
* **Technique:** Smooth
* **Depth:** 200-205%
* **Direction:** Up
* **Size:** 65 px
* **Soften:** 8 px
* **Angle:** 120 degrees
* **Altitude:** 70 degrees
* **Use Global Light:** unchecked
* **Gloss Contour:** Linear (default)
* **Anti-aliased:** checked
* **Highlight Mode:** Screen, White
* **Opacity:** 84%
* **Shadow Mode:** Screen, White
* **Opacity:** 33%

(13) The first toe is going to be blue and will carry varying depths of color to add to the illusion of plastic or semi-transparency. Select Inner Glow and enter the following settings:

* **Blend Mode:** Multiply
* **Opacity:** 75%
* **Noise:** 0%
* **Color:** R = 63, G = 75, and B = 115
* **Technique:** Softer
* **Source:** Edge
* **Choke:** 0%
* **Size:** 170 px
* **Contour:** Linear (default)
* **Anti-aliased:** checked
* **Range:** 50%
* **Jitter:** 0%

(14) Select Color Overlay. Enter the following settings:

* **Blend Mode:** Multiply
* **Color:** R = 18, G = 152, and B= 246
* **Opacity:** 100%

(15) Select Gradient Overlay. Set the Blend mode to Normal. Create a new gradient using the Inner Glow color and the Color Overlay color that you entered in the previous steps. Add a white color stop in the center of the gradient. Save the gradient. Set the Gradient Type to Radial.

(16) Before quitting the styles for this layer, save the Layer Style. Click New Style and name it BlueGloss. Click OK and then click OK again to exit the styles and apply them to the text.

(17) Select the second toe layer and again open the Layer Styles. Select Color Overlay and change the color to R = 246, G = 18, and B = 34.

(18) You may also opt to replace the blue tones in the gradient overlay to red and pink hues, respectively. Again, save the style (RedGloss) in the same set before accepting it.

19 Repeat the process for the other two toes and the palm, but alter the color overlay and gradient overlay for each. Use green for the third toe and purple for the fourth for a mixture of hues. For the palm, alter the gradient overlay to something with a lot of variety, such as the 'Yellow, Violet, Orange, Blue' gradient in the default gradient set. Save each of the styles as you alter the color.

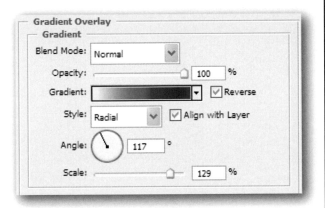

20 Now apply the saved styles that you used for the toes to the letters, only in reverse order. When you are done, you now have your logo, complete with metallic edging.

21 By coupling it with a curved horizon-style effect and the reflection technique from Chapter 1, you can use the new station's logo to endorse all of your great evening breakout hits.

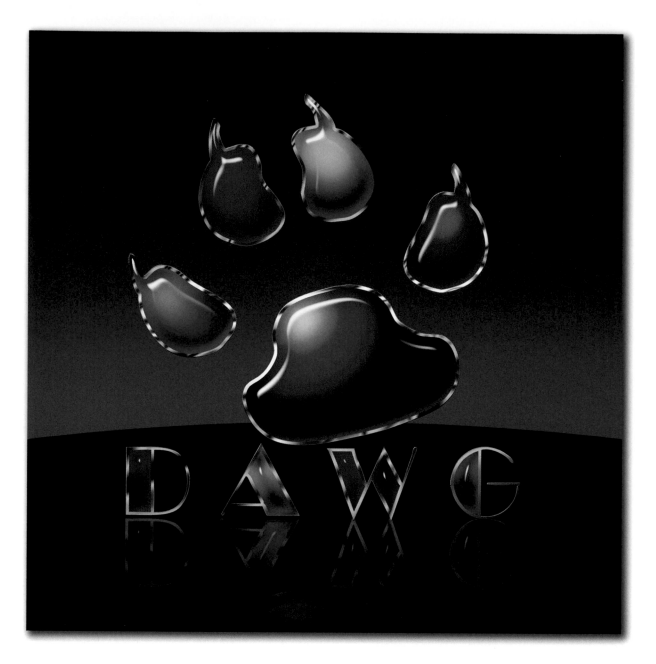

A short recap

We ventured into Layer Styles again this time around, but we coupled variations on the same style with a metallic border. The quality of any type effect resides mainly in the details — could this exist in the real world? The logo here was intended to live only in the digital world, but it still has the illusion of depth. Whether real or not, it attracts the eye with vibrant color and applies it to what the station hopes will become a brand logo that survives for decades.

Weather Woes

As I write this, the Northern Hemisphere is going through what some scientists are calling the warmest summer in recorded history. It definitely seems to be the warmest in my memory. Living in the northwest, we frequently suffer from cooler temperatures than the rest of the nation. For this technique I'm going to turn the tables a bit and create a TV still of a local weather broadcast with the weather turning favorable in my area for a change. Elements from the previous tutorials come into play, with the addition of a transparent PNG file and a couple of other Photoshop tricks. The idea isn't the similarity of these effects to others in the book, but rather how you can apply similar effects in other ways.

THE PLAN

- Add a weather reporter to a mapped 'green-screen' background
- Plug in vector weather icons
- Color the map to reflect temperature ranges
- Create bold, styled temperatures
- Add the station's logo and additional information

(1) Open the images USAMap.jpg and weatherman.png. As the weatherman image is a transparent PNG file, it doesn't require any extractions to separate the man from the background. Simply drag the man into the map image.

(2) Choose Edit⇨Transform⇨Scale and use the scale settings in the Options bar to resize the weatherman. Set both the height and width of the man's layer to 50%. Accept the transformation and reposition him on the left side of the screen.

(3) Open the image weather_elements.eps. This file contains a number of forecast symbols, ranging from a bright sunny day to a midwinter snowstorm. As this is a vector image file, Photoshop asks to rasterize the image before opening it. Click OK, and then select the Rectangular Marquee tool. Make a selection around the sun symbol and hit Command/Ctrl+C to copy it. Return to the weather-map image and paste (Command/Ctrl+V) the sun symbol into a new layer between the map layer and the weather reporter's layer. Resize the layer with the Transform tools again, and position the sun somewhere over the map. Repeat this process with a couple of other weather symbols, moving them to various parts of the country. As I live in the northern Rockies, I could use a little sunshine, and so the northwest is going to be quite a bit warmer than the rest of the country for a change.

(4) As new programs frequently do, you can use color to indicate temperature. Create a new layer just above the background and beneath the weatherman layer. Set the Blend mode to Color. Click the foreground color and enter

NOTE

The PNG format was created as a replacement for GIF when displaying images on the Web. Although not all browsers support it, more are picking it up every day. PNG offers lossless compression for better display and for quicker Web viewing, without the jagged edges associated with those pesky transparent GIF files. PNG also supports 24-bit images; a distinction that the GIF format does not have. The PNG format supports RGB, Indexed Color, Grayscale, and Bitmap mode images without alpha channels, and preserves transparency in grayscale and RGB images. PNG is also patent-free, making it a great alternative to GIF.

the settings R = 242, G = 125, and B = 55 to place orange in the foreground.

5 Select the Paintbrush tool. Using a feathered, round brush, apply some paint to the new layer over the northwestern states (or over the area where you placed the sun symbol).

6 Change the foreground color to something in the bright-yellow range, and paint over the south-central states. Cover a few states in each color application. Change the foreground to turquoise and paint over the southeastern states.

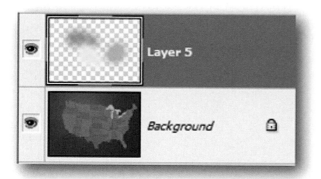

7 Select the sun symbol's layer and open the Layer Styles. Select Outer Glow and enter the following settings:

* **Blend Mode:** Screen
* **Opacity:** 75%
* **Noise:** 0%
* **Color:** R = 254, G = 254, and B = 30

Click OK.

8 The glow suffices for the sun symbol. The symbols with the clouds, however, would benefit from some shading. Select one of the symbols with clouds and open the Styles. Go to Drop Shadow and enter the following:

* **Blend Mode:** Multiply
* **Color:** Black
* **Opacity:** 100%
* **Angle:** 120 degrees
* **Use Global Light:** unchecked
* **Distance:** 20 px
* **Spread:** 0%
* **Size:** 5 px
* **Contour:** Linear (default)
* **Anti-aliased:** checked
* **Noise:** 0%

9 Save the style, and then click OK. Apply this style to each symbol that has clouds attached.

10 Select the Type tool. Open the Character palette and set up the font as follows:

* **Font:** Arial Black
* **Font Size:** 36 pt
* **Leading:** 18 pt
* **Tracking:** 0
* **Vertical Scale:** 100%
* **Horizontal Scale:** 80%
* **Baseline Shift:** 0 pt
* **Color:** Black
* **Faux Italic**
* **Anti-aliasing method:** Smooth

11 Type a temperature somewhere over the sunny portion of the map. The effect used to embolden the type is a variation on those that you created for the logo tutorial. Open the Layer Styles for the new temperature layer. Beginning with Bevel and Emboss, enter the following settings:

* **Style:** Inner Bevel
* **Technique:** Smooth
* **Depth:** 111%
* **Direction:** Up
* **Size:** 3 px
* **Soften:** 0 px
* **Angle:** 120 degrees
* **Use Global Light:** unchecked
* **Altitude:** 70 degrees
* **Gloss Contour:** Linear (default)
* **Anti-aliased:** checked
* **Highlight Mode:** Screen
* **Color:** White
* **Opacity:** 100%
* **Shadow Mode:** Screen
* **Color:** White
* **Opacity:** 33%

Select Color Overlay. Enter the following settings:

* **Blend Mode:** Multiply
* **Color:** R = 254, G = 254, and B = 87
* **Opacity:** 100%

12 Select Gradient Overlay. Create a gradient that spans dark red to white to pink, as in the following example:

* **Blend Mode:** Normal
* **Opacity:** 100%
* **Gradient:** Custom

* **Reverse:** checked
* **Style:** Radial
* **Align with Layer:** checked
* **Angle:** 120 degrees
* **Scale:** 130%

13 To help the temperature stand out from the background, a stroke application does wonders. Open the Stroke settings and enter the following:

* **Size:** 2 px
* **Position:** Outside
* **Blend Mode:** Normal
* **Opacity:** 100%
* **Fill Type:** Color
* **Color:** Black

14 Lastly, add a drop shadow. Open the Drop Shadow settings and enter the following:

* **Blend Mode:** Multiply
* **Color:** Black, 100%
* **Angle:** 120 degrees
* **Use Global Light:** unchecked
* **Distance:** 8 px
* **Spread:** 0%
* **Size:** 0 px
* **Contour:** Linear (default)
* **Anti-aliased:** checked
* **Noise:** 0%

15 Save the style. Add a few more temperatures of varying degrees and place them around the map. Apply the same layer style as the original temperature, but open the Color Overlay for each and change to green, blue, or another hue to vary the tone with temperature. If you would like to use these later, save each style as you alter it — don't forget to save the set!

16 Add some lines of text (for example, Partly Cloudy) on their own layers, and place them next to the areas that they describe. Use the same layer style for each line of text as you applied to the temperature that it sits next to.

17 Set the foreground color to white. Load the Bold Logo brush set that you created earlier in this chapter, and then select the Bold Logo brush. Create a new layer at the top of the layer stack and set the Blend mode to either Screen or Soft Light. Set the brush size to 175 pixels and paint the logo into the lower-left corner of the layer. You can reduce the opacity of the layer if it appears too bright for your taste; subtlety is the key.

18 Select the Type tool again, and create a new type layer in the upper-right area of the document. Use the same settings as the temperatures. Enter **'Storm Team Weather'**. Next, highlight each of the first letters and increase their size to nearly double that of the original text.

19 Apply the layer style that you used for the Hot temperature. A slight alteration of the gradient creates a sunset-style effect. Once you apply the style, double-click it in the palette and select Gradient Overlay. Change the Gradient Type to Linear. Alter the gradient's colors so that the left side is yellow.

20 Change the angle to 90 degrees. Save the layer style and click OK.

21 For a bit of splash, add some warp to the new text. Open the type layer Warp tools and select Arc Upper. Enter the following settings:

* **Horizontal:** checked
* **Bend:** 18%
* **Horizontal Distortion:** -15%
* **Vertical Distortion:** 0%

Click OK.

The final image shows a smarmy, newbie weatherman, something that our local stations seem to cycle through frequently. You know the type: those who are more concerned with how they look on television than with what they are reporting.

A short recap

This chapter was jam-packed with layer style variations, blending mode alterations, and type versus photo positioning. As I mentioned before, the focus wasn't so much on the variety of effects, but rather on how similar effects play differently on varied collage types. Although the images used here are provided on the CD, I encourage you to experiment with your own photos. I think you will find the results far more satisfying.

beyond these four walls

Up to this point, the book has focused mainly on type treatments that you would find in the home. Once you leave the front step, you are inundated with logos, messages, signs, billboards, advertisements – you simply can't get away from them. Even here in the Rockies, deep in the woods, you find that someone there before you had some message to convey, whether it is forest fire prevention posters or "No Access" signs.

This chapter takes you for a drive around the neighborhood. You slap an embedded logo on tires, advertise on a blimp, and create a billboard that uses shock value to get its point across. You also paint with light, chisel stone, advertise a business in a strip mall, and add chrome to a car. Let's get out of the house for awhile and see what the world has to say.

Burn Rubber

This technique imprints a logo into the sidewall of a tire. Using a path, some bold text, and a layer style adjustment, you quickly imprint a brand name in the rubber. Stay tuned, because later in the chapter you'll see what happens when the brand becomes popular and takes its advertisements to the extreme.

THE PLAN

- Use a path to curve a brand name on a sidewall tire
- Embed the text into the tire
- Blend it for a real-world feel

① Open the image tire.jpg. Notice that rather than a straight-shot photograph, the tire is angled so that the type won't be applied to a simple round path: the path in this case needs to be warped a bit or the text appears out of place.

② Select the Pen tool. Click the Paths button in the Options bar and select the standard Pen tool option (rather than the Freeform pen). Create a new layer in the Layers palette.

③ Click on a point in the center of the black area of the tire, on the left-hand side of the image. Think of a good place where type of this sort may start and be imprinted into the rubber. Create another point farther along the curve of the tire, the same distance from the rim. This second point should be up and to the right of the first point — not quite a quarter of the way around the tire's curve. Drag the curve horizontally after making the second point and stretch the curve so that it follows the rotation

of the tire. Create another point somewhere below this point, and then click on the original point, closing the curve. Look at the examples here to get the gist of what the curve should look like.

④ Select the Type tool. Open the Character palette and set up the font as follows:

* **Font:** Arial Black
* **Style:** Regular
* **Font Size:** 48 pt
* **Leading:** 18 pt

* **Tracking:** 0
* **Vertical Scale:** 100%
* **Horizontal Scale:** 100%
* **Baseline Shift:** 0 pt
* **Color:** White
* Normal
* **Anti-aliasing method:** Smooth

(5) Set the justification to Center in the Options bar. Move the type cursor over the path line curve at the top of the path. The cursor changes as you move it over the path, telling Photoshop that the type is to follow the path. Click on the path and enter the name of the tire company: in this case, I'm using HANK'S TIRES.

(6) Choose Edit⇨Transform Path⇨Skew. Reposition the text as needed to match it to the curve of the tire. Accept the transform settings.

(7) To blend the letters so that they appear stamped onto the tire, you could simply adjust the opacity of

the layer so that the rubber and texture appear through the type. This works to a degree, but not as effectively as you may think. There is a slight highlight on the rubber that follows the curve of the tire, and you need to see this highlight through the text, however faintly. In this instance, Blend If is going to give the better result, in my humble opinion.

(8) Open the Layer Styles for the type layer and select Blending Options. Choose the Blend If area at the bottom and select Blend If: Gray. Hold down the Alt/Option key to separate the black slider halves found on the bottom, and click on the innermost black slider half. Move it to the 0/100 position. This allows some of the black to appear through the type along the curve.

(9) Now you may stamp the text into the sidewall. Open the Bevel and Emboss style settings and enter the following:

* **Style:** Emboss
* **Technique:** Smooth
* **Depth:** 600%
* **Direction:** Down
* **Size:** 0 px
* **Soften:** 0 px
* **Angle:** 120 degrees
* **Use Global Light:** unchecked
* **Altitude:** 25 degrees
* **Gloss Contour:** Linear (default)

* **Anti-aliased:** checked
* **Highlight Mode:** Screen
  * **Color:** White
  * **Opacity:** 100%
* **Shadow Mode:** Multiply
  * **Color:** Black
  * **Opacity:** 75%

Click OK.

10 If the type appears too big for your liking, you may select it and reduce the font size. In the final example, I've reduced the font size to 36 points and repositioned it with the Move tool to better fit the tire. Once the type fits the sidewall, the effect is complete.

A short recap

Simplicity and subtlety — those are the keywords for this tutorial. Although the warp tools often allow for realistic placement on curved surfaces, sometimes perspective doesn't work in your favor. In instances such as this, typing on paths works wonders.

On the Hood

Let's stay with the automotive theme and produce a chrome logo for a classic auto. There are many methods that people use to create chrome, and each is usually dependent on where they apply the chrome and under what light. The secret to chrome is not so much in the color, but in how the material reflects the light in its surroundings.

THE PLAN

- Affix type to the side panel of a car
- Chrome the text

① Open the image car-side.jpg. This appears, if I don't miss my guess, to be the side panel of a '50s-era Corvette, but I could be wrong. Whatever the case, you can create your own brand.

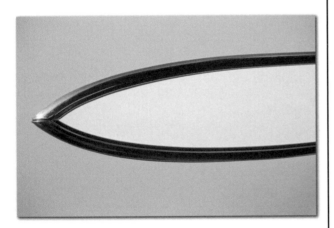

② Select the Type tool and open the Character palette. Enter the following type characteristics:

- **Font:** Edwardian Script (or some other script-style font)
- **Style:** Regular
- **Font Size:** 160 pt
- **Leading:** 18 pt
- **Tracking:** 0
- **Vertical Scale:** 90%
- **Horizontal Scale:** 110%
- **Baseline Shift:** 0 pt
- **Color:** Black
- **Normal**
- **Anti-aliasing method:** Smooth

③ Type the name of your car over the white portion of the photo. I'm calling mine the Styler.

④ Choose Layer⟹Rasterize and turn the type layer into a standard layer. Because this photo is not a straight-on shot, some warping of the text needs to occur. Choose Edit⟹Transform⟹Perspective and decrease the height of the right side of the text. Once it fits well within the confines of the white area and appears to follow the perspective of the side panel, accept the transformation.

⑤ Now it is time to prep the letters that you want to chrome. Turn it off in the Layers palette and select the type layer.

⑥ Open the Channels palette and duplicate the Blue channel. Choose Image⟹Adjustments⟹Invert so that the text appears white and the surrounding area black. Duplicate the Blue copy channel and choose Filter⟹Blur⟹Gaussian Blur. Set the Radius of the blur to 10 pixels and click OK.

7 Return to the Layers palette and duplicate the type layer. Command/Ctrl-click the new layer and fill the selection with 50% gray. Why? When working with metallic effects such as chrome, especially when the Lighting Effect filter and channels become involved (as is about to happen), gray just works better than black at getting to the final effect.

8 Choose Filter➪Render➪Lighting Effects. Enter the following settings:

* **Style:** Default
* **Light Type:** Spotlight
* **On:** checked
* **Intensity:** 39
* **Focus:** 69
* **Color:** White
* **Properties:**
  * **Gloss:** 92
  * **Material:** 100 (Metallic)
  * **Exposure:** 0
  * **Color:** White
* **Ambience:** 8
* **Texture Channel:** Blue copy 2
* **White is High:** checked
* **Height:** 50

Position the light so that it is shining from the upper left. Click OK.

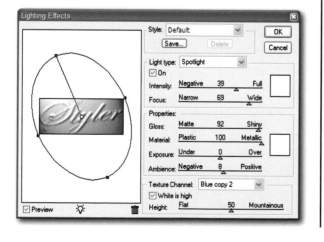

9 Apply the Lighting Effects filter again, but this time alter the settings:

* **Style:** Three Down
* **Light Type:** Spotlight
* **On:** checked
* **Intensity:** 35
* **Focus:** 96
* **Color:** White
* **Properties:**
  * **Gloss:** 100
  * **Material:** 100 (Metallic)
  * **Exposure:** 0
  * **Color:** White
  * **Ambience:** 6
* **Texture Channel:** Blue copy 2
* **White is High:** checked
* **Height:** 50

Position the three lights so that they are striking the image from three distinct directions with minimal overlap of the beams. Click OK.

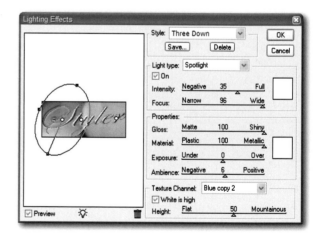

10 Create a Curves adjustment layer. Make a new curve that looks like a sine wave that slowly increases in intensity. This helps to bring the detail out of the reflections on the metal.

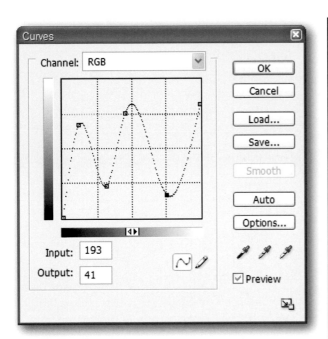

(12) Create another copy of the type layer and place it just beneath the Curves adjustment layer. Change the Blend Mode to Soft Light.

(13) Command/Ctrl-click a type layer and create a Gradient Fill adjustment layer. Create a gradient of alternating grays, white, and green/turquoise (to match the tone of the car's paint) as shown here.

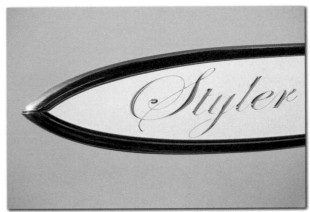

(14) Enter the following Gradient Fill settings:

* **Gradient:** Custom
* **Style:** Linear
* **Angle:** 100 degrees
* **Scale:** 100%
* **Reverse:** unchecked
* **Dither:** unchecked
* **Align with Layer:** checked

Click OK.

(15) The gradient may be a bit overpowering, but rather than altering the gradient again, ensure that the selection is still active and create a Hue/Saturation adjustment layer. Reduce the saturation to -50% and click OK.

(11) Duplicate the type layer, and select the version just above the background. Set the opacity to 60%. Choose Filter⇨Artistic⇨Plastic Wrap and enter the following settings for the filter:

* **Highlight Strength:** 20
* **Detail:** 7
* **Smoothness:** 15

Click OK. This adds to the reflection factor of the metal, as you will see shortly.

16 Select the bottom type layer and open the Layer Styles. Select Drop Shadow and enter the following:

* **Blend Mode:** Multiply
* **Color:** Black
* **Angle:** 130 degrees
* **Use Global Light:** unchecked
* **Distance:** 6 px
* **Spread:** 0%
* **Size:** 8 px
* **Contour:** Linear (default)
* **Anti-aliased:** checked
* **Noise:** 0%

Click OK. The type is really starting to shine now.

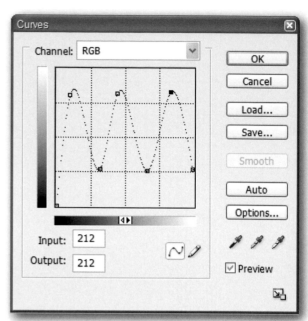

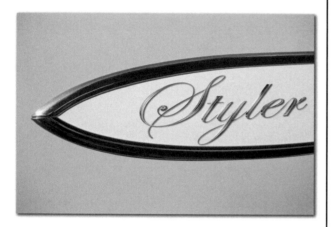

17 At this point, for this project at least, you are basically left with finishing touches. For instance, there is some additional color (reddish tints and so forth) in the reflection that you may want to remove. You can do this by adding a Hue/Saturation adjustment layer above the text with the following settings:

* **Hue:** 203
* **Saturation:** 14
* **Lightness:** 0
* **Colorize:** checked

TIP

The addition of a Curves adjustment layer can help as well. Just keep the sine-wave arrangement, and work with it while watching the text change as you move the shadow, midtones, and highlight points.

18 The last touch that I'd suggest is to collapse all layers except the background into a single layer, and then apply the Dodge tool to points along the text where reflections might occur. Set the Dodge tool options to Highlights before you do this.

A short recap

If possible, keep an eye on other chrome elements in the photo that you are working on and try to match them in color and reflection. Ensure that your reflections match the direction of the reflections that would hit real-world metal. There are hundreds of chrome tutorials online, but most stop after applying the chrome filter or a single pass of the Lighting Effects filter. To really get your metal to shine, you need a combination of filters, adjustment layers, and plain old hard work, even if you are using a preset filter package such as Alien Skin's Eye Candy (which is a great program, by the way — find out more at www.alienskin.com).

Signs of the Times

Occasionally the message itself doesn't quite have the impact required to get its point across. This is particularly true with public service-style ads. Although words alone can easily be dismissed, adding something visual and shocking can motivate more people to act. In the past few months, our state has adopted an ad campaign to make the residents aware of a drug problem. Rather than using the old "egg in a frying pan" commercials of years ago, they have adopted very graphic ads for both television and print showing young people suffering the effects of addiction.

This tutorial follows that approach, although it is not as shocking as what we have been seeing. You take a stark, emotional photo, add a message to garner public interest, and apply it to a billboard. One thing to note is the use of color: sometimes less is more.

THE PLAN

- Create a public awareness ad
- Add a bold header to the ad
- Distress the text
- Include additional text to better convey the point
- Place the ad on a billboard for all passersby to see

1 Open the image billboard.jpg. This ultimately serves as the resting place for the final ad. Minimize it for now, as you will be returning to it soon.

2 Open the image anger.jpg. This photo conveys the emotion, both in the man's expression and in the restrictive use of stark red and black, that gives this billboard its shock factor. Imagine this image meeting you on the side of the road at 50 feet high!

3 Double-click the background layer to transform it into a normal, editable layer. Create a new layer and move it beneath the face layer. Choose Image➪Canvas Size and increase the width of the canvas to 200%.

4 Select the face layer again and press Command/Ctrl+A to select the entire document. Click on the Move tool, and then click the Align Left Edges icon in the Options bar. This moves the face layer to the left edge of the image, leaving the right side blank.

5 Select the Type tool and open the Character palette. Set up the font as follows:
- ✳ **Font:** Arial Black
- ✳ **Style:** Regular
- ✳ **Font Size:** 200 pt

* **Leading:** 18 pt
* **Tracking:** 0
* **Vertical Scale:** 90%
* **Horizontal Scale:** 110%
* **Baseline Shift:** 0 pt
* **Color:** White
* Normal
* **Anti-aliasing method:** Smooth

6 Type **RAGE** at the top of the document. Center the text so that the *RA* rests over the red portion, and the *GE* over the black. It's starting to get the point across already, and the actual message hasn't even been included yet.

7 There are a number of ways to distress the text, but the method that I find easiest and often most satisfying is the use of a textured, or "grunge," brush. As you know, you can create a brush from any photo, so long as the longest side does not exceed 2500 pixels. Open the image rock-03.jpg. This image shows up in another tutorial later in the chapter, but it serves as an excellent brush for this technique.

8 Because the width of the image is 2400 pixels, it will have no trouble becoming a brush. Choose Edit⇨

Define Brush Preset. Name the new brush and click OK. If you would like to save this brush for later use, hold down the Alt/Option key, click on the other brushes in the Brushes palette to delete them, and save the new brush as a set. You may add to the set later and create an entire set of rock texture brushes.

9 Create a mask for the type layer and set the foreground color to a median gray (#666666 should do fine). Select the Brush tool and ensure that the new brush is selected. Increase the size to 2500 pixels. Set the Brush opacity to 75-100% and paint in the mask over the text.

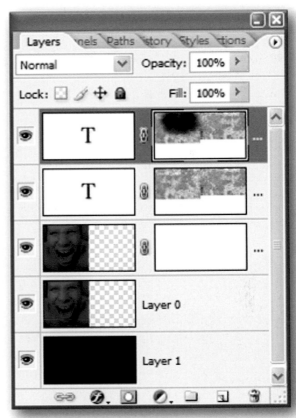

10 It's time to add the rest of the message. Select the Type tool again. Open the Character palette and set up the font as follows:

* **Font:** Arial
* **Style:** Regular
* **Font Size:** 36 pt
* **Leading:** 36 pt
* **Tracking:** 0
* **Vertical Scale:** 90%
* **Horizontal Scale:** 110%
* **Baseline Shift:** 0 pt
* **Color:** White
* **Italic**
* **Anti-aliasing method:** Smooth

NOTE

Depending on how dark the paint application was, you may find that the text is hard to read in some areas. You can correct this problem by doing the following: duplicate the type layer and mask (this is done automatically when you create the duplicate layer), and then manipulate the opacity of the text in specific areas by painting with black in the mask using a standard round or feathered brush. You must reset the brush beforehand. In this manner you can control how much white appears and how much of the backdrop shows through the text.

11 Draw a paragraph box along the lower half of the right side. It should cross over the red portion as well, but not too far. Type the message in the bounding box. In this example, my message is: "Your child says there's a monster in the house. Is it you? GET HELP... for both your sakes." Once you type the message, space the text so that the three sentences are dispersed vertically on separate lines. This adds a dramatic pause feel, as though the message is being spoken straight to the person. Position the text with the Move tool as needed.

12 Duplicate the document and choose Layer⇨Flatten Image. Select the entire image, copy it, and then open billboard.jpg again. Paste the ad into the billboard image. Choose Edit⇨Transform⇨Scale and reduce the size of the ad so that it fits within the confines of the billboard photo.

13 In order to place the photo over the billboard with accuracy, you actually need to see the sign through the ad. Reduce the opacity of the ad layer to 60-70% so that you can see the area where you are pasting the ad beneath the layer.

14 To conform the ad to the billboard, choose Edit⇨ Transform⇨Distort. Move the corners of the transform box to the corners of the sign area on the billboard. Once it is in place, accept the transformation.

15 Almost there! Increase the opacity of the ad layer to 100% again.

16 The final touch is to take some of the characteristics of the billboard and apply them to the ad that overlays it. This gives some semblance that the ad has been in place for a while and suffered from the elements.

Set the Blend mode of the ad layer to Overlay. If the ad appears too faint, duplicate the ad layer, but reduce the opacity of the second layer to 50–60%. The texture, warps, and dents of the billboard appear through the layers, giving the impression of age to the ad and a real-world quality that wouldn't be there if the ad was left in its original state.

A short recap

This effect is full of distress. Distressed text, distressed by the elements, and distressing in content and imagery. Each of these elements combines to convey a chaotic urgency.

Graphic design is more than simple splashes of color: there is a definite human emotional element that you must take into consideration. Yes, I'm saying it: graphic design is a mind game. What seems shocking and powerful to you most likely has the same effect on others.

Neon at Night

Glowing type is not a new thing to the Photoshop crowd. Neon effects have been circulating for years now, some very basic, and some incredibly realistic. This tutorial, while dealing with neon, gives it an advertising twist. Instead of simply creating a marquee, let's reverse it and reflect it off a surface. Even with the text thus distorted, the message comes across just fine, providing you can read in reverse.

THE PLAN

- Create neon-style text from scratch
- Apply it to a car window in reverse to imitate a reflection

(1) Create a new image with the following characteristics:

- **Name:** Neon
- **Preset:** Custom
- **Width:** 10 inches
- **Height:** 5 inches
- **Resolution:** 300 pixels/inch
- **Color Mode:** RGB, 8 bit
- **Background Contents:** White

Click OK.

(2) Fill the background layer with black, at 100% opacity.

(3) Select the Type tool. Open the Character palette and set the following font characteristics:

- **Font:** Register Sans BTN – If this font is not installed on your system, try to find one that is relatively thin with rounded angles and ends
- **Style:** Regular
- **Font Size:** 200 pt
- **Leading:** 18 pt
- **Tracking:** 0
- **Vertical Scale:** 90%
- **Horizontal Scale:** 110%
- **Baseline Shift:** 0 pt
- **Color:** White
- **Bold**
- **Italic**
- **Anti-aliasing method:** Smooth

(4) Type your text and center it in the image. In this example, I'm using "Eatery," but you may certainly write something like "BAR" or "PIZZA" if you want. To generate the neon effect, or a reasonable facsimile thereof that serves for this technique, open the Layer Styles for the type layer and select Outer Glow. Enter the following attributes:

- **Blend Mode:** Normal
- **Opacity:** 75%
- **Noise:** 0%
- **Glow Style:** Gradient (Custom) – Create a gradient that has bright orange on both sides and a wide percentage of white in the center. (See image below.)
- **Technique:** Softer
- **Spread:** 25%
- **Size:** 45 px
- **Contour:** Linear (default)
- **Anti-aliased:** checked
- **Range:** 50%
- **Jitter:** 0%

(5) Select Inner Glow from the style list. Enter the following characteristics:

- **Blend Mode:** Normal
- **Opacity:** 75%
- **Noise:** 0%
- **Glow Type:** Gradient (Custom) - Create a gradient as before, only use white at the ends and orange in the middle section.

* **Technique**: Softer
* **Source**: Center
* **Choke**: 0%
* **Size**: 32 px
* **Contour**: Custom (see below)
* **Anti-aliased**: checked
* **Range**: 50%
* **Jitter**: 0%

6 The contour should have a wave in the center. Create a contour that resembles the one shown here:

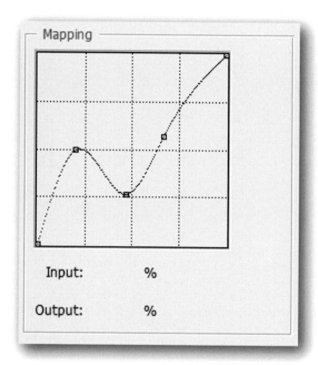

7 Save the layer style for future use if you like, and click OK. You end up with glowing type that has several alternating color characteristics.

8 Open the image carwindow.jpg. There is already some neon reflecting from the window, but you replace that with the text that you just created.

9 Duplicate the background layer, and then create a new layer at the top of the layer stack. Press the D key to set black as the foreground color, and then paint over the area of the window where the neon reflects. Don't cover the reflection of the woman or her hat.

10 Return to the type image and turn off the background layer. Choose Layer⇨Merge Visible. Drag and drop the newly merged layer into the car image. Use the transform tools to resize it (Transform⇨Scale) to fit over the window. Once you resize it, choose Edit⇨Transform⇨Flip Horizontal.

11 The transform tools once again help to conform the reflection to the image. First, rotate the layer so that the left side is higher than the right side. The window curves a bit, so choose Edit⇨Transform⇨Warp. Distort the corners of the image so that the right side is higher than the left, and add a bit of wobble to the type. See the example to get the idea. Once you are happy with the distortion, accept the transformation.

12 Duplicate the type layer. Set the Blend mode of the lower type layer to Screen, and reduce the opacity to 60-75%.

13 The lower type layer serves as a blur, roughly where the characters of the letters are. To achieve this, you must bypass the standard Gaussian Blur. Instead, ensure that you select the lower type layer, and choose Filter⇨Blur⇨Shape Blur. Select one of the shapes from the list. I'm using Grass 3 from the default shape set. Set the Blur Radius to 100 pixels and click OK. This gives the neon an extra kick, expanding the glow.

If you prefer to have the neon vary in color, simply create a Hue/Saturation adjustment layer and adjust the hue, saturation, and lightness. Then paint with black in the Adjustment Layer's mask over the areas that you want to retain their original color. For the final example, I altered the Hue/Saturation as follows:

* **Hue:** 25
* **Saturation:** 25
* **Lightness:** -30
* **Colorize:** unchecked

A short recap

When reflecting off of a surface, analyze closely the surrounding elements in the photo, the surface that the reflection plays on, the lighting, and so forth. Reflections on moving glass, such as in this example, have a blurred quality, while a reflection on still water or glass has a very crisp, clean feel. The surroundings dictate which style of reflection works best in your masterpiece.

Old Paint

This technique is inspired by my love of nostalgia. Did you ever have a band that you listened to constantly and that had your parents convinced you were being enticed to the dark side? I did. My walls were plastered with cheap band posters that I "won" at the county fair, and I demanded every new LP as a birthday present. Not to mention the decals, the temporary tattoos, the action figures, and the comics. Although the members of the band in question have passed beyond retirement age, their legacy lives on.

You can paint a logo reflecting a semi-imaginary band on a brick wall, conform it to the wall, and apply age by fading it into the contours. I'm sure that you recognize some similarity to an actual band logo, but I assure that you this is almost entirely accidental. (Almost.)

THE PLAN

- Create text resembling the logo of a popular '70s rock band
- Apply the type to a wall
- Manipulate the text to fade the paint, applying it to the bricks and mortar

1 Open the image colored-bricks.jpg.

2 Before getting to the text, you need to create a displacement map. The process goes like this:

- Choose the Channels palette
- Duplicate the Blue channel

- Choose Image⇨Adjustments⇨Brightness/Contrast and increase the contrast of the channel until there is a clear separation between whites and blacks
- Choose Filter⇨Blur⇨Gaussian Blur and blur the channel by 2-5 pixels
- Right-click the channel and select Duplicate
- In the Duplicate dialog box, name the new image and select New as the destination so that the image opens as a new document
- Save the new, blurred image to your hard drive as a PSD file. Remember where you put it, because you will need it shortly

- Close the blurred image
- Return to the first image and delete the Blue copy channel

The image is now saved, and you can use it as a displacement map.

③ Select the Type tool. Open the Character palette and set up the font as follows:

* **Font:** Die Nasty — This font is patterned after the logo of that '70s band to which I alluded earlier. You can download this font for free. Simply do a Google search for "Die Nasty font." Google offers several links where you can acquire it.
* **Style:** SuperBold
* **Font Size:** 140 pt
* **Leading:** 36 pt
* **Tracking:** 0
* **Vertical Scale:** 120%
* **Horizontal Scale:** 110%
* **Baseline Shift:** 0 pt
* **Color:** Black
* **Anti-aliasing method:** Smooth

④ Type the name of your band. For this example, I'm calling them MISS, and yes, the pun is intended. They were a hair band that wore incredible amounts of makeup, after all! Change the foreground color to R = 235, G = 195, and B = 85. Change the background color to R = 135, G = 10, and B = 7.

⑤ Open the Layer Styles for the type layer and select Gradient Overlay. Enter the following settings:

* **Blend Mode:** Normal
* **Opacity:** 100%
* **Gradient:** Foreground to Background
* **Reverse:** unchecked
* **Style:** Linear
* **Align with Layer:** checked
* **Angle:** 90 degrees
* **Scale:** 100%

⑥ For the outline around the text, both white and black are used. Select Stroke from the Layer Styles list and create a new black-to-white gradient. Move the color stops so that they meet at about one-third the width of the gradient window from the left-hand side. Set the rest of the Stroke options as follows:

* **Size:** 6 px
* **Position:** Outside
* **Blend Mode:** Normal
* **Opacity:** 100%

* **Fill Type:** Gradient (as described above)
* **Gradient:** Custom
* **Style:** Shape Burst
* **Angle:** 90 degrees
* **Scale:** 100%

⑦ Save the layer style and click OK. You now have a reasonable knock-off of a very-recognizable band logo (at least to my age group, anyway).

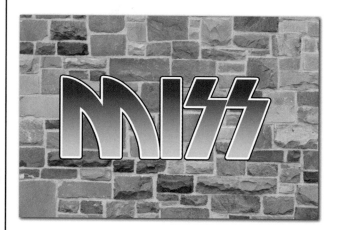

The next step is to distort the text somewhat so as not to appear a total copycat. Create a new layer just above the background and select the type layer. Choose Layer⇨Merge Down. This collapses the style and rasterizes the text. Next choose Edit⇨Transform⇨Warp and tweak the logo so that the corners bow up while the horizontal centers pinch closer together.

8 Choose Filter⇨Distort⇨Displace. Enter the following settings:

- **Horizontal Scale:** 2
- **Vertical Scale:** 2
- **Displacement Map:** Stretch To Fit
- **Undefined Areas:** Repeat Edge Pixels

Click OK.

9 In the window that pops up, navigate to the folder where you saved the displacement map, select it, and click OK. The text ripples to conform to the light and dark areas of the map. You will see the importance of this shortly.

10 Open the Layer Styles for the type layer and select Blending Options. In the Blend If section, enter the settings shown here, and click OK.

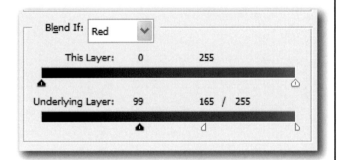

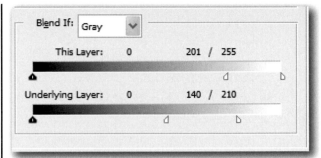

11 Set the foreground color to R = 106, G = 106, and B = 106. The color change is used to help distress the text further.

12 Create a layer mask for the type layer. Load the rock brush that you created earlier in this chapter. Maximize the size of the brush, increase the opacity of the brush to 100%, and paint over the type in the mask by holding the brush in place (this is important) and clicking once. Change the Blend mode of the layer to Multiply.

13 Duplicate the type layer and change the Blend mode to Overlay. Reduce the opacity to 50%. This simply enriches the color of the remaining paint while leaving it distressed and displaced, thus matching the contours of the bricks and mortar.

A short recap

This is one of my favorite effects, and one that will really test your Blend If abilities. This is a very powerful tool that is often overlooked or simply misunderstood. It can, however, help you achieve some dynamic blending that opacity changes and blending mode alterations simply can't perform. In short, Blend If rocks... 'nuf said.

Merging Worlds

In the past two techniques, you have created neon and aged paint. So here's an interesting twist: how about taking a photo of neon and turning it into aged paint? What happens when those two worlds collide? This time you don't have to create the neon from scratch, but can use an existing photograph of a neon sign to generate the final effect. Because you have been through most of the steps for this one already, it will be quick and, I assure you, relatively painless.

THE PLAN

- Create a displacement map
- Convert a photo of a neon sign to paint
- Apply the type to a wall

(1) Open the images brickwall.jpg and pizzaneon.jpg.

(2) Begin with the brick wall image. Create a displacement map as per the instruction given in Step 1 of the Old Paint tutorial.

(3) Select the pizza sign photo. The dark background works in your favor, as it makes it a simple task to select the colored areas. Choose Select⇨Color Range. Set up the following options:

- **Select:** Sampled Colors
- **Fuzziness:** 40
- **Selection:** checked
- **Eyedropper tool selected
- **Invert:** checked

(4) Click somewhere in the dark background of the image. Click OK. Because you checked Invert, the glowing sign is selected instead of the background.

(5) Press Command/Ctrl+C to copy the selection. Go to the wall photo and press Command/Ctrl+V to paste the selection into a new layer.

6 Choose Edit⇨Transform⇨Scale and reduce the size of the new layer so that the sign resides to the left of the shutter.

7 Accept the transformation. Choose Filter⇨Distort⇨ Displace. Enter the following:

* **Horizontal Scale:** 2
* **Vertical Scale:** 2
* **Displacement Map:** Stretch To Fit
* **Undefined Areas:** Repeat Edge Pixels

Click OK.

8 Select the displacement map you created in Step 1. Change the Blend mode of the paint/light layer to Multiply.

9 To finish things off, open the Layer Style Blending Options and find your way down to Blend If. Change the settings as follows:

* **Blend If:** Gray
* **This Layer**
  * **Black Stops:** 0 / 110
  * **Red Stops:** 255 (both)
* **Underlying Layer:**
  * **Black Stops:** 0 / 110
  * **Red Stops:** 220 / 255

If the text becomes too transparent, adjust the sliders as needed. Click OK. Your pizza sign is now converted from neon to paint.

A short recap

Although the selection looked rough to start with, espe-cially with the blurred glow tagging along, it actually works in the favor of the final shot. That the green of the neon matches the paint on the shutter — well, that was a total accident, but it works. Try performing this technique using a portrait instead of neon. The process is the same, but it can be far more satisfying to see faces that you know painted on the wall.

How Convenient

When I was growing up in rural Montana, we had to drive nearly 15 miles to get to the store, to church, to a restaurant, or to any kind of civilization. If we wanted to stock up and save some money, we had to travel an additional 100+ miles to get to the big city — population 20,000. There were no corporate coffee shops, no strip malls, and none of the modern conveniences that we have today. I'm not so sure that we were worse off then than now, but I digress.

Because the mom-and-pop stores are fast fading into oblivion, this tutorial recognizes the mega-store. They are springing up everywhere, and their name alone inspires fear in the hearts of small business owners. You can create a sign for one of these chains and prominently place it on the building's façade.

THE PLAN

- Create a logo for a chain store
- Render the logo in 3D
- Attach it to the store's façade
- Add highlights and shadows to bring it to life in the real world

① Create a new image with the following attributes:

- **Name:** Store Sign
- **Preset:** Custom
- **Width:** 10 inches
- **Height:** 5 inches
- **Resolution:** 300 pixels/inch
- **Color Mode:** RGB, 8 bit
- **Background Contents:** White

② Press the D key to place black in the foreground, and select the Type tool. Open the Character palette and set up the font as follows:

- **Font:** Arial Black
- **Style:** Regular
- **Font Size:** 140 pt
- **Leading:** 36 pt
- **Tracking:** 0
- **Vertical Scale:** 120%
- **Horizontal Scale:** 110%
- **Baseline Shift:** 0 pt

- **Color:** Black
- **Anti-aliasing method:** Smooth

③ Type your text. I'm calling the new store Q-MART. Sound familiar? Nah...

Q-MART

④ Open the Layer Styles for the type layer. Select Color Overlay. Enter the following settings:

- **Blend Mode:** Normal
- **Color:** R = 33, G = 22, and B = 178
- **Opacity:** 100%

⑤ Move down to the Stroke settings. Set up the stroke as follows:

- **Size:** 21 px
- **Position:** Outside
- **Blend Mode:** Normal
- **Opacity:** 100%
- **Fill Type:** Gradient
- **Gradient:** Custom (see below)
- **Reverse:** checked
- **Style:** Shape Burst
- **Angle:** 90 degrees
- **Scale:** 100%

TIP

Bold, bright color combinations are the key to making the signs and logos stand out from the competition.

6 Open the Gradient Editor from the stroke settings and create a gradient that is red to black with no transitional blending. Take a look at the example below and set up your gradient in a similar manner.

7 Save the layer style if you want to use it later, and click OK.

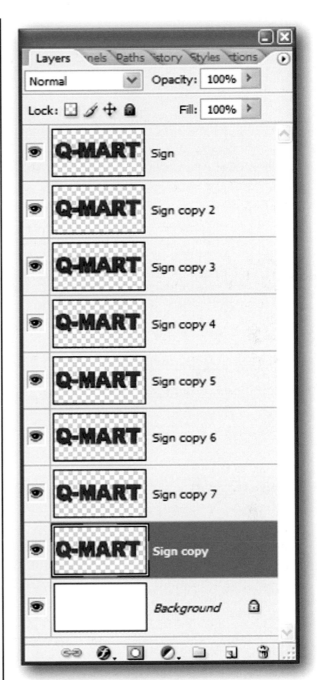

8 Create a new layer beneath the type layer. Select the type layer and choose Layer⇨Merge Down. The type is now ready to be made '3D.'

9 Duplicate the type layer, and select the version on the bottom, just above the background. Select the Move tool. Using the arrow keys on the keyboard, move the layer two clicks to the left and one click down. Duplicate the bottom layer again. Then, once again select the version just above the background and move it two clicks to the left and one click down. Repeat the process until the text is several layers thick. Be sure to always duplicate the bottom layer, then select and move the bottom layer. This is very important to get the 3D effect to look right.

10 Once you have the depth that you want, merge all but the top layer and the background layer together. This leaves the background untouched and the top layer editable and separate from the 3D layers.

13 Set up the remainder of the gradient overlay as follows:

* **Blend Mode:** Normal
* **Opacity:** 100%
* **Gradient:** Custom
* **Reverse:** checked
* **Style:** Linear
* **Align with Layer:** checked
* **Angle:** 95 degrees
* **Scale:** 100%

14 Select the Stroke options. Set up the stroke as follows:

* **Size:** 6 px
* **Position:** Inside
* **Blend Mode:** Normal
* **Opacity:** 100%
* **Fill Type:** Color
* **Color:** Black

11 Command/Ctrl-click the top layer to generate a selection. Select the bottom type layer and press Delete.

12 Open the Layer Styles for the bottom type layer and choose Gradient Overlay from the list. Open the Gradient Editor and create a gradient of alternating shades of gray, as shown in the example below.

15 Save the layer style and click OK. The 3D area now has a reflective quality, with a dark outline further distinguishing it from the background. You may have seen a logo similar to this stage in a print ad.

16 Create a new layer beneath the bottom type layer, then select the bottom type layer. Select Layer⇨ Merge Down to flatten the layer effects into the text, Merge the two type layers together as described above, and then copy the newly merged type layer to the Clipboard. Open the image mall.jpg. This serves as your superstore. Paste the text into a new layer, and use the Transform tools to position the text on the façade above the entryway.

17 Choose Select⇨Color Range. Select the blue fill area, click OK, and then choose Layer⇨New⇨Layer via Copy. Select the Dodge tool and enter the following settings in the Options bar:

* **Brush:** Round, Feathered
* **Brush Size:** 30
* **Range:** Midtones
* **Exposure:** 70%

18 Use the Dodge tool to lighten a few semi-horizontal streaks in the surface of the sign. Don't go overboard; simply lighten a few bright spots and lines on each of the letters.

19 Select the Burn tool. Enter the following settings in the Options bar:

* **Brush:** Feathered, Round
* **Brush Size:** 10
* **Range:** Midtones
* **Exposure:** 70%

The sun is coming from the upper right in the photo, so burn shadows along the right edges of the blue type to give the impression that it is recessed from the border.

20 Choose Filter⇨Artistic⇨Plastic Wrap. Set Highlight Strength to 20, Detail to 14, and Smoothness to 8.

21 Click OK. Set the Blend mode for the layer to Screen and the opacity to 30%. Duplicate this layer once to increase the effect.

22 Select the bottom-most type layer and then generate a selection around the text by Command/ Ctrl-clicking the layer. Create a Brightness/Contrast adjustment layer. Set Brightness to -60 and Contrast to +75.

The 3D portion of the sign is considerably darker now, and blends better with its surroundings.

(23) Open the Layer Styles for the bottom type layer. Select Drop Shadow and enter the following:

* **Blend Mode:** Multiply
* **Color:** Black
* **Opacity:** 55%
* **Angle:** 65 degrees
* **Use Global Light:** unchecked
* **Distance:** 12 px
* **Spread:** 0%
* **Size:** 5 px
* **Contour:** Linear (default)
* **Anti-aliased:** checked
* **Noise:** 0%

(24) Now select the Stroke settings:

* **Size:** 5 px
* **Position:** Outside
* **Blend Mode:** Normal
* **Opacity:** 100%
* **Fill Type:** Gradient, Black to White (default)
* **Style:** Linear
* **Align with Layer:** checked
* **Angle:** 105 degrees
* **Scale:** 100%

Click OK.

(25) You should apply these settings only to the 3D portion and not the background. Command/Ctrl-click the bottom type layer to generate a selection.

(26) Click on the adjustment layer's mask and choose Select⊃Inverse. Fill the selection with black to mask the adjustment from the non-sign portions of the image.

A short recap

This is a tricky one, in that getting the reflections and shading to match the real-world setting can be taxing on the brain cells. Still, you were able to see the logo develop through three stages: standard 'vector' logo, 3D, and then real-world 3D. How you apply the logo is up to you, but please, DON'T start another chain of stores!

Meet the Flintstones

I could have called this "Meet the Caesars," "Message for Moses," or any number of things, but you get the idea. This technique chisels type into solid rock. Once again, you get a workout conforming the text to the surface of the rock, and you even change the quality of the stone in the photo. Who said playing with rocks had to be boring? My son would definitely disagree.

THE PLAN

- Manipulate a rock face, giving it more features
- Etch text into the rock face

1 Open the image rock.jpg. Although a fine rock in its own right, I prefer my rocks with a bit of character.

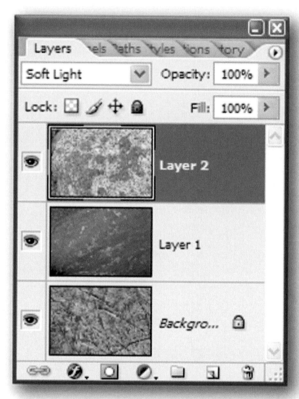

2 It can and will be dressed up, but first you need to create a displacement map. Using this image, follow the process in Step 1 of the "Old Paint" project in this chapter.

3 Open the images rock-02.jpg and rock-03.jpg. Copy each of these two images and paste them into the original rock document on their own layers. Change the Blend mode for the two new layers to Soft Light. This adds some of their color and texture to the original rock face, creating a stone-age makeover.

4 Select the Type tool. Open the Character palette and set up the font as follows:

* **Font:** BoogieWoogie – if this font is not installed on your system, find a thick, comic-style font
* **Style:** Regular
* **Font Size:** 100 pt
* **Leading:** 18 pt
* **Tracking:** 0
* **Vertical Scale:** 90%
* **Horizontal Scale:** 110%
* **Baseline Shift:** 0 pt
* **Color:** Black
* **Anti-aliasing method:** Smooth

5 Type **Bedrock** across the image. Choose Edit⇨ Transform⇨Rotate and rotate the type layer so that it runs from lower left to upper right.

6 Accept the transformation.

7 As with so many type effects, the easiest way to get from point A to Pi (if there can be such a line) is via Layer Styles. Open the styles for the type layer and select Bevel and Emboss. Enter the following settings:

* **Style:** Inner Bevel
* **Technique:** Chisel Hard
* **Depth:** 100%
* **Direction:** Down
* **Size:** 250 px
* **Soften:** 0 px
* **Angle:** 140 degrees
* **Use Global Light:** unchecked

* **Altitude:** 16 degrees
* **Gloss Contour:** Linear (default)
* **Anti-aliased:** checked
* **Highlight Mode:** Screen
* **Color:** R = 192, G = 183, and B = 165
* **Opacity:** 90%
* **Shadow Mode:** Multiply
* **Color:** R = 95, G = 76, and B = 63
* **Opacity:** 55%

8 Select the Blending Options. Choose Blend If and enter the following:

* **Blend If:** Gray
* **This Layer:**
  * Black Stops: 0 / 10
  * White Stops: 255
* **Underlying Layer:**
  * Black Stops: 0
  * White Stops: 255

9 Save the layer style. The text is beginning to take on a carved and chiseled appearance.

10 Before the type can be displaced, you need to rasterize it. Choose Layer⇨Rasterize⇨Type and convert the text from vector to raster.

11 Command/Ctrl-click the type layer to generate a selection, and then click on the top rock layer. Create a mask and fill the selection with black, at 50% opacity. This reduces the color without removing it from the text completely.

(12) Choose Filter⇨Distort⇨Displace. Enter the following:

* **Horizontal Scale:** 2
* **Vertical Scale:** 2
* **Displacement Map:** Stretch To Fit
* **Undefined Areas:** Repeat Edge Pixels

(13) Select the map that you created from the original rock texture and click OK.

(14) To deepen the shadows and highlights a bit more, Command/Ctrl-click the type layer again and create a Curves adjustment layer at the top of the layer stack. Create three points and adjust them as in the example below. Once you are done, click OK.

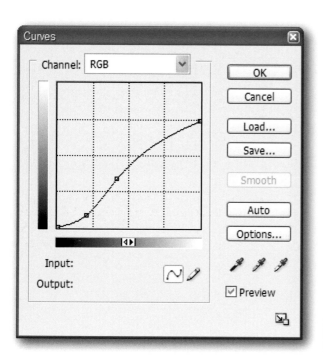

(15) Select the type layer. Set the Fill opacity to 0%.

You may want to experiment with the layer order to get the best rock appearance for your text. For instance, turn the background layer into a standard layer and move it up one position. Change the Blend mode of the bottom layer to Normal and the Blend mode of the moved layer to Overlay.

If the color inside the text is still a bit too vibrant, open the Layer Styles for the type layer and select Color Overlay. Set the Blend Mode to Hue, Color to R = 118, G = 118, B = 118, and Opacity to 65%.

You can experiment with the layers and the Blend modes to reveal variations that you may like better.

A short recap

As with everything in Photoshop CS2, this is only one way to chisel rock. Again, experiment with the style settings, with lighting effects, with blending modes, and with variations of color. Displacing the type and the shadows and highlights in the bevel really makes this effect come to life, but the rock that you use also enhances the effect. If you are unhappy with the rock, then by all means, make your own! You now have the technology.

Fire on the Mountain

When the table of contents for this book was in development, I didn't realize how topical this tutorial would be. As I'm writing this, evacuations are taking place five miles from my home as two fires are roaring through the mountain ranges to the east and west. When I look out my window, I can see the glow from the closer of the two. Both blazes have been determined to be caused by Man.

This tutorial creates a public service-style poster for those who take the time to read it. Using text and a torn and aged photo, it will hopefully grab the attention of the campers who read it. Better still that they heed it.

THE PLAN

- Create text filled with flame from the photo that it accentuates
- Tear the photo
- Include a safety message
- Alter the photo's tone

1. Open the image fire.jpg. Because this photo is also used to enhance the text, choose Edit⇨Define Pattern. Name the new pattern and click OK.

2. The poster needs a big, bold, attention-getting title (as with the billboard effect from earlier in the chapter). Select the Type tool and open the Character palette. Enter the following font settings:

   * **Font:** Arial Black
   * **Style:** Regular
   * **Font Size:** 140 pt
   * **Leading:** 36 pt
   * **Tracking:** 0
   * **Vertical Scale:** 120%
   * **Horizontal Scale:** 110%
   * **Baseline Shift:** 0 pt
   * **Color:** Black
   * **Anti-aliasing method:** Smooth

3. Type **FIRE** at the top of the poster. Open the Layer Styles for the type layer. Select Gradient Overlay and enter the following:

   * **Blend Mode:** Overlay
   * **Opacity:** 100%
   * **Gradient:** White to Black (default)

* **Reverse:** checked
* **Style:** Linear
* **Align with Layer:** checked
* **Angle:** 90 degrees
* **Scale:** 100%

(4) Next, go to Pattern Overlay:

* **Blend Mode:** Normal
* **Opacity:** 100%
* **Pattern:** Fire image pattern
* **Scale:** 140%
* **Link with Layer:** checked

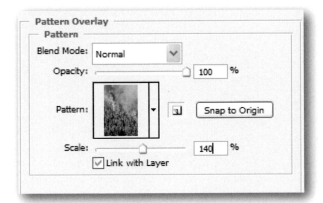

(5) Click in the text with the cursor and position the pattern in the text so that the fire appears in the letters, with none of the seams visible along the edge of the pattern.

(6) Double-click the background layer and turn it into a normal, editable layer. Create a new layer and move it beneath the photo layer. Fill the new background with black, at 100% opacity.

(7) Select the Paintbrush tool. Open the Brushes menu and load the brush set called PageSplatBrushes.abr, found on this book's companion CD-ROM. Select one of the brushes that appear as a torn page corner.

(8) Increase the brush size to 2500 pixels. Create a mask for the photo layer and change the foreground color to black.

(9) Set the Brush opacity to 100% in the Options bar, and then click once over the lower half of the layer in the mask. This renders the lower portion of the photo invisible, revealing the black beneath.

(10) Open the Brushes menu and select Reset Brushes to return to the default set.

11 Select the Dodge tool. This tool is going to enhance the torn look in the lower part of the page. Set up the Dodge tool options as follows:

* **Brush:** Round
* **Hardness:** 70
* **Brush Size:** 50
* **Range:** Midtones
* **Exposure:** 70%

12 Dodge the edge of the tear until narrow, uneven lengths of the tear appear white or nearly white. This gives the photo the illusion of being torn away.

13 Click OK. The image now has a sepia tone. However, this isn't quite as dramatic as it could be, so select the Paintbrush tool. With black in the foreground and a large feathered brush selected, paint over the mask beneath the letters, returning some of the natural color to the upper portion of the photo.

14 Select the Type tool again. Draw a paragraph box over the left side of the image, beginning about two-thirds of the way from the top of the photo and going almost to the bottom. Open the Character palette and change the type settings as follows:

* **Font:** Arial
* **Style:** Regular
* **Font Size:** 48 pt
* **Leading:** 60 pt
* **Tracking:** 0
* **Vertical Scale:** 120%
* **Horizontal Scale:** 110%
* **Baseline Shift:** 0 pt
* **Color:** White
* **Anti-aliasing method:** Smooth

15 Justify the text to the left, and then type **Prevention is our responsibility**. Position the text so that it primarily covers the black background, although some can overlay the remainder of the photo.

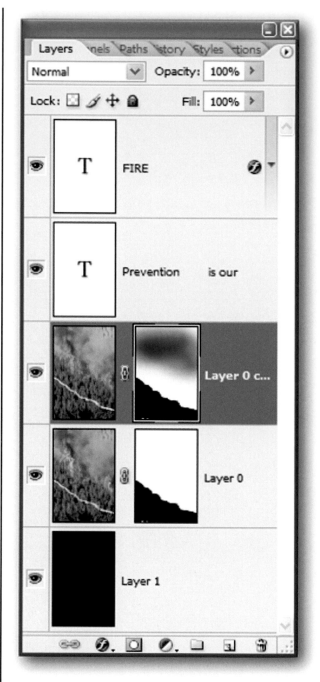

16 The final touch for this technique is to give the letters an infernal little glow. Select the FIRE text layer and choose Inner Glow. Enter the following:

* **Blend Mode:** Screen
* **Opacity:** 100%
* **Noise:** 0%
* **Color:** R = 250, G = 168, and B = 24
* **Technique:** Softer

* **Source**: Edge
* **Choke:** 0%
* **Size:** 24 px
* **Contour:** Linear (default)
* **Anti-aliased:** checked
* **Range:** 50%
* **Jitter:** 0%

Click OK to accept the style settings.

A short recap

I love how the fire from the photo seems to explode inside the text in the final example. You can see how the subtle inner glow makes the lettering stand out, and the sepia-to-color transition works to add a touch of drama. Notice also that, as in the billboard that you created earlier, the message is effective without additional bells and whistles: the header text grabs the attention, the image dramatizes it, and once the viewer's eyes are captured, the message itself is delivered in a no-nonsense, straight-to-the-point fashion.

Blimp Advertising

Remember our buddy Hank? He's the guy with the tire company. Earlier in this chapter, you slapped his name on a sidewall tire. It turns out that Hank's tire company has been doing very well for itself, but he would like to increase exposure for his brand. The answer? Jump on the bandwagon and buy space on a blimp.

In this tutorial, you take Hank's logo and add it to the side of a blimp for everyone at the Superbowl to see. This is fast, easy, and hopefully for Hank, effective.

THE PLAN

- Advertise on a blimp
- Conform the text to the curved structure of the blimp
- Blend the text for real-world appeal

(1) Open the image blimp.jpg.

(2) Select the Type tool. Open the Character palette and enter the following:

- ✳ **Font:** Arial Black
- ✳ **Style:** Regular
- ✳ **Font Size:** 140 pt
- ✳ **Leading:** 36 pt
- ✳ **Tracking:** 0

- ✳ **Vertical Scale:** 90%
- ✳ **Horizontal Scale:** 110%
- ✳ **Baseline Shift:** 0 pt
- ✳ **Color:** Black
- ✳ **Normal**
- ✳ **Anti-aliasing method:** Sharp

(3) Type **HANK'S TIRES** across the face of the blimp.

(4) Open the Warp tools for the type layer and enter the following:

- ✳ **Style:** Squeeze
- ✳ **Horizontal**
- ✳ **Bend:** -5%
- ✳ **Horizontal Distortion:** -14%
- ✳ **Vertical Distortion:** 0%

5 Click OK. Position the text so that it doesn't cover anything but the side of the blimp. Pay close attention that it does not overlay the prop sticking out of the side.

6 Open the Layer Styles for the type layer and select Gradient Overlay. Use all of the default settings, but change the angle to 90%. Create a gradient that transitions from dark blue to turquoise to white, as shown in the example.

7 Select the stroke settings, and enter the following:

* **Size:** 5 px
* **Position:** Outside
* **Blend Mode:** Overlay
* **Opacity:** 100%
* **Fill Type:** Color
* **Color:** Black

8 Would you believe it is almost done? Open the Blending Options for the style. In the Blend If section, change the settings as follows:

* **Blend If:** Blue
* **This Layer:** Default Settings
* **Underlying Layer:**
  * **Black Stops:** 0
  * **Red Stops:** 95 / 255

9 Save the style and click OK.

A short recap

I certainly hope that Hank is happy and has a long, fruitful life. As you can see, it is easier to create photo-realistic advertising on a blimp than for a mega-store façade. As always, the key is in the lighting, the shading, and the blending. Isn't that how we already perceive the world? Life, my friend, is a series of gradients. Here's hoping that our lives aren't only shades of gray.

leisure time

There comes a time in every person's daily routine when a break in the monotony is not only desired but required. What activities we partake in to unwind vary greatly (and that is an understatement). Some take comfort in quiet walks on the beach, while others yearn for the adrenaline rush of a roller coaster. Whatever the extreme, you can bet that fancified fonts are lurking in the background somewhere.

This chapter delves into our leisure time and dissects the type that we find there. Write a message on a sandy beach, create your own candy, and snack at the movies by creating a popcorn box from scratch. Take a stroll with someone whom you care about and etch a message in a tree, or just relax with a video game. Surf the Web, or get a tattoo. Photoshop allows you to relax and have fun for a bit.

At the Beach

There are few things more relaxing than the sound of breaking waves. When my son was still a babe, we purchased a number of cassettes (remember those?) with soft music and sounds to aid in him slipping off to dreamland. I don't know if it ever helped him, but those tapes certainly knocked his daddy out. What I found interesting is all these tapes had a subtle track of wave noises in the background. This technique demonstrates one way to draw a message in a soggy, sandy beach. You don't require a stick for this bit of text, however. Photoshop is all you need.

THE PLAN

- Write a message on a sandy beach image
- Change the perspective to match the photo
- Blend the text into the sand

1 Open the image beach-01.jpg. This photo has an off-kilter perspective, and *you need to distort your text* to match the angle of the photo.

2 Select the Type tool. Open the Character palette and set up the font as follows:

- **Font:** Blackadder ITC (if this font is not installed, find a font that appears roughly drawn)
- **Style:** Regular
- **Font Size:** 140 pt
- **Leading:** 36 pt
- **Tracking:** 0
- **Vertical Scale:** 90%
- **Horizontal Scale:** 110%
- **Baseline Shift:** 0 pt

- **Color:** White
- Italic
- **Anti-aliasing method:** Smooth

3 Enter your message. Something short like "Hi!" will suffice.

4 Choose Layer⇨Rasterize⇨Rasterize Type. This frees up the transform tools that you need to change the perspective of the text to match the photo.

5 Choose Edit⇨Transform⇨Perspective. Narrow the top of the text to about three-quarters of the original width. Accept the transformation.

6 Choose Edit⇨Transform⇨Perspective again, and shorten the right side of the text a bit. Accept the transformation.

7 Choose Edit⇨Transform⇨Distort. Move the upper-right corner toward the center about one-quarter of the width. Accept the transformation.

8 Finally, choose Edit⇨Transform⇨Rotate. Rotate the text about 45 degrees counterclockwise and accept the transformation.

9 Command/Ctrl-click the type layer to create a selection. Select the Background layer and choose Layer⇨New⇨Layer via Copy.

10 Select the Background layer again. Choose Select⇨Modify⇨Expand. Increase the size of the selection by 20 pixels and click OK. Next, choose Select⇨Feather and enter a feather radius of 15 pixels. Press Command/Ctrl+C to copy the selection, and then press Command/Ctrl+V to paste it into a new layer. Turn off the original white type layer.

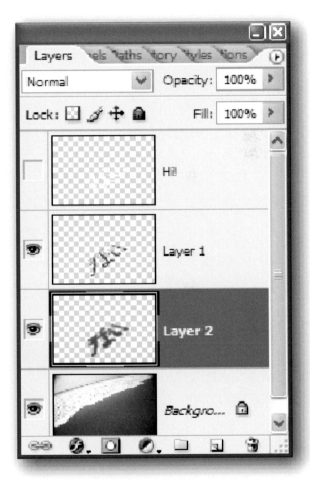

11 Ensure that the sandy type layer just above the background is selected, and open the Layer Styles dialog box. Choose the Bevel and Emboss settings, and enter the following to imprint the sandy text into the beach.

* **Style:** Inner Bevel
* **Technique:** Smooth
* **Depth:** 100%
* **Direction:** Down
* **Size:** 9 px

* **Soften:** 0 px
* **Angle:** 120 degrees
* **Use Global Light:** unchecked
* **Altitude:** 30 degrees
* **Gloss Contour:** Linear (default)
* **Anti-aliased:** checked
* **Highlight Mode:** Screen
    * **Color:** R = 105, G = 98, and B = 98
    * **Opacity:** 80%
* **Shadow Mode:** Multiply
    * **Color:** Black
    * **Opacity:** 95%

Click OK. The bottom layer is now depressed into the sand, giving a washed-away feel to the text.

(12) Select the sandy type layer just above the newly depressed layer. Open the Layer Styles, and again select Bevel and Emboss. Enter the following settings:

* **Style:** Inner Bevel
* **Technique:** Smooth
* **Depth:** 510%
* **Direction:** Down
* **Size:** 10 px
* **Soften:** 0 px
* **Angle:** 135 degrees
* **Use Global Light:** unchecked
* **Altitude:** 37 degrees
* **Gloss Contour:** Linear (default)

* **Anti-aliased:** checked
* **Highlight Mode:** Screen
* **Color:** R = 105, G = 98, and B = 98
* **Shadow Mode:** Screen
    * **Color:** Black
    * **Opacity:** 27%

(13) The text is still a bit light, even with this second depressed layer. Select the Gradient Overlay settings. Enter the following:

* **Blend Mode:** Overlay
* **Opacity:** 30%
* **Gradient:** Black to White gradual (default gradient)
* **Reverse:** unchecked
* **Style:** Linear
* **Align with Layer:** checked
* **Angle:** 125 degrees
* **Scale:** 100%

(14) Click OK. If the text is too deep or sharp in some areas, then create a layer mask and paint over those areas with gray, or with black with the opacity of the brush set to about 50%.

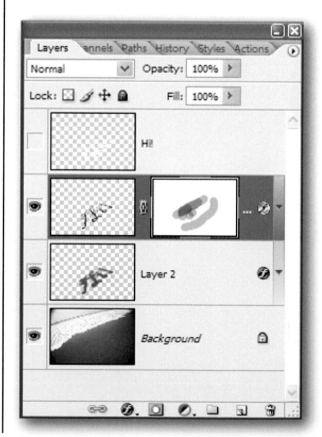

A short recap

This tutorial makes me yearn for a trip to the coast. Not to discredit the mountains surrounding my home, but I'm an old Navy man and always found comfort in the sights and smells of the surf. The key is to have two separate type layers: one for the soft outer depressions and one for the slightly sharper inner etchings. You can manipulate the layers to increase the amount of bevel and the sharpness, and this makes the type appear fresher and not recently washed away by the waves. As always, experiment!

Sweet Tooth

Chocolate is one of my favorite food groups. Okay, maybe it isn't a 'group' per se, but it should be grouped right up there with coffee as a daily requirement. This tutorial creates a chocolate bar from scratch, including the confectioner's name stamped in the bar. Heck, we'll even sample the wares and taste a bite of velvety yumminess.

THE PLAN

- Create a candy bar from scratch
- Divide the bar into four sections
- Stamp the confectioner's name in the bar
- Take a bite out of the bar

1 Create a new image with the following dimensions and specifications:

- **Name:** Candy
- **Preset:** Custom
- **Width:** 10 inches
- **Height:** 5 inches
- **Resolution:** 300 pixels/inch
- **Color Mode:** RGB, 8 bit
- **Background Contents:** White

The layout of the candy bar needs to be as symmetrical as possible, and the rulers can help you with this. If the rulers are not turned on, choose View⇨Rulers (Command/Ctrl+R). Right-click one of the rulers and select Percent from the list that appears.

2 Change the foreground color to R = 65, G = 45, and B = 15.

3 Create a new layer. Select the Rectangular Marquee tool and create a selection beginning at the 10% point, both horizontally and vertically. Draw the selection out to the 90% point, horizontally and vertically. Use the position indicators that appear on the rulers as your guides.

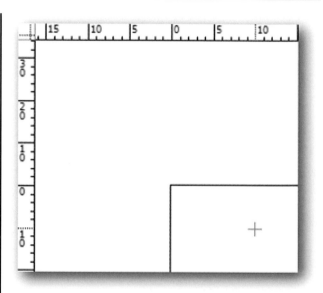

4 In the new layer, fill the selection with the foreground color.

5 Grab the Selection tool and pull out guides from the vertical ruler, positioning them at 27.5%, 50%, and 72.5% positions on the horizontal ruler. These guides visually divide the candy bar into four sections.

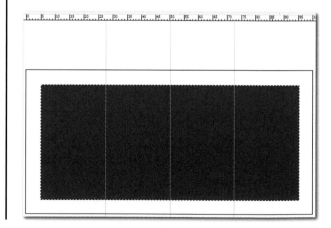

6 Using the Rectangular Marquee tool again, select a rectangular area that covers most of the first section of the candy bar. Leave a narrow border between the outside edge of the selection and the edges of the candy bar and the first guide. Choose Layer⇨New⇨Layer via Copy to isolate the selection on its own layer.

7 With the new section's layer selected, open the Layer Styles and select Bevel and Emboss. Enter the following settings:

* **Style:** Inner Bevel
* **Technique:** Smooth
* **Depth:** 159%
* **Direction:** Down
* **Size:** 8 px
* **Soften:** 7 px
* **Angle:** 120 degrees
* **Use Global Light:** unchecked
* **Altitude:** 30 degrees
* **Gloss Contour:** Linear (default)
* **Anti-aliased:** checked
* **Highlight Mode:** Screen
  * **Color:** White
  * **Opacity:** 75%
* **Shadow Mode:** Multiply
  * **Color:** Black
  * **Opacity:** 75%

8 Now to put some molded designs into the face of the candy. Duplicate the section's layer. Choose Image⇨Rotate Canvas⇨90 degrees CW to orient the candy bar

vertically. Choose Filter⇨Sketch⇨Halftone Pattern. Set Size to 6, Contrast to 50, and Pattern Type to Line. Click OK.

9 Choose Select⇨Color Range. Set the Fuzziness to 40, and then ensure that Selection is checked. Using the Eyedropper tool, select the light areas of the pattern. Click OK and press Delete.

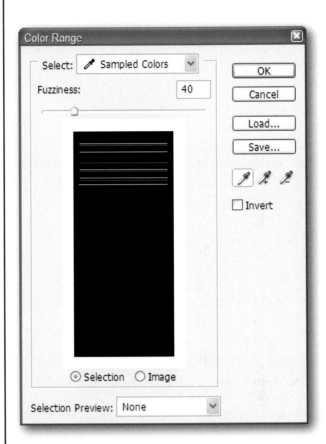

10 Open the Layer Styles dialog box and apply the following Bevel and Emboss settings:

* **Style:** Inner Bevel
* **Technique:** Smooth
* **Depth:** 55%
* **Direction:** Up
* **Size:** 0 px
* **Soften:** 0 px
* **Angle:** -130 degrees
* **Use Global Light:** unchecked
* **Altitude:** 40 degrees

* **Gloss Contour:** Linear (default)
* **Anti-aliased:** checked
* **Highlight Mode:** Screen
  * **Color:** White
  * **Opacity:** 100%
* **Shadow Mode:** Multiply
  * **Color:** Black
  * **Opacity:** 100%

(11) Save the layer style. If there are a few points that remained white along the left edge, then create a mask for the layer and cover these points with black in the mask.

(12) Create a new layer. Select the Rectangular Marquee tool again, create a rectangular selection in the center of the lined area, and fill it with the foreground color. Open the Layer Styles again and enter the following Bevel and Emboss settings:

* **Style:** Inner Bevel
* **Technique:** Chisel Hard
* **Depth:** 130%
* **Direction:** Down
* **Size:** 5 px
* **Soften:** 0 px
* **Angle:** -124 degrees
* **Use Global Light:** unchecked
* **Altitude:** 32 degrees
* **Gloss Contour:** Linear (default)
* **Anti-aliased:** checked
* **Highlight Mode:** Screen
  * **Color:** White
  * **Opacity:** 85%
* **Shadow Mode:** Multiply
  * **Color:** White
  * **Opacity:** 75%

(13) To stamp the logo into the bar, select the Type tool and open the Character palette. Enter the following font settings:

* **Font:** Times New Roman
* **Style:** Regular
* **Font Size:** 30 pt
* **Leading:** 36 pt

* **Tracking:** 0
* **Vertical Scale:** 90%
* **Horizontal Scale:** 100%
* **Baseline Shift:** 0 pt
* **Color:** Foreground Color
* Normal
* **Anti-aliasing method:** Sharp

(14) Type the name of the candy bar over the centered rectangle. I'm naming mine HARRY's.

(15) Open the Layer Styles for the type layer. Again, the Bevel and Emboss settings come into play, this time to stamp the name into the chocolate.

* **Style:** Inner Bevel
* **Technique:** Smooth
* **Depth:** 51%
* **Direction:** Up
* **Size:** 0 px
* **Soften:** 0 px
* **Angle:** -130 degrees
* **Use Global Light:** unchecked
* **Altitude:** 40 degrees
* **Gloss Contour:** Linear (default)
* **Anti-aliased:** checked
* **Highlight Mode:** Screen
  * **Color:** White
  * **Opacity:** 65%
* **Shadow Mode:** Multiply
  * **Color:** Black
  * **Opacity:** 100%

Save the layer style and click OK.

16 Choose Image⇨Rotate Canvas⇨90 degrees CCW to place the candy bar back on its side. Hold down the Command/Ctrl key and click on each layer that makes up the quarter section that you just created.

17 Choose Layer⇨Smart Objects⇨Group into New Smart Object. The candy section retains the settings that you applied when it is rotated.

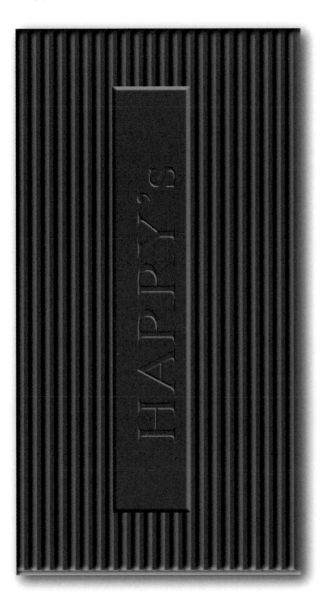

18 Select Layer 1, or the large candy bar layer. Because the bar also needs to have depth, open the Layer Styles one more time and select Bevel and Emboss. Enter the following:

- **Style:** Inner Bevel
- **Technique:** Smooth
- **Depth:** 300%
- **Direction:** Up
- **Size:** 16 px
- **Soften:** 0 px
- **Angle:** 120 degrees
- **Use Global Light:** unchecked
- **Altitude:** 40 degrees
- **Gloss Contour:** Linear (default)
- **Anti-aliased:** checked
- **Highlight Mode:** Screen
  - **Color:** White
  - **Opacity:** 75%
- **Shadow Mode:** Multiply
  - **Color:** Black
  - **Opacity:** 75%

Save the style and click OK.

19 Select the Move tool. Duplicate the smart object three times. Using the arrow keys, move an object to the other three quarters of the candy bar. Leave some space between the guides and edges of the big bar. When you are done, render the background invisible and choose Layer⇨Merge Visible. This places the entire candy bar on a single layer.

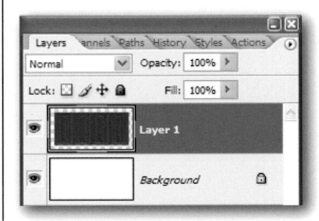

20 Let's sample the wares and take a bite out of the bar. Select the Lasso tool. Set the Feather to 0 in the Options bar and make a rough selection in the form of a bite mark in the upper-left corner. Use the example below as a guide. Once you select it, press Delete.

21 Once more with Bevel and Emboss. Open the Layer Styles and select the Bevel and Emboss settings. Enter the following:

* **Style:** Inner Bevel
* **Technique:** Chisel Hard
* **Depth:** 140%
* **Direction:** Up
* **Size:** 3 px
* **Soften:** 0 px
* **Angle:** 103 degrees
* **Use Global Light:** unchecked
* **Altitude:** 42 degrees

* **Gloss Contour:** Linear (default)
* **Anti-aliased:** checked
* **Highlight Mode:** Screen
  * **Color:** White
  * **Opacity:** 75%
* **Shadow Mode:** Multiply
  * **Color:** Black
  * **Opacity:** 100%

Save the layer style and click OK.

22 Do you recall the 3D type from the previous chapter? The same technique adds depth to the candy bar. Duplicate the layer, then select the version on the bottom. Select the Move tool. With the arrow keys, move the layer two clicks left and one down. Duplicate the bottom candy layer again, select the one beneath the new duplicate, and again move it two clicks to the left and one down. Repeat the process until you have about six layers adding to the depth of the candy bar.

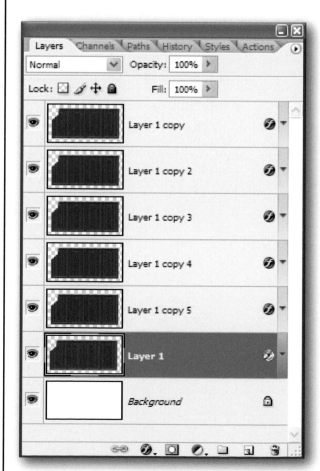

(23) Merge all of the candy layers together. Open the Layer Styles and select Drop Shadow. Enter the following:

* **Blend Mode:** Multiply
* **Color:** Black
* **Opacity:** 75%
* **Angle:** 120 degrees
* **Use Global Light:** unchecked
* **Distance:** 20 px
* **Spread:** 0%
* **Size:** 40 px
* **Contour:** Linear (default)
* **Anti-aliased:** checked
* **Noise:** 0%

Click OK.

(24) Command/Ctrl-click the candy bar layer to generate a selection around it. Select the Burn tool and darken the areas of the bite where they need to blend the bite together better.

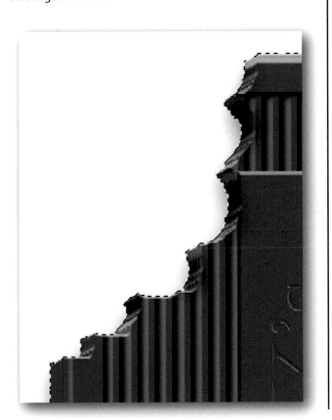

(25) Duplicate the candy bar layer, and then choose Filter⇨ Render⇨Lighting Effects. Enter the following:

* **Style:** Default
* **Light Type:** Spotlight
* **On:** checked
* **Intensity:** 25
* **Focus:** 69
* **Color:** White
* **Properties:**
  * **Gloss:** 50
  * **Material:** 69 (Metallic)
  * **Exposure:** 0
  * **Color:** White
  * **Ambience:** 8
* **Texture Channel:** None
* **White is High:** checked
* **Height:** 50

Click OK.

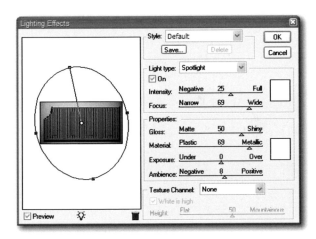

(26) Reduce the opacity of the new layer to 55%.

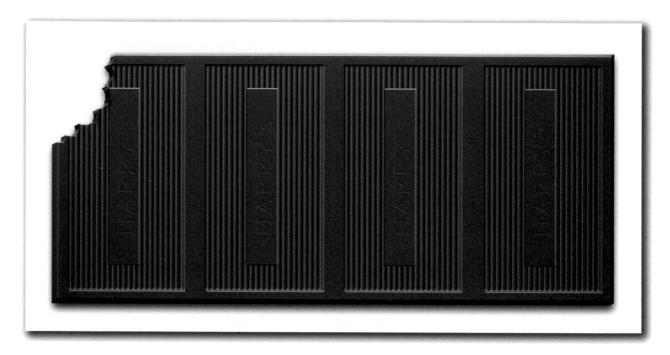

A short recap

I lost count of how many times we applied the Bevel and Emboss settings in this tutorial. As you can see, they were key in producing the realism of the candy bar, including the manufacturer's stamp on each section. This tutorial demonstrates the creation of a plain milk chocolate bar, but I prefer mine with almonds. That tutorial will have to wait for another day.

Let's Go Out to the Lobby

Because we are on the subject of snacks and relaxation, this tutorial ventures where those two subjects merge: the movie theater. Even in these days of video on demand, TIVO, and the Internet, movie theaters still retain a fond spot in the hearts of millions. I go for the whole experience: the huge screen, the thunderous audio and, yes, the overpriced snacks.

In this tutorial, you create the kind of campy popcorn box that adorned the floors of movie theaters everywhere a few decades ago. Don't forget to grab a pop to wash it down!

THE PLAN

- Create a popcorn box from scratch
- Render the box in a 3D perspective
- Add stylized type
- Place the box in a cartoonish 3D setting
- Add some popcorn-like embellishments

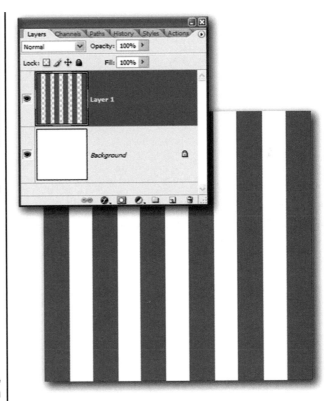

(1) Create a new image with the following dimensions and attributes:

* **Name:** Popcorn Pattern
* **Preset:** Custom
* **Width:** 10 inches
* **Height:** 10 inches
* **Resolution:** 300 pixels/inch
* **Color Mode:** RGB, 8 bit
* **Background Contents:** White

(2) The first item to tackle is the pattern for the box, which is usually in festive red-and-white pattern combinations. Make a new layer and change the foreground color to R = 250, G = 54. and B = 1.

(3) Select the Rectangular Marquee tool and make a narrow vertical selection along the left side of the image, about an inch wide. Fill this selection with red. Select the Move tool and move the selection to the right with the arrow keys until the amount of space between the selection and the bar equals about the width of the bar. Fill the selection with the foreground color again. Do this until you have a series of red bars across the layer. You may also adjust the layer with the Edit⇨Transform⇨Scale settings to ensure that the bars are symmetrical across the face of the layer.

(4) Choose Edit⇨Define Pattern. Name the pattern ('Popcorn' works well) and click OK to add it to the active pattern set. Close the pattern image.

(5) Create a new image with the following specifications:

* **Name:** Popcorn Box
* **Preset:** Custom
* **Width:** 15 inches
* **Height:** 15 inches
* **Resolution:** 300 pixels/inch
* **Color Mode:** RGB, 8 bit
* **Background Contents:** White

6 Make a new layer. Grab the Rectangular Marquee tool in the toolbar and make a vertical rectangular selection that spans about three-quarters of the height of the image, leaving more room at the top of the selection than the bottom in relation to the edge. Select the Elliptical Marquee tool. Click the Add To Selection button in the Options bar and create a circle selection at the top of the rectangular selection so that the circular selection is cut in half by the top edge of the rectangular selection. Look at the example and use it as a guide.

8 Choose Edit➪Transform➪Perspective. Click on one of the bottom corners and move it slightly toward the center to give the box face a shape that you would find at the movie theater. The old popcorn boxes were generally wider at the top than at the bottom.

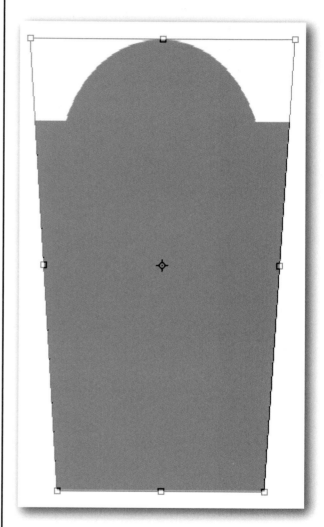

9 Accept the transformation.

7 Choose Edit➪Fill, and fill the selection with 50% gray. Click OK.

10 To add the stripes to the box face, you could simply create a selection and fill it with the pattern. However, this doesn't give you any control over how the pattern lays on the box. Open the Layer Styles and choose Pattern Overlay. Enter the following settings:

* **Blend Mode:** Normal
* **Opacity:** 100%
* **Pattern:** Popcorn Stripes Pattern
* **Scale:** 100%
* **Link with Layer:** checked

Before you close the Layer Styles, take a look at how the stripes lay on the face of the box. Select the Move tool and position the pattern so that the stripes are even across the face and edges. Once you are happy with their position, click OK.

11 Create a new layer beneath the box face layer. Select the box face and choose Layer⇨Merge Down, collapsing the style.

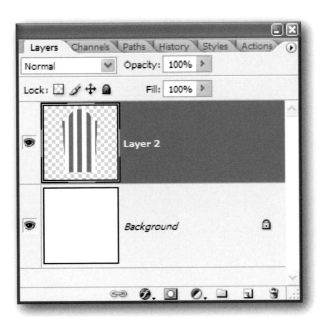

12 Choose Edit⇨Transform⇨Distort. Shorten the right side of the box by moving the lower-right corner up slightly, and narrow the bottom slightly more by moving the two bottom corners toward the center. The idea is to give the box face the perspective that it would have if you were looking down at it and at an angle. Take a look at the example as a guide, and accept the transformation.

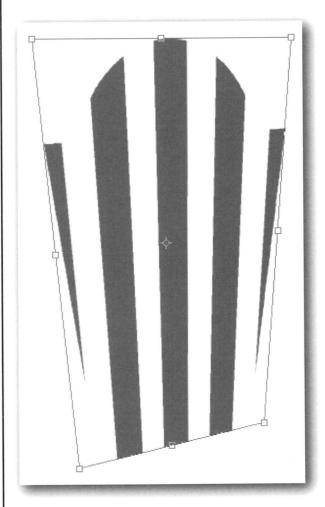

It may be difficult to see the development of the box over the white background. For that reason, I'm adding a stylized gradient background for the remainder of this effect to make the box stand out.

13 Create a new layer. Select the Rectangular Marquee tool and make a vertical rectangle roughly the height of the left edge of the box front and half the width. Fill the selection with the red that you used as the foreground. Deselect the rectangle.

14 Choose Edit➪Transform➪Distort. Align the right edge of the box with the left edge of the box front. Distort the image (as shown in the following example) to create the side of the box as though you were viewing it at an angle. Accept the transformation.

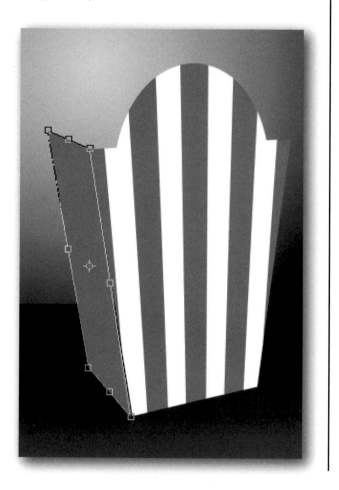

15 Create a new layer beneath the box face layer. Select the Polygonal Lasso tool and draw a triangular selection that serves as the right side of the box. Fill the selection with light gray.

16 Command/Ctrl-click the box face layer. Select the Move tool and position the selection so that you can use it as the back of the box. Use the upper-left corner on the box side as a positioning reference. Once it is in place, fill the selection with the same gray that you used before. Grab the Polygonal Lasso tool and select the areas that extend beyond where the box edges would normally reside. Delete these areas.

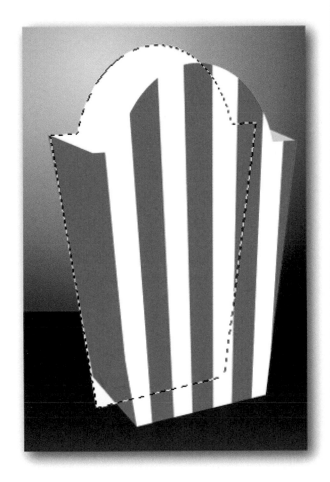

17 The box is almost finished now. To shade the layer that you just created, a Gradient Overlay layer style helps to bring it into the semi-real world. Open the Layer Styles, select Gradient Overlay, and enter the following:

* **Blend Mode:** Normal
* **Opacity:** 50%
* **Gradient:** Black to White (default)
* **Reverse:** unchecked
* **Style:** Radial
* **Align with Layer:** checked
* **Angle:** 140 degrees
* **Scale:** 140%

Click OK to accept the style settings.

18 Select the box side layer and choose the Burn tool. Enter the following settings in the Options bar:

* **Brush:** Feathered, Round
* **Master Diameter:** 800
* **Range:** Highlights
* **Exposure:** 40%

Run the Burn tool over the most distant edge of the box side. Slightly darken the side where the corner of the box joins the side and the face. Shade the lower area of the box side a bit darker to create the illusion of shadow. For even darker shading, change the range from Highlights to Midtones.

19 Repeat the same process on the box face. Use the example shown here as a visual guide. Remember, use light applications of the Burn tool for the best results, and do not linger too long on one area.

20 The text effect in this tutorial is actually the easiest technique. Select the Type tool and open the Character palette. Enter the following type settings:

* **Font:** WallowHMKBold (a rounded, hand-drawn substitution also works well)
* **Style:** Regular
* **Font Size:** 36 pt
* **Leading:** 0 pt
* **Tracking:** 0
* **Vertical Scale:** 90%
* **Horizontal Scale:** 110%
* **Baseline Shift:** 0 pt
* **Color:** Black
* Normal
* **Anti-aliasing method:** Smooth

21 Type **POPCORN** on the face of the box. Choose Edit⇨Transform⇨Rotate and turn the text to fit the perspective of the box.

(22) Choose Layer➪Rasterize➪Rasterize Type. Open the Edit menu and select Transform➪Warp. Move the corner points so that the text better fits the perspective of the box. You may also opt to give it a cartoonish curve using the Warp option. Accept the transformation.

(23) Open the Layer Styles and click Color Overlay. Change the color to the red that you used for the stripes. Next, select Stroke. Enter the following settings:

* **Size:** 27 px
* **Position:** Outside
* **Blend Mode:** Normal
* **Opacity:** 100%
* **Fill Type:** Gradient (Black to White, with the center color stops set to 50% each)
* **Style:** Shape Burst
* **Align with Layer:** checked
* **Angle:** 90 degrees
* **Scale:** 100%

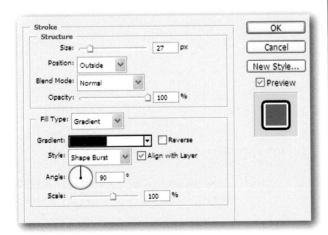

Click OK.

(24) As a final touch, a few popcorn shapes added to the box and background should get those taste buds working. Select the Custom Shape tool. Open the Shapes menu and load the Nature set. Select the cloud shape — it should be the ninth icon. Click the Fill Shape button in the Options bar.

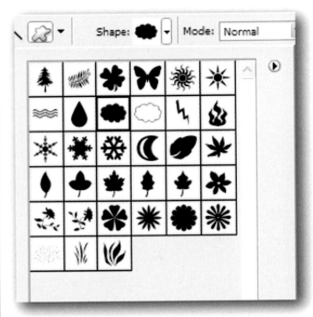

Change the foreground color to white. Create a new layer beneath the type layer. Draw a few popped kernels on the face of the box. Edit with the Transform tools as you did with the text, to conform the kernels to the box face.

If you created a background for the box as I did, you may also add a few faded shapes to the wall behind the box.

A short recap

Boxes, pyramids, buildings, and spheres — Photoshop is masterful for tackling basic geometric shapes. Again, the key is the lighting and the shading that add the required dimension to the piece. This tutorial doesn't make an object that one would believe is a photo, but the effect does give a vector-style illusion as though it were created in Adobe Illustrator or another drawing program. When you can't find a billboard for your message, sometimes it is simply easier to make one.

Carved in the Tree

When I was a kid, oh so long ago, everyone had a pocketknife; you never knew when the urge to make sharp, pointy sticks might arise. My son the cub scout recently earned his whittling badge and received his first pocketknife. His first masterpiece? A sharp, pointy stick. These days, the scouts have to pass certain saftey procedures before getting their badge. When I was young, there were no such restrictions. I have the scar to prove it.

This tutorial isn't about making pointy sticks, but it does involve some digital whittling. Using two photos and opening your Photoshop pocketknife, you carve a message in the side of an old pine tree. Nothing shouts affection like defacing nature for your soulmate.

THE PLAN

- Create a layered image consisting of a surface (the bark) and an interior (the wood grain)
- Carve a message through the bark and into the tree

① Begin by opening two images: bark.jpg and wood-grain.jpg. Select the entire bark image and paste it into a new layer in the wood grain photo.

② With the bark layer active, create a displacement map and save it to your hard drive as outlined in Chapter 4.

③ Grab the Type tool and open the Character palette. Set up the font as follows:

* **Font:** StarbabeHMKBold (any substitution will do, but try to used a rough, uneven font)
* **Style:** Regular
* **Font Size:** 80 pt
* **Leading:** 36 pt
* **Tracking:** 0
* **Vertical Scale:** 90%
* **Horizontal Scale:** 200%
* **Baseline Shift:** 0 pt
* **Color:** White
* **Anti-aliasing method:** Smooth

4 Type your message across the face of the tree. A simple "I Luv U" will suffice.

5 Open the Warp dialog box for the type layer and set up the following:

* **Style:** Bulge
* **Horizontal**
* **Bend:** +26%
* **Horizontal Distortion:** -20%
* **Vertical Distortion:** 0%

Click OK. This helps to add a slight curve to the text, as though it is following the curve of the tree.

6 Rasterize the type layer. Choose Filter⇨Distort⇨ Displace, and enter the following:

* **Horizontal Scale:** 4
* **Vertical Scale:** 4
* **Displacement Map:** Stretch To Fit
* **Undefined Areas:** Repeat Edge Pixels

7 Use the map that you just created to displace the text, and then click OK.

8 Command/Ctrl-click the type layer, select the bark layer, and delete the selection. Select the type layer again and decrease the fill opacity to 0%.

9 Open the Layer Styles for the type layer and select Inner Bevel. Enter the following settings:

* **Style:** Inner Bevel
* **Technique:** Chisel Hard

* **Depth:** 650%
* **Direction:** Down
* **Size:** 40 px
* **Soften:** 0 px
* **Angle:** 120 degrees
* **Use Global Light:** unchecked
* **Altitude:** 25 degrees
* **Gloss Contour:** Linear (default)
* **Anti-aliased:** checked
* **Highlight Mode:** Screen
  * **Color:** R = 141, G = 136, and B = 127
  * **Opacity:** 75%
* **Shadow Mode:** Multiply
  * **Color:** R = 97, G = 75, and B = 62
  * **Opacity:** 75%

10 Select Color Overlay. Set the Blend Mode to Color. Specify a color of R = 75, G = 74, and B = 74. Set Opacity to 44%. Save the layer style and click OK.

11 To peel away the bark from the edges of the text, a simple application of the Eraser tool works wonders. Select the Eraser tool. In the Options bar, choose a rough brush from the default set, and set the size to about 70 points. Set up the rest of the options as follows:

* **Mode:** Brush
* **Opacity:** 100%
* **Flow:** 100%
* **Erase to History:** unchecked

12 Apply the eraser roughly around the perimeter of the text. The idea is to create some jagged wearing of the edges as though they are being peeled away by the knife or by time and the elements.

13 Select the bark layer. Open the Layer Styles, select Bevel and Emboss, and enter the following:

* **Style:** Inner Bevel
* **Technique:** Chisel Hard
* **Depth:** 320%
* **Direction:** Up
* **Size:** 15 px
* **Soften:** 0 px
* **Angle:** 120 degrees
* **Use Global Light:** unchecked
* **Altitude:** 25 degrees
* **Gloss Contour:** Linear (default)
* **Anti-aliased:** checked
* **Highlight Mode:** Multiply
  * **Color:** R = 75, G = 74, B = 74
  * **Opacity:** 55%
* **Shadow Mode:** Multiply
  * **Color:** Black
  * **Opacity:** 55%

14 Click OK and apply the style.

A short recap

As you have probably deduced already, etching text into surfaces is similar in each case, but the final settings are dependent on the material itself. As with the sand and stone tutorials, you should ask yourself at the outset, 'Just what would type look like on a tree?' and proceed with that final image in mind. To carve directly into a piece of grained wood, the process is very similar to that of chiseled stone. But to cut through another surface first, such as the bark in this case, adds another layer of interesting detail to the final image.

Under Your Skin

Tattooing has been a part of human expression for nearly all of recorded history. Research points to the Egyptians as having actively practiced tattooing nearly 6,000 years ago, when it migrated to other cultures around the globe. The significance placed on modern skin art is deeply personal, and in many areas of the globe, it retains a spiritual connotation.

Whether for personal or spiritual reasons, the decision to get a tattoo is something that one needs to consider seriously. Not only are they painful to apply (so I've been told — this author remains tattoo-free), but they are also permanent unless you opt for surgery to have them removed. Wouldn't it be a fantastic service for the tattoo enthusiast to have a visual beforehand of what the tattoo would look like affixed to his or her body?

THE PLAN

- Make a displacement map to conform the type to the contours of the skin
- Affix the type to the body
- Use Layer Styles and Blend If settings to finish the tattoo, making it appear embedded into the skin
- Add embelishments

1 Open the image Bareback.jpg from your book's CD. I have made displacement maps a few times earlier in this book, but skin is a slightly different medium, and so I will go through it one more time.

2 Open the Channels palette. The channel with the greatest variation between the light and darks areas creates the best displacement maps — in this case, the Blue channel. Drag the Blue channel to the Create New Channel icon to create a duplicate. Be sure to select the Blue copy channel. Choose Image⇨Adjustments⇨Brightness/Contrast and increase the Contrast setting to +35. Click OK.

3 Choose Filter⇨Blur⇨Gaussian Blur. Enter 7 for the Blur radius and click OK.

4 Right-click on the Blue copy channel and select Duplicate Channel from the drop-down menu that appears. In the Duplicate Channel dialog box, set the document destination to New, name the map, and click OK. The document opens in Photoshop. Save the displacement map image to a folder on your hard drive (the desktop is also fine). Once you save it, close the displacement map image in Photoshop, and delete the Blue copy channel from the original document.

⑤ Once you have created and saved the displacement map, it is time to design your text. Set the foreground color to black (Command/Ctrl+D). Select the Type tool and choose a calligraphy or script-style font. If the photo were of a man, then we would choose a more masculine font. As this image is of a young lady, a script font better reflects the theme. Enter two lines of text on two separate type layers, in two different font sizes. For the first line, use a font size of 36 points, and for the second line, use 48 points. Select the Move tool and manually position the type layers in the center of the back.

⑥ With the text in position, it is time to add some ink. Select the topmost type layer and open the Layer Styles for that layer. Select Gradient Overlay from the list, and then click in the Gradient window to open the Gradient Editor. Change the first color stop (black) to dark red, and the second stop (white) to light red, or pink. Leave the rest of the gradient settings alone.

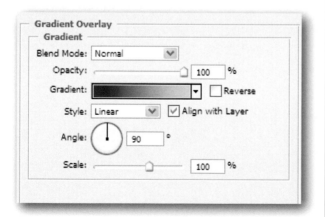

⑦ Select the Stroke setting. Enter the following:

* **Size:** 3 px
* **Position:** Outside
* **Blend Mode:** Normal
* **Opacity:** 100%
* **Fill Type:** Color
* **Color:** R = 5, G = 72, B = 118

⑧ Open the Blending options. Change the Blend If channel to red. As you are working on a canvas of skin, the pink tone of the skin allows for Blend If to work exceptionally well when you embed the ink. Enter the following:

* **Blend If:** Red
* **This Layer:** Default Settings
* **Underlying Layer:**
  * **Black Stops:** 0 / 130
  * **Red Stops:** 91 / 255

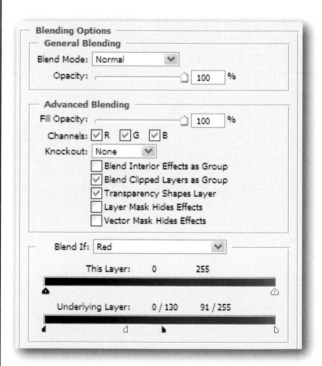

9 Because the stroke around the text is blue, you need to blend it into the skin separately. Open the Blue channel Blend If settings:

* **Blend If:** Blue
* **This Layer:** Default Settings
* **Underlying Layer:**
  * **Black Stops:** 0 / 113
  * **Red Stops:** 255 (default)

Click OK.

10 It's time to conform the type to the contours of the body. First, right-click on each type layer and select Rasterize Type. Once you rasterize the text, it is no longer editable by the Type tool. Select the topmost type layer and choose Edit➪Merge Down to combine the two type layers together.

11 Choose Filter➪Distort➪Displace. By default, the horizontal and vertical scales are both set to 10. Leave all Displace settings at default and click OK. Navigate to the folder on your hard drive where you saved the displacement map, select it, and click OK. The text warps slightly to conform to the light and dark areas of the displacement map, thus also making it conform to the contours of the photo.

12 Some additional blending is often required at this stage, simply because you can now see what areas need further alteration to enhance the realism of the tattoo. For instance, the red fill color in the type is a bit dominant, which gives the feeling that either the ink is extremely fresh or it is merely painted on. Open the Layer Styles for the merged type layer again, and select Gradient Overlay. Reduce the opacity of the gradient to 45%. This allows some of the original black to show through, thus fading the red and revealing additional skin texture.

13 Open the Blending options once again. You can further enhance the effect by changing the Blending Mode to Overlay and tweaking the blend and fill opacities. Reduce the General Blending, or Layer, opacity to 85%, and the Fill opacity under Advanced Blending to 55%.

14 Before closing the Layer Styles dialog box, save the layer style again as a new style. Now you have two layer styles that can assist you in duplicating the effect later.

15 You can now add additional elements and flourishes to the tattoo. For instance, following the same process as above for custom shapes (applying the saved layer style, applying the displacement map, and so forth), you can add interesting designs to accompany the message.

A short recap

The key to tattooing in Photoshop lies in two primary areas: conforming the tattoo to the contours of the body, and the absolute necessity of having the skin appear within the tattoo. Any hair or blemishes that would reside within the bounds of the artwork should be present once you apply the ink. Fading the tattoo with blending options adds to the illusion that time has passed since the subject went under the needle; this also contributes to the realism. Once you have the technique down, you can apply the process to any manner of objects and art, some of which you see in this book. With these steps firmly in mind, your painting skills are limited only by your imagination.

movies gone wild

Movies are a passion of mine. That's not to say that I spend hours in arthouse theaters watching foreign films that hardly anyone has heard of. I'm not that cultured. My passion lies more with well-done thrillers, campy comedy, or film noir. Okay, I admit it — I'm somewhat of a Trekkie, as well.

Many of the movies today do not rely much on plot or character development, let alone a masterful marriage of the two. Special-effects technology being the order of the day, a movie rarely has to deliver much more than realism in unrealistic effects to deliver a multi-million-dollar payday at the box office. My rule of thumb is this: if it is a book first, then read the book before seeing the movie — unless the book in question is a comic or "graphic novel," as the kids like to call them today.

Another key to box-office success is the advertising, and this chapter takes a look at some of the hits that have made their way to DVD over the past few years. Yes, type effects play a very prominent role in said advertising, and so you will try to mimic some of the styles that are used by studio designers. This is not intended to duplicate the styles exactly, but to give you an idea of how they may have been created. Grab your popcorn box from Chapter 5 and let's head to the show.

We Come in Peace

Although there was actually a movie by this title, the idea for this technique doesn't follow that movie's style. Rather, it pays homage (somewhat) to another classic space-horror film that was popular in my teen years. You will create a glowing egg, surround it with stars, and add the title and catch phrase, with some visual splash thrown in for good measure.

To follow this tutorial completely, you should first go to the Website `http://simplythebest.net/fonts/` and download the Alien League font. Install this font on your computer, open Photoshop, and proceed with this section.

THE PLAN

- Create a glowing egg on a dark background
- Add a title and some text
- Add stars to the background

(1) Open the image goldegg.jpg. This image is set up to become an eerie black color, because it is already white. How? Simply by creating an Invert Adjustment layer.

(2) Click on the mask for the adjustment layer, and then set the foreground color to black. With a soft, feathered brush set to 400 pixels or so, paint over the egg in the mask. This restores the original gold on the egg but leaves the hand blue and the background black. Extend the paint slightly beyond the edges of the egg to make the egg appear to glow.

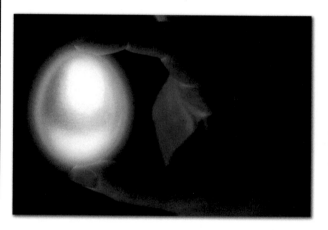

(3) Create a new layer and set the Blend mode to Color and the opacity to 50%. Change the foreground color to R = 25, G = 228, B = 58.

(4) Paint around the outside of the egg in the new layer using the same soft brush as before. This changes the glow to a pale green.

(5) Create a new layer and change the Blend mode to Hue. Paint over the right side of the eggshell, slightly altering the color to green to 'reflect' the glow. Also paint over the palm of the hand, making it appear that the glow is reflecting off the palm as well.

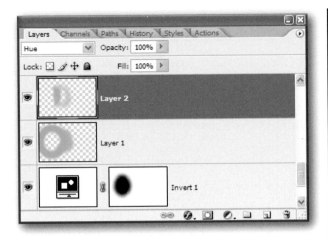

Select the Type tool and open the Character palette. Enter the following font settings:

* **Font:** Alien League
* **Style:** Regular
* **Font Size:** 72 pt
* **Leading:** Auto
* **Vertical Scale:** 100%
* **Horizontal Scale:** 115%
* **Color:** White
* Normal
* **Anti-aliasing method:** Smooth

⑦ Type **AVIANS** at the top of the image, and then open the Layer Styles for the type layer. Select Outer Glow and enter the following settings:

* **Blend Mode:** Screen
* **Opacity:** 75%
* **Noise:** 0%
* **Color:** R = 99, G = 251, B = 128
* **Technique:** Softer
* **Spread:** 0%
* **Size:** 50%
* **Quality Settings:** Default

⑧ Select Inner Glow and enter the following settings:

* **Blend Mode:** Normal
* **Opacity:** 75%
* **Noise:** 0%
* **Color:** R = 205, G = 189, B = 15
* **Technique:** Softer

* **Source:** Edge
* **Choke:** 0%
* **Size:** 20 px
* **Contour:** Linear (default)
* **Anti-aliased:** checked
* **Range:** 50%
* **Jitter:** 0%

⑨ Save the layer style if you want to add it to your toolbox, and click OK.

⑩ Create a new layer. With the foreground color set to white, select the Paintbrush tool. Use a soft, round brush set to 100-150 pixels, and click once over the *I* in *AVIANS*. Choose Blur⇨Motion Blur and enter the following:

* **Blur:** 100 px
* **Angle:** 0 degrees

Click OK.

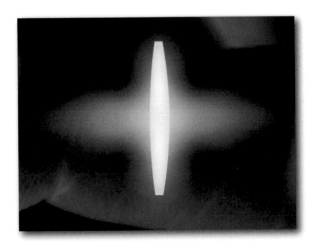

If you would like to increase the intensity of the glow, simply duplicate the blurred layer a few times until you are happy with the effect.

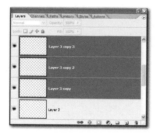

(11) Select the Type tool and open the Character palette. Enter the following font settings:

* **Font:** Alien League
* **Style:** Regular
* **Font Size:** 18 pt
* **Leading:** Auto
* **Vertical Scale:** 100%
* **Horizontal Scale:** 115%
* **Color:** White

* Normal
* **Anti-aliasing method:** Sharp

(12) Along the bottom of the image, type **IN SPACE, NO ONE CAN HEAR YOU CLUCK.**

IN SPACE, NO ONE CAN HEAR YOU CLUCK

(13) To add stars to the image, create a new layer and choose Filter⇨Render⇨Clouds. Next choose Filter⇨Noise⇨Add Noise. Set the Amount to 15-20% and the Distribution to Gaussian, and ensure that Monochromatic is checked. Click OK. Set the Blend mode for the layer to Screen and reduce the opacity to 35%.

(14) Create a Layer Mask for the stars layer. Set the foreground color to black and, with a soft, round brush, paint over the hand and the egg in the mask so that the stars are primarily in the background.

(15) To add a star, choose Filter⇨Render⇨Lens Flare. Create a flare (I'll allow you to choose the style and size) and place it in the upper-right corner of the star layer. Click OK. To brighten the star, simply create a new layer with the Blend mode set to Screen, and paint lightly over the star with white.

When you are finished, there will be no question of the movie to which you are paying homage!

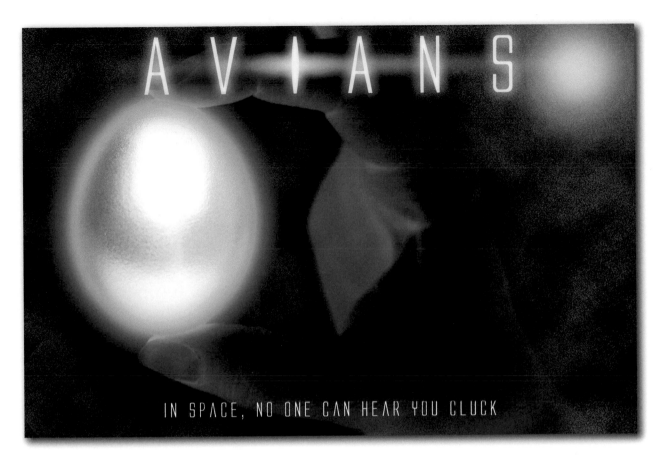

IN SPACE, NO ONE CAN HEAR YOU CLUCK

A short recap

Although not a duplicate of the original poster by any stretch of the imagination, the imagery does give viewers an idea of the movie that is being satirized. One thing that I would like you to note is how simply inverting the color on the original image made a huge difference in the photo: it effectively did most of the work for us in one quick step. Nifty!

Space Fights

I'm one of those late-season baby boomers. That is to say my formative years occurred during the time when things people consider "Retro" today were new, fresh, and innovative. Toys I used to beat to mockeries of their former selves are now sold for small fortunes to collectors, providing they haven't been beaten to husks. The comics I once paged through are now worth thousands . . . but again, who knew or cared back then about meticulous care for toys and comics? Comics were meant to be read, and toys meant to be played with.

Back in those days, cinematic storytelling also took a giant leap. One of the most easily recognizable text effects in the history of the movies is that of a story overview fading into the depths of space. Photoshop is a master of tackling this effect, and this tutorial shows you how.

THE PLAN

- Add paragraph-style text to an image
- Distort the text's perspective
- Fade the text into the great beyond

and extending about twice the height of the image beyond the bottom border. The width of the text box should leave an equal space on either side of the box.

1 Open the image space.jpg.

2 Change the foreground color to R = 250, G = 242, B = 165.

3 Press Command/Ctrl+- to zoom out in the image. In order to get the paragraphs to line up correctly, they should have their perspective altered at the same time, rather than a paragraph at a time. Select the Type tool and draw a paragraph box beginning in the upper-left corner

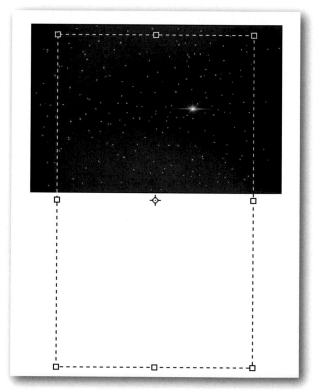

4 Open the Character palette and set up the font as follows:

- **Font:** Arial
- **Style:** Regular

- ✱ **Font Size:** 18 pt
- ✱ **Leading:** 30 pt
- ✱ **Tracking:** 5
- ✱ **Vertical Scale:** 160%
- ✱ **Horizontal Scale:** 100%
- ✱ **Baseline Shift:** 0 pt
- ✱ **Color:** Foreground Color
- ✱ Normal
- ✱ **Anti-aliasing method:** Smooth

(5) Open the Paragraph palette. Set the indents on both the right and left to 4 points, and set the space between paragraphs to 4 points. Click the Justify Last Centered icon.

(6) Click in the text box and begin typing. I have created two paragraphs for this example. The text should extend well beyond the bottom edge of the image, because much of that text will come into view shortly.

(7) Choose Layer⇨Rasterize⇨Type. Now you can change the perspective on the text by choosing Edit⇨Transform⇨Perspective. Widen the bottom of the type layer and narrow the top so that the type appears to be moving away from the foreground. As you alter the perspective, more text comes into view.

(8) To fade the text into space, create a layer mask for the type layer. Select the Gradient tool and press the D key. Select the standard foreground-to-background gradient from the Options bar, and ensure that Linear Gradient is selected as the gradient type. Draw the gradient from top to bottom in the mask.

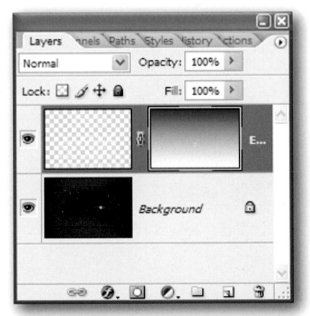

NOTE

Move the text around with the Move tool to check the spelling! Once you have checked it out, reposition the text box. The example here has errors, but they are corrected in the next figure.

Episode I: An empire in crisis

'Twas a time of peace in the known galaxies. For nearly a millenia law and order reigned under the tender guidance of the Imperial Guard. Commerce prospered, health and well-being was known by all. A virtual utopia existed for eons, but such was not to continue.

An Evil known only as 'The Rebels' unleashed a campaign of terror across the charted territories, attacking and killing innocent civilians and heroic Imperial Troopers alike. Even Droids were not safe from the carnage spread by the so-called 'freedom fighters'.

A short recap

That was not too difficult at all — short and sweet. Those poor Imperial Troopers! It's about time that someone told their side of the story.

Where No Designer Has Gone Before

That is not actually true, as many designers have sought to create the perfect sci-fi logo for their favorite star travellers. Do a search for *Star Trek* online and you will be inundated with fan sites, many of which have tried to add their own twist to the logo, the uniform, or with the creation of their own adventures using that future setting. This tutorial is just my take on how a popular franchise could advertise its newest series.

Rather than try to match a font already installed, there are a few free font sites with reasonable replicas of famous font that you can download and use. To follow this tutorial completely, you should first go to the Website `http://simplythebest.net/fonts/` and download the Final Frontier font. Install this font on your computer, open Photoshop, and proceed with this section.

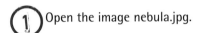

THE PLAN

- Add a spacecraft to a nebula photo
- Create an insignia that will one day be worn by conventioners everywhere
- Add and stylize the franchise name

2 Duplicate the background layer, and then choose Filter⇨Blur⇨Gaussian Blur. Set the Blur Radius to 6 and click OK.

3 Create a mask for the blurred layer, and then fill it from top to bottom with a black-to-white linear gradient.

1 Open the image nebula.jpg.

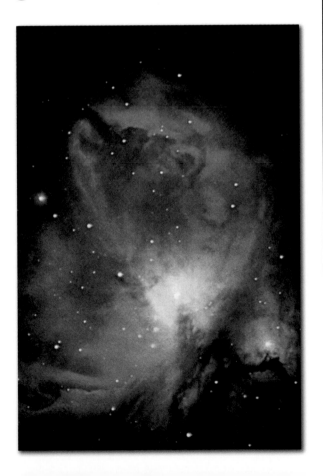

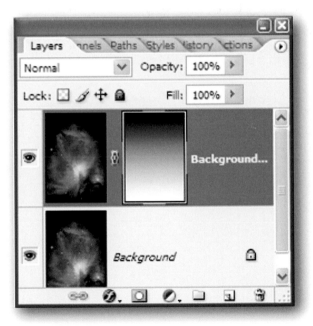

4 Open the image shuttle.png. Drag-and-drop the shuttle from the PNG image to the nebula photo. Create a mask for the shuttle layer, and with a black brush, paint lightly over the edges of the shuttle and the landing gear so that you can see some of the nebula on the shuttle's fringes. Duplicate the blurred nebula layer and place it above the shuttle. Change the Blend mode to Multiply.

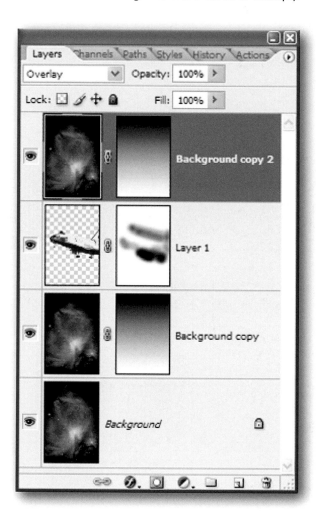

5 Select the Custom Shape tool and load the Nature set from the Custom Shape menu. Select the shape Fire. Create a new layer. In the Options bar, click on the Fill Pixels button and draw the shape in the new layer. Center it in the bottom portion of the image below the shuttle.

6 Open the Layer Styles for the shape layer. Beginning with Bevel and Emboss, enter the following settings:

* **Style:** Inner Bevel
* **Technique:** Smooth
* **Depth:** 380%
* **Direction:** Down
* **Size:** 13 px
* **Soften:** 0 px
* **Angle:** 120 degrees
* **Use Global Light:** unchecked
* **Altitude:** 25 degrees
* **Gloss Contour:** Sawtooth 1 (from the default set)
* **Anti-aliased:** checked
* **Highlight Mode:** Screen
* **Color:** White
* **Opacity:** 100%
* **Shadow Mode:** Multiply
* **Color:** Black
* **Opacity:** 84%

7 Select Outer Glow and enter the following settings:

* **Blend Mode:** Screen
* **Opacity:** 75%
* **Noise:** 0%
* **Color:** R = 255, G = 255, and B = 190

* **Technique:** Softer
* **Spread:** 0
* **Size:** 80
* **Quality:** default settings

8 Select Satin and enter the following settings:

* **Blend Mode:** Soft Light
* **Opacity:** 50%
* **Angle:** 20 degrees
* **Distance:** 8 px
* **Size:** 14 px
* **Contour:** Gaussian (default)
* **Anti-aliased:** checked
* **Invert:** checked

9 Select Color Overlay and enter the following settings:

* **Blend Mode:** Multiply
* **Color:** R = 124, G = 86, and B = 5
* **Opacity:** 100%

10 Just a few more style settings to go. Open the Gradient Overlay and apply the following settings:

* **Blend Mode:** Normal
* **Opacity:** 100%
* **Gradient:** Copper (from default gradient set)
* **Reverse:** unchecked
* **Style:** Linear
* **Align with Layer:** checked
* **Angle:** 90 degrees
* **Scale:** 100%

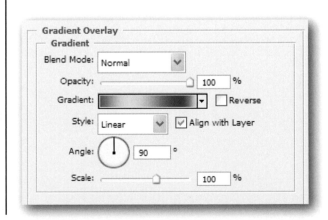

11 Lastly, open Stroke and apply the following settings:

* **Size:** 32 px
* **Position:** Inside
* **Blend Mode:** Normal
* **Opacity:** 100%
* **Fill Type:** Color
* **Color:** R = 246, G = 210, and B = 40

Save the layer style and click OK.

 12 Select the Type tool and open the Character palette. Enter the following font settings:

* **Font:** Final Frontier
* **Style:** Regular
* **Font Size:** 72 pt
* **Leading:** 30 pt
* **Tracking:** 5
* **Vertical Scale:** 100%
* **Horizontal Scale:** 100%
* **Color:** Black
* **Normal**
* **Anti-aliasing method:** Smooth

13 Type the name of the franchise (in this case, **SPACE TRIP**) on two separate layers, and position them one above the other. Apply the Layer Style that you just created for the logo to the text.

A short recap

You will notice that when you apply the style to the lettering, the fill that you see in the styled shape does not appear. That is simply because the text is so narrow that the fill does not have room to make an appearance. The font style plays an important role in these franchise-themed posters, and will continue to do so throughout this chapter.

Tales of Blarnia

One movie was released recently that had its origins in novel form, and it is one of the few that I was actually pleased to see created in "real life." It did not sacrifice the story or the characters to the special effects, but retained the notion that the story and the characters involved were at the heart of the matter. Special effects certainly played a part in this particular film, but only when driven by the story.

This tutorial pays homage to that movie. You will not find the font effect to be particularly difficult. The primary focus of this tutorial, as well as the one to follow, is the canvas on which the type displays.

THE PLAN

- Create a collage using several images
- Render the collage as an artist's rendering
- Add text and stylize it for display

1 Open the images tigerface.jpg and snow_kid.jpg.

2 Select the image of the boy and choose Filter⇨ Extract. Select the Highlighter tool and set the Brush size to 14 pixels. Outline the boy, fill the selection with the Paintbucket tool, and then click Preview. Clean up the edges as needed, and click OK.

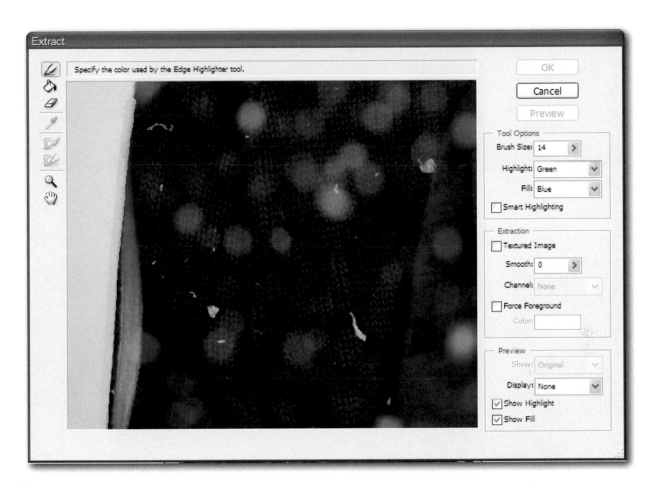

③ Drag-and-drop the boy to the tiger image. Choose Edit⇨Transform⇨Scale and resize the boy so that he takes up less than a quarter of the tiger image. Position him in the lower-right area of the image.

4 Open the image knight.jpg. Double-click the background layer and convert the background to a standard layer. Drag-and-drop the knight into a new layer in the tiger image. Position the knight so that his head and shoulders rest in the upper-left area of the image.

5 Open the Layer Styles for the knight and select Blending Options. In the Blend If area, use the following settings:

* **Blend If:** Blue
* **This Layer:**
    * *Black Stops:* 0
    * *Blue Stops:* 119 | 255

* Underlying Layer:
    * *Black Stops:* 0
    * *Blue Stops:* 255

To further blend the knight layer, create a mask and paint over the areas with black, using a soft brush where the knight covers the tiger.

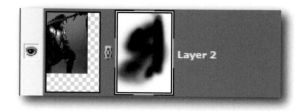

6 Open the image snow_building.jpg. Copy the image and paste it into a new layer in the tiger image. Position the building below and to the left of the tiger.

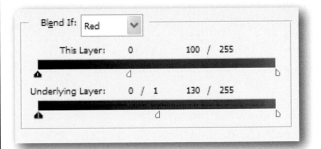

⑨ Create a Hue/Saturation adjustment layer at the top of the Layers palette and enter the following settings:

* **Hue:** 200
* **Saturation:** 33
* **Lightness:** 0
* **Colorize:** checked

Click OK.

⑩ Select the mask for the adjustment layer. Set black as the foreground color and paint over the tiger in the mask. This leaves the tiger with his original color while adding a blue cast to the surrounding images.

⑦ Open the Layer Styles for the building layer and select Blending Options. In the Blend If area, enter the following settings:

* **Blend If:** Gray
* **This Layer:**
  * **Black Stops:** 0
  * **White Stops:** 108 / 255
* **Underlying Layer:**
  * **Black Stops:** 0
  * **White Stops:** 199 / 255

⑧ Select the Red channel in the Blend If settings, and enter the following:

* **Blend If:** Red
* **This Layer:**
  * **Black Stops:** 0
  * **Red Stops:** 100 / 255
* **Underlying Layer:**
  * **Black Stops:** 0 / 1
  * **Red Stops:** 130 / 255

Click OK.

11 Now we can turn this into a painting. Choose Image⇨ Duplicate. Name the duplicate image, click OK, and then choose Layer⇨Flatten Image.

12 Working with the new duplicate image, choose Filter⇨ Artistic⇨Cutout. Enter the following settings:

* **Number of Levels:** 8
* **Edge Simplicity:** 1
* **Edge Fidelity:** 3

Click OK.

13 Choose Filter⇨Artistic⇨Dry Brush. Enter the following settings for the filter:

* **Brush Size:** 5
* **Brush Detail:** 8
* **Texture:** 2

Click OK.

14 Choose Filter⇨Artistic⇨Poster Edges. Enter the following settings for the filter:

* **Edge Thickness:** 0
* **Edge Intensity:** 0
* **Posterization:** 3

The image now appears painted rather than simply as a series of pasted photos.

NOTE

For the final image, I have added an additional line of white text stroked with black to describe the story.

15 Select the Type tool and open the Character palette. Enter the following font settings:

* **Font:** Cloister Black BT (some other gothic-style calligraphy font can work as a substitute)
* **Style:** Regular

* **Font Size:** 90 pt
* **Leading:** 30 pt
* **Tracking:** 5
* **Vertical Scale:** 100%
* **Horizontal Scale:** 100%
* **Color:** R = 133, G = 9, B = 6
* Normal
* **Anti-aliasing method:** Smooth

(16) Type **Tales of**. Create a new type layer and increase the font size to 120 points. Type **Blarnia**. Position the type layers on the lower half of the image, one above the other.

(17) Open the Layer Styles for either type layer and select Bevel and Emboss. Enter the following settings:

* **Style:** Inner Bevel
* **Technique:** Smooth
* **Depth:** 380%
* **Direction:** Down
* **Size:** 5 px
* **Soften:** 0 px
* **Angle:** 120 degrees
* **Use Global Light:** unchecked
* **Altitude:** 25 degrees
* **Gloss Contour:** Linear (default)
* **Anti-aliased:** checked
* **Highlight Mode:** Screen
    * **Color:** White
    * **Opacity:** 100%
* **Shadow Mode:** Multiply
    * **Color:** Black
    * **Opacity:** 84%

(18) Select Outer Glow from the Layer Styles list and enter the following settings:

* **Blend Mode:** Screen
* **Opacity:** 75%
* **Noise:** 0%
* **Glow Type:** Color
* **Color:** R = 255, G = 255. and B = 190
* **Technique:** Softer
* **Spread:** 0%
* **Size:** 81 px
* **Contour:** default
* **Anti-aliased:** checked
* **Range:** 50%
* **Jitter:** 0%

(19) Select Gradient Overlay and enter the following settings:

* **Blend Mode:** Normal
* **Opacity:** 100%
* **Gradient:** Custom - Gradual foreground to background
* **Foreground Color:** R = 254, G = 9, and B – 2
* **Background Color:** R = 246, G = 98, and B = 3
* **Reverse:** unchecked
* **Style:** Linear
* **Align with Layer:** checked
* **Angle:** 90 degrees
* **Scale:** 100%

(20) Open Stroke and enter the following settings:

* **Size:** 10 px
* **Position:** Outside
* **Blend Mode:** Normal
* **Opacity:** 100%
* **Fill Type:** Color
* **Color:** Black

(21) Save the layer style and click OK.

A short recap

I love the way that the filters play with the colors in the final image. Again, the image was really the focus, rather than the font. The next tutorial follows the same idea, tackling yet another book-turned-movie.

Larry Blotter

The font for this one is another variation of reflective metal. You will notice elements of other tutorials, such as the process of creating chiseled wood from earlier in this book. The collage for this technique is as important to the final image as the font effect, because it displays thematic elements found in the movie. Granted, the movie in this case is imaginary, but take a look at the posters that this tutorial attempts to mimic and you will see what I mean.

To follow this tutorial completely, you should first go to the Website `http://simplythebest.net/fonts/` and download the Harry Potter font. Install this font on your computer, open Photoshop, and proceed with this section.

THE PLAN

- Collage several images together
- Alter the lighting to create a gothic feel to the piece
- Create metallic text for the series name
- Stylize the movie title font to reflect the theme of the film

① Open the images castle.jpg and wizard.png.

② Duplicate the background layer in the castle photo. As the wizard image is a PNG file, just click on the boy wizard and drag-and-drop him in a new layer in the castle image. Resize the boy using Edit⇨Transform⇨Scale so that he appears at the bottom of the image.

205

3 Select the castle layer and choose Filter⇨Distort⇨ Lens Correction. Enter the following adjustments:

* **Vertical Perspective:** -78
* **Horizontal Perspective:** 0
* **Angle:** 0
* **Edge:** Transparency
* **Scale:** 126

Click OK.

Edit⇨Transform⇨Rotate. Rotate the glasses to match the angle of the boy's head, and then accept the rotation.

5 Open the image goblet.png and drag-and-drop the goblet image to the castle image. Move the goblet layer beneath the boy's layer. Resize the goblet (Edit⇨ Transform⇨Scale) so that it is about half the height of the castle image. Select the Move tool and position the goblet in the lower half of the image.

4 Open the image glasses.png. Drag-and-drop the glasses into the castle image, over the boy's layer. Choose Edit⇨Transform⇨Scale and resize the glasses to fit the boy's face. Accept the transformation, and then choose

6 You are now going to fill the cup, but not with liquid. The one thing that these types of movies are best at generating is cool, hard cash. Why not let our movie poster depict that?

Open the image cashwad.jpg. Copy the entire image, and then paste it into the castle image beneath the goblet layer.

7 Select the Move tool, and move the layer so that the hand is covered by the goblet, with the money extending above the rim. Resize the image with the Transform tools as needed.

8 Open the Layer Styles for the money layer and select the Blending options. In the Blend If area, using the following slider settings:

* **Blend If:** Gray
* **This Layer:**
  * **Black Stops:** 0 / 55
  * **White Stops:** 255
* **Underlying Layer:**
  * **Black Stops:** 0
  * **White Stops:** 255

9 Create a mask for the money layer and paint with black over the areas of the hand that are still visible. If the background of the money layer is still faintly visible, then paint over these areas as well.

10 Create a mask for the goblet layer. Paint with black over the inside of the cup where the money underlays it, so that it appears that the cash is springing forth from the cup.

11 Duplicate the image (Image⇨Duplicate). Choose Layer⇨Flatten Image, and then make two copies of the background layer. Name the top copy Lit Version and the one beneath Blue Version. Turn the top layer off and select the Blue Version layer.

12 Choose Image⇨Adjustments⇨Hue/Saturation. Enter the following settings:

* **Hue:** 220
* **Saturation:** 40
* **Lightness:** 0
* **Colorize:** checked

Click OK.

13 Choose Filter⇨Render⇨Lighting Effects. Enter the following settings:

* **Style:** default
* **Light Type:** Spotlight
* **On:** checked
* **Intensity:** 28
* **Focus:** 28
* **Color:** White
* **Properties:**
  * **Gloss:** 0
  * **Material:** 69 (Metallic)
  * **Exposure:** 0
  * **Color:** White
  * **Ambience:** 8
* **Texture Channel:** None

14 Use the example provided as a guide for where you should position the light. Once it is in place, click OK.

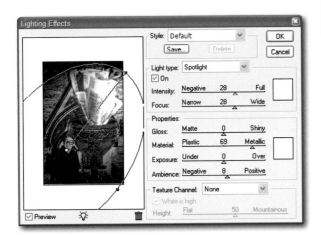

15 Select and enable the Lit Version layer. Choose Filter⇨ Render⇨Lighting Effects. Enter the following settings:

* **Style:** default
* **Light Type:** Spotlight
* **On:** checked
* **Intensity:** 28
* **Focus:** 28
* **Color:** R = 230, G = 175, and B = 119
* **Properties:**
  * **Gloss:** 0
  * **Material:** 69 (Metallic)
  * **Exposure:** 0
  * **Color:** White
  * **Ambience:** 8
* **Texture Channel:** None

16 Use the example provided as a guide for where you should position the light. Once it is in place, click OK.

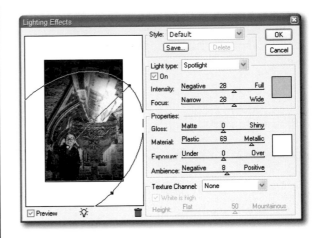

17 Create a mask for the Lit Version layer. Ensure that black is the foreground color, and then select the Paintbrush tool. Select a round, feathered brush from the default set. Set the Brush Size to 350 pixels or so. Paint over the left side of the image, the left side of the goblet, the left side of the boy's face, and so forth until it appears that the right sides of the objects are lit, with the rest under a blue shadow cast.

19 Select the Type tool and open the Character palette. Enter the following font settings:

* **Font:** Harry Potter
* **Style:** Regular
* **Font Size:** 72 pt
* **Leading:** 60 pt
* **Tracking:** 5
* **Vertical Scale:** 100%
* **Horizontal Scale:** 100%
* **Color:** White
* Normal
* **Anti-aliasing method:** Smooth

20 Type **Larry Blotter** on two lines. They can be in the same type layer, so just press Enter after you type **Larry**. Open the Layer Styles for the type layer and select Bevel and Emboss. Enter the following settings:

* **Style:** Inner Bevel
* **Technique:** Chisel Hard
* **Depth:** 550%
* **Direction:** Up
* **Size:** 21 px
* **Soften:** 0 px
* **Angle:** 63 degrees
* **Use Global Light:** unchecked
* **Altitude:** 32 degrees
* **Gloss Contour:** Custom (see example below)
* **Anti-aliased:** checked
* **Highlight Mode:** Normal
* **Color:** R = 228, G = 189, and B = 114
* **Opacity:** 100%
* **Shadow Mode:** Multiply
* **Color:** R = 90, G = 52, and B = 27
* **Opacity:** 75%

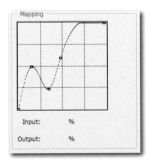

21 Set the foreground color to R = 126, G = 96, B = 77. Set the background color to R= 214, G = 176, B = 44.

22 Select Gradient Overlay and enter the following settings:

* **Blend Mode:** Multiply
* **Opacity:** 100%
* **Gradient:** Foreground to Background
* **Reverse:** unchecked
* **Style:** Linear
* **Align with Layer:** checked
* **Angle:** 0 degrees
* **Scale:** 100%

23 Save the Layer Style and click OK.

24 Create a new layer beneath the type layer, and then reselect the type layer. Choose Layer⇨Merge Down to collapse the style and rasterize the text. Rename the new layer Larry.

25 Choose Filter⇨Render⇨Lighting Effects.

* **Style:** Default
* **Light Type:** Spotlight
* **On:** checked
* **Intensity:** 53
* **Focus:** 14
* **Color:** R = 230, G = 175, and B = 119
* **Gloss:** 100
* **Material:** 100 (Metallic)
* **Exposure:** 0
* **Color:** White
* **Ambience:** -4
* **Texture Channel:** Blue
* **White is High:** checked
* **Height:** 69

26 Position the light as shown in the example.

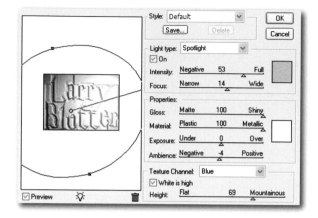

You may want to add reflections and deepen shadows on the text. You can do this by applying the Dodge and Burn tools to the lettering.

27 Create a new type layer with the same settings as before. Type in **Chalice of Cash** on three lines, and then open the Layer Styles for the new type layer. Select Outer Glow and enter the following settings:

* **Blend Mode:** Screen
* **Opacity:** 100%
* **Noise:** 0%

* **Glow Type:** Color
* **Color:** R = 46, G = 98, and B = 96
* **Technique:** Softer
* **Spread:** 0%
* **Size:** 130 px
* **Contour:** default
* **Anti-aliased:** checked
* **Range:** 50%
* **Jitter:** 0%

28 Select Stroke and enter the following settings:

* **Size:** 50 px
* **Position:** Inside
* **Blend Mode:** Soft Light
* **Opacity:** 72%
* **Fill Type:** Color
* **Color:** R = 11, G = 238, and B = 33

29 Select Outer Glow and enter the following settings:

* **Blend Mode:** Screen
* **Opacity:** 100%
* **Noise:** 0%
* **Fill Type:** Color
* **Color:** R = 245, G = 190, and B = 5
* **Technique:** Softer
* **Spread:** 0%
* **Size:** 81 px
* **Contour:** default
* **Anti-aliased:** checked
* **Range:** 50%
* **Jitter:** 0%

30 Save the layer style and click OK.

A short recap

Is this technique a statement on how I view these movies? I suppose it could be said that I am not a fan of making mega-franchises that market their product directly to children. As for the effects in the poster, the text in the logo is usually consistent from one movie to the next, while the title can take detours, depending on the subject of the book.

Back in a Minute

Fast cars, beautiful women, and an antihero with a chip on his shoulder and a big heart. We saw this formula in the '50s, the '60s, the '70s, and the '80s; I am not so sure about the '90s, but the new millennium has repackaged the genre with great box office success. This tutorial takes a look at this popular movie theme by creating a poster for *Back in a Minute*, the newest adrenaline-pumping racing movie to get teens to open their wallets for a ticket. Hopefully, it is just a movie ticket and not a donation to the highway patrol.

THE PLAN

- Create grungy text over a stylized time-delay photo
- Dress up the image as a movie poster

1 Open the image streetnight.jpg.

2 Select the Type tool and open the Character palette. Enter the following font settings:

- ✻ **Font:** Arial Black
- ✻ **Style:** Regular
- ✻ **Font Size:** 24 pt
- ✻ **Leading:** Auto
- ✻ **Vertical Scale:** 200%
- ✻ **Horizontal Scale:** 100%

- ✻ **Color:** R = 221, G = 28, and B = 37
- ✻ **Font Style:** Faux Italic
- ✻ **Anti-aliasing method:** Smooth

3 Type two lines of text, **BACK IN** and **MINUTE**, on two layers. Position these layers on the right portion of the screen, and vertically centered. Offset the lines of text a bit, with space in between them for additional text. Use the example as a guide.

4 Create a new type layer and open the Character palette. Enter the following font settings:

* **Font:** Arial Black
* **Style:** Regular
* **Font Size:** 72 pt
* **Leading:** Auto
* **Vertical Scale:** 200%
* **Horizontal Scale:** 100%
* **Color:** White
* **Font Style:** Faux Italic
* **Anti-aliasing method:** Smooth

5 Type **01** in the new layer and position it with the Move tool so that it rests between the previous two lines of text.

6 Open the Layer Styles for any of the type layers and select Drop Shadow. Enter the following settings:

* **Blend Mode:** Multiply
* **Color:** Black

* **Opacity:** 100%
* **Angle:** 120 degrees
* **Use Global Light:** unchecked
* **Distance:** 8 px
* **Spread:** 0%
* **Size:** 0 px
* **Contour:** Linear (default)
* **Anti-aliased:** checked
* **Noise:** 0%

7 Save the style and apply it to the other two type layers as well.

8 Create a new layer above the background but below the type layers.

9 Open the image tiretracks.jpg.

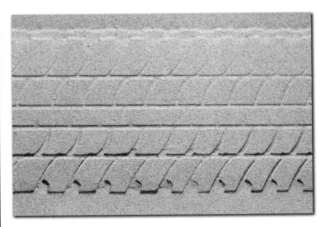

10 Press the D key to place black in the foreground. Choose Edit⇨Define Brush Preset, to create a paintbrush from the tire tracks image.

11 Return to the original document and select the Paintbrush tool. Set the opacity to 60% or so, and select the tire tracks brush. Click in the new layer without moving the brush so that the brush covers the entire layer: resize the brush as needed.

12 Change the Blend mode of the painted layer to Color Burn. Adjust the opacity until you can see the tracks faintly, as in the example.

13 To grunge the text up, you can use the same brush, only smaller. Create a new layer above the type layers. Reduce the brush size to 1200 pixels. Open the brush settings in the Options bar, and rotate the brush to an angle of 180 degrees.

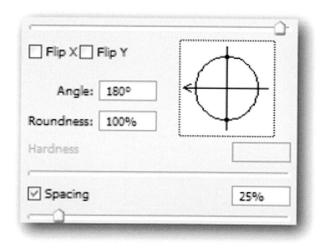

14 In the Options bar, set the opacity to 60%. Paint with black over the type in the new layer.

15 Turn off all layers except for the type layers and the top brushes layer. Choose Layer⇨Merge Visible. Command/Ctrl-click the newly merged layer to generate a selection. Create a Curves adjustment layer and create a curve with darker blacks and lighter whites, as shown in the example.

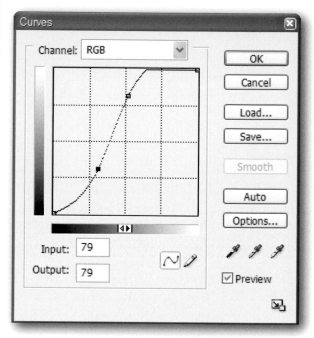

16 As we spent quite a bit of time creating a collage of the previous two images, I will avoid that this time. In the final example, I have added two people (a primary and secondary) to reflect the actors in the film. I lightened the area around the text by selecting the text, increasing the selection size by 100 pixels, and then adjusting the brightness and contrast of the background layer.

An Al Ward Production

BACK IN
01
MINUTE

A short recap

In this example, the primary effect to the text was simply to grunge it up – that is, to add spotty lines and dots, making the text appear as if it had been run over at some point.

Grunge is one of the more popular effects these days, and you will see a few more examples of this in the next few techniques.

Frantic 5

A number of years ago, I remember wishing that some movie studio would embark on creating movies that were based on my favorite comics. Looking back, I am glad that they waited, as the few that were made in my younger days were hardly special effects-laden extravaganzas. Now that technology has advanced, the studios have been pushing ahead with incredibly cool versions of the heroes that I grew up with.

This tutorial acknowledges one of these features, creating a super-hero (sort of) from scratch and then adding effects to the title and logo of the piece. I bring to you The Frantic 5. Okay, only one hero is going to make the cut, but there are actually five. No, really . . . .

THE PLAN

- Create a stoney hero using two images and a displacement map
- Affiix the texture image to the hero's skin and color it
- Create and emboss a logo for the heroic group

1 Open the image muscle.jpg.

2 Create a displacement map of the man by going to the Channels palette and duplicating the Blue channel. Choose Image⇨Adjustments⇨Brightness/Contrast, and set Brightness to +8 and Contrast to +70. Click OK.

3 Choose Filter⇨Blur⇨Gaussian Blur. Set the Radius value to 20 pixels and click OK.

4 Right-click the Blue copy channel and select Duplicate Channel. In the dialog box that appears, set the Destination: Document to New and click OK. Save the displacement map to your hard drive as a PSD file.

5 Open the image cracked_earth.jpg.

6 Select the entire texture image and copy it (Command/Ctrl+A, Command/Ctrl+C). Paste it into a new layer in the muscle image (Command/Ctrl+V). Change the Blend mode for the new layer to Overlay.

7 Choose Filter⇨Distort⇨Displace. Enter the following settings:

* **Horizontal Scale:** 10
* **Vertical Scale:** 10

* **Displacement Map:** Stretch To Fit
* **Undefined Areas:** Repeat Edge Pixels

Click OK.

8 In the dialogue box that appears, navigate to the displacement map that you just created, select it, and click OK.

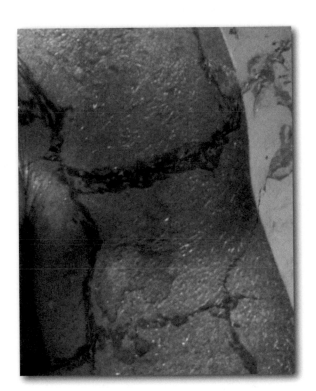

9 Create a layer mask for the texture layer, and then render the layer invisible. Select the Polygonal Lasso tool and depress the Add To Selection icon in the Options bar, with the Feather set to 0. Select the areas around the man. Turn on the texture layer again and fill these areas with black in the layer mask.

10 Duplicate the texture layer three times.

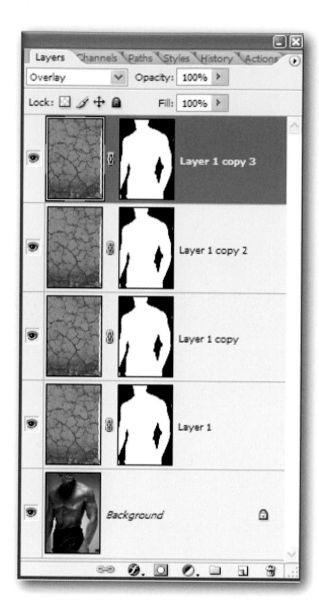

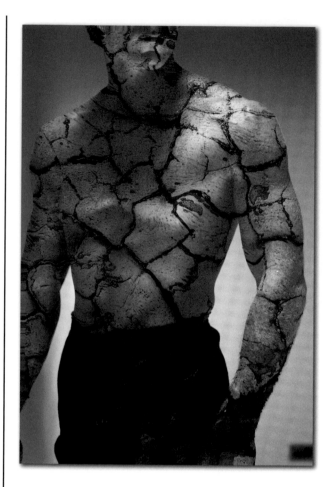

11 If the selection is no longer active, choose Select⇨ Reselect and then create a Solid Color adjustment layer. Set the color to R = 250, G = 135, B = 30. The man now has a rocky, orange texture to his skin. He still has a way to go, but he is getting there!

12 Choose Layer⇨Flatten Image. To take care of some of the distortions and stretching, you can now apply some lighting effects. This also adds a mood to the poster.

13 Choose Filter⇨Render⇨Lighting Effects. Enter the following settings, and use the example provided as a guide for where to place the spotlight:

* **Style:** default
* **Light Type:** Spotlight
* **On:** checked
* **Intensity:** 25
* **Focus:** 69
* **Color:** White

* **Properties:**
  * **Gloss:** 0
  * **Material:** 69 (Metallic)
  * **Exposure:** 0
  * **Color:** White
  * **Ambience:** 8
* **Texture Channel:** None

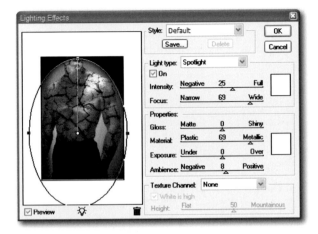

(14) Select the Type tool and open the Character palette. Enter the following font settings:

* **Font:** Arial Black
* **Style:** Regular
* **Font Size:** 120 pt
* **Leading:** Auto
* **Vertical Scale:** 200%
* **Horizontal Scale:** 180%
* **Color:** White
* **Font Style:** Faux Italic
* **Anti-aliasing method:** Smooth

(15) Type a large **5** on the image and center it with the Move tool.

(16) Open the Layer Styles for the type layer and select Bevel and Emboss. Enter the following settings:

* **Style:** Inner Bevel
* **Technique:** Smooth
* **Depth:** 1000%
* **Direction:** Down
* **Size:** 16 px
* **Soften:** 0 px
* **Angle:** 120 degrees
* **Use Global Light:** unchecked
* **Altitude:** 25 degrees
* **Gloss Contour:** Ring (from default set)
* **Anti-aliased:** checked
* **Highlight Mode:** Screen
  * **Color:** White
  * **Opacity:** 37%
* **Shadow Mode:** Multiply
  * **Color:** Black
  * **Opacity:** 100%

17 Select Inner Shadow, and enter the following settings:

* **Blend Mode:** Multiply
* **Color:** Black
* **Opacity:** 75%
* **Angle:** 120 degrees
* **Use Global Light:** unchecked
* **Distance:** 5 px
* **Choke:** 0%
* **Size:** 76 px
* **Contour:** default
* **Anti-aliased:** unchecked
* **Noise:** 0%

18 Select Gradient Overlay and enter the following settings:

* **Blend Mode:** Normal
* **Opacity:** 100%
* **Gradient:** Custom (See figure below)
* **Reverse:** unchecked
* **Style:** Linear
* **Align with Layer:** checked
* **Angle:** 90 degrees
* **Scale:** 100%

19 When creating the gradient, use the color values R = 127, G = 139, B = 216 for the blue on the ends.

> # NOTE
> Save the gradient! You will need it shortly.

20 Save the layer style and click OK.

21 Command/Ctrl-click the type layer to generate a selection, and then create a new layer. Select the Gradient tool and create a gradient of alternating grays and whites, as shown in the example:

22 Fill the selection from top to bottom with the gradient. Change the Blend mode of the new layer to Overlay.

23 Choose Filter⇨Sketch⇨Chrome. Set Detail to 0 and Smoothness to 9, and then click OK.

24 Select the Type tool and open the Character palette. Enter the following font settings:

* **Font:** Arial Black
* **Style:** Regular
* **Font Size:** 48 pt
* **Leading:** Auto
* **Vertical Scale:** 200%
* **Horizontal Scale:** 100%
* **Color:** White
* **Font Style:** Faux Italic
* **Anti-aliasing method:** Smooth

25 Create two new type layers, Frantic and FIVE. Overlay these layers on the large number five, as shown in the example.

26 The font effect for these two layers is relatively simple. Open the Layer Styles for one of the new type layers and select Gradient Overlay. Enter the following settings:

* **Blend Mode:** Normal
* **Opacity:** 100%
* **Gradient:** Custom (use the gradient that you created and applied to the '5')
* **Reverse:** checked
* **Style:** Linear
* **Align with Layer:** checked
* **Angle:** 90 degrees
* **Scale:** 100%

27 Select Stroke and enter the following settings:

* **Size:** 10 px
* **Position:** Outside
* **Blend Mode:** Normal
* **Opacity:** 100%
* **Fill Type:** Color
* **Color:** R = 2, G = 11, and B = 130

28 Save the layer style and click OK. Select the other type layer and apply the style.

29 As a final embellishment, create a medallion to go behind the logo. Select the Elliptical Marquee tool and create a new layer beneath the *5*. Draw a circular selection that is roughly the size of the number, and fill the selection with black. Choose Select⇨Modify⇨Contract, and reduce the selection by 50 pixels. Choose Layer⇨New⇨ Layer via Cut.

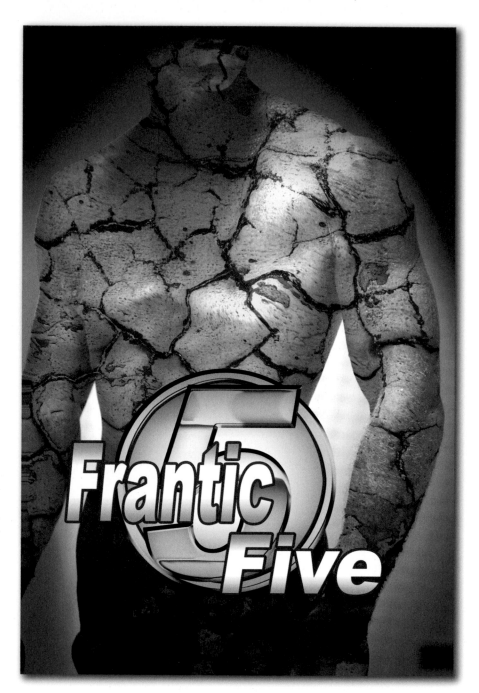

A short recap

So what made The Thing look so cool? Definitely the best member of the Fantastic Four (for those who are unaware of comic-book mythology), the Thing is a hero made of bright-orange stones. I do not believe that the choice in color was an accident, for either the stone he was composed of or the deep-blue tones of the costumes. The two go together naturally, being at opposite ends of the color wheel.

You Cannot Pick Your Neighbors

Okay, maybe you can — especially if you are the landlord. If you are not, or if you have no viable means to relocate to a new place, you may just have to put up with some undesirables.

This tutorial has its roots in a popular movie about extraterrestrial neighbors who are determined to destroy mankind. As we do not seem to have any looming threats of aliens wanting to exterminate us, the final image will actually be an opinion piece. This is not intended as a political statement: it is simply a statement.

THE PLAN

- Set a globe on fire
- Generate text from a textured image
- Create a 3D effect for the type

1. Open the images globe.jpg and flames.jpg.

2. Copy the fire photo and paste it into a new layer in the globe photo. Reduce the opacity of the flames to 60% so that you can see the globe, and then choose Edit⇨ Transform⇨Scale. Increase the size of the flames so that they completely engulf the globe, and also extend above the globe. Accept the transformation. Set the Blend mode to Overlay and the opacity back to 100%.

3 Duplicate the flames layer and set the Blend mode to Soft Light.

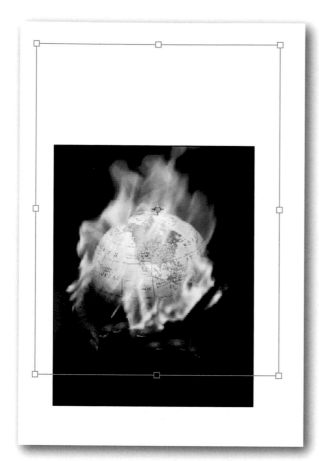

4 Open the image steel_shine.jpg.

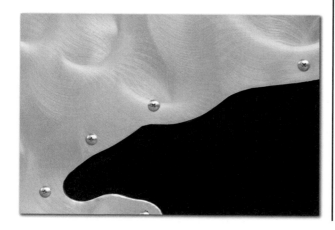

5 Copy the image and paste it into a new layer in the globe image. Choose Edit⇨Transform⇨Scale and resize it so that the steel takes up most of the area above the globe.

6 Select the Type Mask tool. Open the Character palette and set up the font as follows:

* **Font:** Arial Black
* **Style:** Regular
* **Font Size:** 120 pt
* **Leading:** Auto
* **Tracking:** 0
* **Vertical Scale:** 200%
* **Horizontal Scale:** 100%
* **Baseline Shift:** 0 pt
* **Color:** Anything (this is a type selection – the color is moot)
* Normal
* **Anti-aliasing method:** Smooth

7 Center-justify the type in the Options bar, and then type **WAR** over the steel in the upper part of the image. Choose Select⇨Inverse and press Delete.

8 Create a new layer beneath the WAR layer. Change the foreground color to R = 132, G = 36, B = 6. Change the background color R = 196, G = 13, B = 4.

9 Select the Polygonal Lasso tool. In the Options bar, depress the first icon, set the Feather to 0 pixels, and select the Anti-aliased option.

10 You have to rely a bit on your own imagination for this next part. On the bottom of the *W*, create a selection beneath the first *V* of the *W*, as shown in the example. The selection will be the base of the letter. Imagine that you are looking at a 3D version of the *WAR* text, with the *A* in the center. The selections should all gravitate toward that central point.

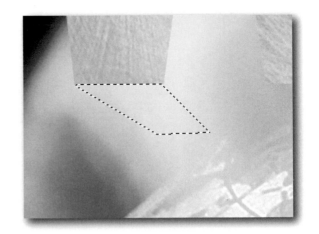

11 Select the Gradient tool. Choose the standard foreground-to-background gradient, and fill the selection from lower right to upper left, or vice-versa.

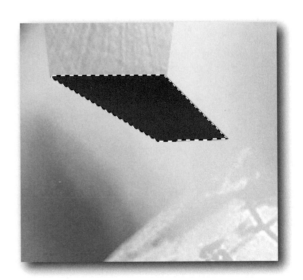

12 Repeat this process for the entire letter, creating a filled selection wherever there would be a plane extending away toward the background.

13 With the center of the *A* as the point where your vision is centered, create filled selections, one plane at a time, for the other two letters.

14 To add some shine to the 3D areas, duplicate the layer that you have been working on, and choose Image⇨ Adjustments⇨Desaturate. Change the Blend mode to Multiply and reduce the opacity to 30%. Command/Ctrl-click the layer, and then create a Curves adjustment layer. Create a multipoint curve, as shown in the example provided.

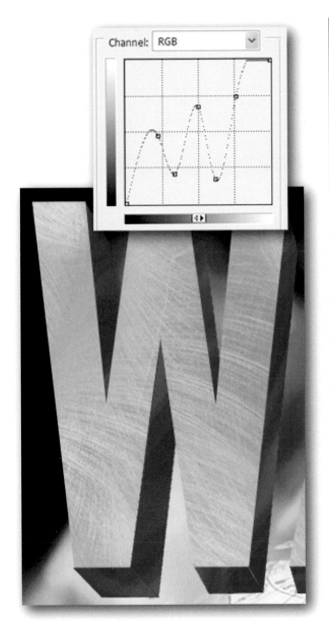

15 Select the steel type layer again and open the Layer Styles for the layer. Select Bevel and Emboss and enter the following settings:

* **Style:** Inner Bevel
* **Technique:** Chisel Hard
* **Depth:** 710%
* **Direction:** Up
* **Size:** 10 px
* **Soften:** 0 px
* **Angle:** 120 degrees
* **Use Global Light:** unchecked
* **Altitude: 30** degrees
* **Gloss Contour:** Linear (default)
* **Anti-aliased:** checked
* **Highlight Mode:** Screen
* **Color:** Foreground Color (see step 1 in this tutorial)
* **Opacity:** 100%
* **Shadow Mode:** Multiply
* **Color:** Background Color (see step 1 in this tutorial)
* **Opacity:** 100%

Click OK.

16 Duplicate the flame layer again, and drag the new copy above the type layer. Set the Blend mode to Overlay and the opacity to 100%. Create a mask and paint with black over all areas except where the flames would naturally extend over the text.

17 The actual poster on which this is based had additional 3D text with veins or tentacles interwoven with the letters — something that would take more pages than are available for the technique. However, you can turn this into a poster that would garner a lot of attention in these troubled times with the addition of a single word.

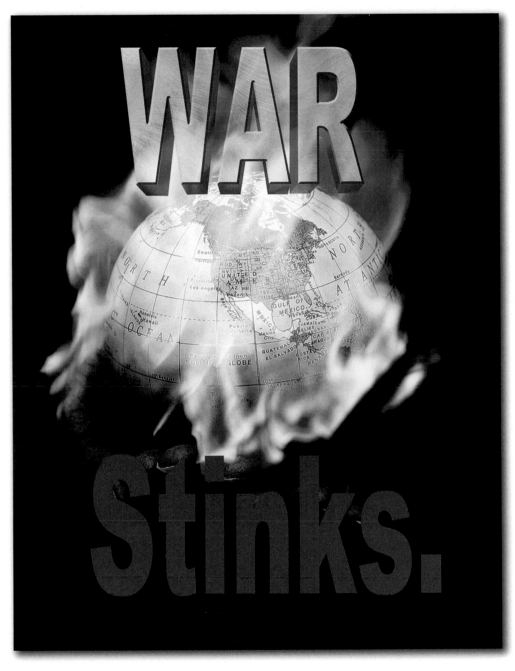

A short recap

As most people really do not want war, regardless of their end of the political spectrum, I think that the final image is safe. As for the effect, note that some type effects do require a bit more detailed work than simply using styles. Not that styles are bad — far from it. It is just that they can use some help occasionally. They are an ingredient, but not the meal.

Gotta Love Camp

By "camp" I mean cheesy movies — those B-list cult classics that do not take themselves too seriously and are just plain fun to watch. If you have never taken time out to attend a midnight showing of one of these gems at a movie theater, you are missing out. A DVD simply is not the same as a theater packed with all manner of oddballs enjoying a film that probably is not that good without the atmosphere of the crowded theater. Thus, I bring you *The Randy Terror Movie Flick.*

To follow this tutorial completely, you should first go to the Website `http://simplythebest.net/fonts/` and download the Rocky AOE font. Install this font on your computer, open Photoshop, and proceed with this section.

THE PLAN

- Create stark, bright-red lips on a black background
- Add stylized text

(1) Open the image lips.jpg

Create a new image with the following attributes:

* **Name:** Randy Terror
* **Preset:** Custom
* **Width:** 8.5 inches
* **Height:** 11 inches
* **Resolution:** 300 pixels/inch

* **Color Mode:** RGB, 8 bit
* **Background Contents:** Transparent

(2) Fill the new image with black. Create a copy of the lips image, paste it into a new layer on the new black background, and then choose Edit⇨Transform⇨Scale. Resize the lips so that they dominate the upper half of the black background.

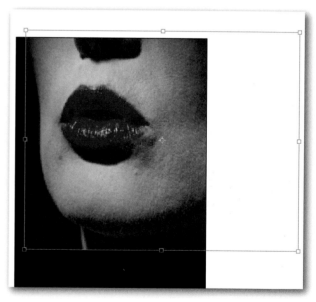

(3) Create a layer mask for the lips layer. Select the Polygonal Lasso tool and set the Feather to 3 pixels. Make a selection around the lips. Choose Select⇨Inverse, ensure that the mask is selected, and fill the selection with black.

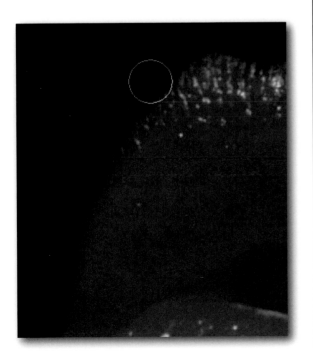

④ With the mask still selected, choose Filter➪Blur➪ Gaussian Blur. Enter a blur radius of 24 pixels and click OK. Paint around the lip edges in the mask with black as needed to get a distinct, red-black edge with just a slight feather.

⑤ To better define the edges, keep the mask selected and choose Image➪Adjustments➪Threshold. Move the slider until the edges of the mouth are clearly defined.

⑥ Command/Ctrl-click the mask, and then click on the actual lips layer (not the mask). Choose Layer➪ New➪Layer via Copy. Another way to define the edges of the lips is by using Layer Styles. Open the styles for the new lips layer and select Outer Glow. Enter the following settings:

* **Blend Mode:** Multiply
* **Opacity:** 75%
* **Noise:** 0%
* **Glow Type:** Color
* **Color:** Black
* **Technique:** Softer
* **Spread:** 0%
* **Size:** 5 px
* **Contour:** default
* **Anti-aliased:** checked
* **Range:** 50%
* **Jitter:** 0%

⑦ Choose Inner Glow and enter the following settings:

* **Blend Mode:** Color Burn
* **Opacity:** 35%
* **Noise:** 0%
* **Color:** Black
* **Technique:** Softer
* **Source:** Edge
* **Choke:** 0%
* **Size:** 140 px
* **Contour:** Linear (default)
* **Anti-aliased:** checked
* **Range:** 50%
* **Jitter:** 0%

8 Save the style in case you want to use it later, and click OK.

9 Now that the lips are basically done, you can tackle the text. There is really nothing difficult about the font effect, as the actual font takes care of the effect for us. Change the foreground color to R = 175, G = 2, B = 6.

10 Select the Type tool and open the Character palette. Enter the following font settings:

* **Font:** Rocky AOE
* **Style:** Regular
* **Font Size:** 100 pt
* **Leading:** Auto
* **Vertical Scale:** 90%

* **Horizontal Scale:** 100%
* **Color:** Foreground Color
* **Normal**
* **Anti-aliasing method:** Smooth

11 Type **The Randy Terror Movie Flick** on three lines that are centered horizontally beneath the lips.

12 Increase the size of the lip layer further by choosing Edit⇨Transform⇨Scale. Increase them so that they take up nearly the entire top half of the image.

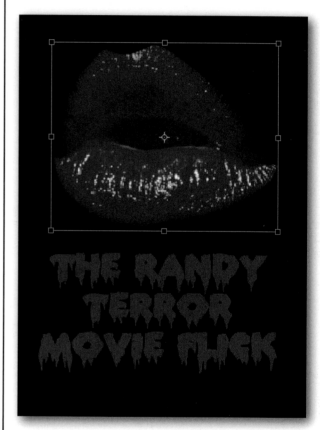

You can also use the Dodge tool to brighten the teeth a bit.

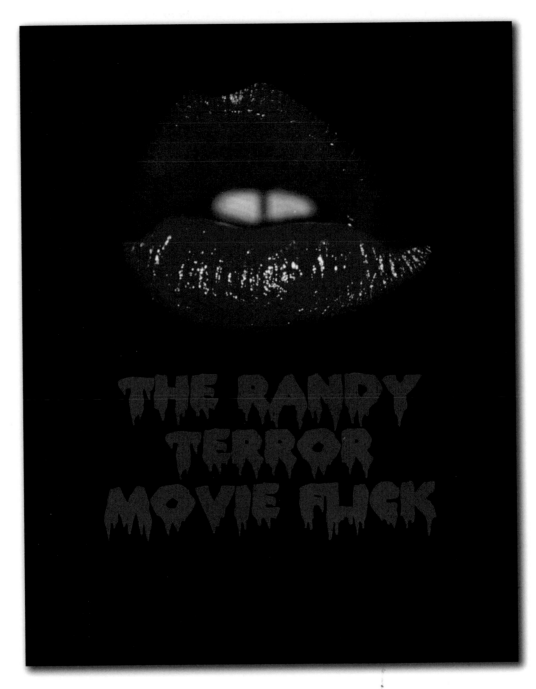

A short recap

Great Scott! The effect in this case was the lips, as the font did the work for us as far as the text is concerned. I hope that you have enjoyed this little trip through the time warp.

Quiet Knob

I have seen most of the movies that this chapter has lovingly tried to capture, but this last one has yet to find its way to my DVD player. I am not much of a fan of straight-out horror movies — I prefer suspense without gore. For me, the original *House on Haunted Hill* is a masterpiece in its simplicity and ability to make me jump without the shock and blood of modern horror movies. I say that with a disclaimer: zombie flicks are not horror movies, but are just plain great viewing!

This poster makes another attempt at a creepy poster that, in reality, had nothing to do with the film itself. You will texture another human form as with the hero poster, but this poster has a decidedly more sinister side to it.

THE PLAN

- Texturize the face of a child
- Heighten the sinister nature of the piece with tricks of color and lighting
- Add the text
- Manipulate the font sizes
- Grunge up the fonts with the Smudge and Eraser tools

1 Open the image girl.png.

2 Create a new layer and place it beneath the girl layer. Fill the new layer with black.

3 Select the girl layer and click on the Clone Stamp tool. To begin on the path to the dark side, you must erase the girl's mouth. In the Options bar, set up the Clone Stamp tool as follows:

- **Brush:** Round, Feathered
- **Brush Size:** 250 px
- **Mode:** Normal
- **Opacity:** 75%
- **Flow:** 100%
- **Airbrush:** depressed
- **Aligned:** unchecked
- **Sample All Layers:** unchecked

4 Hold down the Option/Alt key, sample an area close to the young lady's mouth, and then stamp the selection over an area of the lips close to where you took the sample. Continue doing this until the entire mouth has vanished.

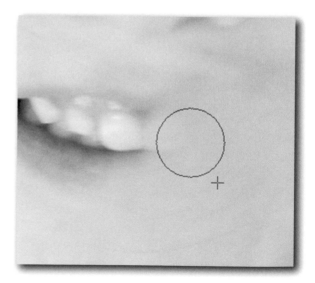

9 Find the girl displacement map and use it for the displacement. Select the girl's layer and choose Filter⇨Distort⇨Displace again. This time, use the following settings:

* **Horizontal Scale:** 4
* **Vertical Scale:** 4
* **Displacement Map:** Stretch To Fit
* **Undefined Areas:** Repeat Edge Pixels

Click OK.

10 Find the textured map and use it for the distortion. Change the Blend mode for the texture layer to Multiply. Create a mask for the texture layer. With a black paintbrush, mask the areas where the texture covers the hair, eyes, shirt, and so forth. The texture should only be visible on the skin of the girl. Reduce the opacity of the texture layer to 50-55%.

5 Create a displacement map of the girl as you did with the hero earlier in this chapter. When adjusting the Brightness/Contrast of the channel, set Brightness to -42 and Contrast to +64.

6 Once you have created the displacement map, save it to your hard drive.

7 Open the image texture.jpg. Create a displacement map for this image as well, and save it to your hard drive.

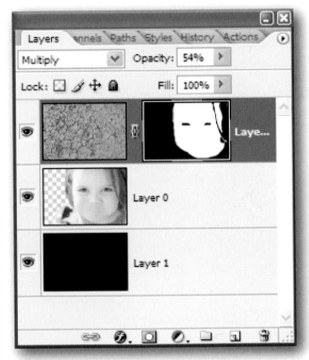

8 Copy the texture image and paste it into the girl's image. Choose Filter⇨Distort⇨Displace and enter the following settings:

* **Horizontal Scale:** 10
* **Vertical Scale:** 10
* **Displacement Map:** Stretch To Fit
* **Undefined Areas:** Repeat Edge Pixels

Click OK.

11 Duplicate the texture layer. Change the Blend mode for the new layer to Soft Light and the opacity to 50%.

12 Create a new layer. Paint with black over areas that could be further blended into the background, such as the hair on the left side of her face. Reduce the opacity as needed to get a good blend.

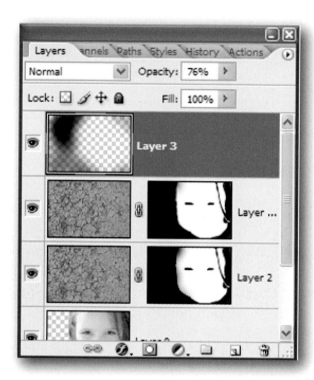

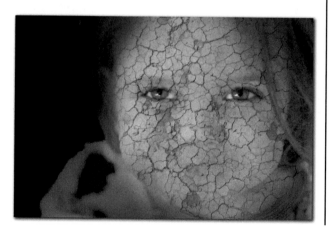

13 Getting creeped out yet? Just wait — it gets better! Create a Hue/Saturation adjustment layer with the following settings:

* **Hue:** -7
* **Saturation:** -50
* **Lightness:** 0
* **Colorize:** unchecked

Click OK.

14 Now create a Curves adjustment layer. Use the image shown as a guide:

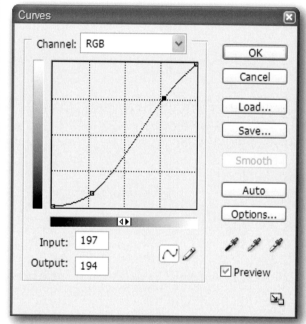

15 To give the girl's eyes an eerie glow, select the Dodge tool. Set the brush size to 100 pixels or so, and the Range to Midtones. Click over the areas where the pupils and irises are in both child layers. Apply the tool several times between the layers, keeping an eye on the image until you have a nice creepy glow in both eyes.

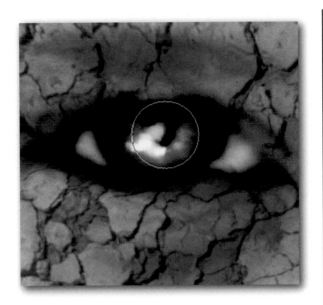

16 Open the Hue/Saturation adjustment layer again and decrease the saturation to -75. You may also decrease the Lightness to -10 or so.

17 Select the Type tool and open the Character palette. Enter the following font settings:

* **Font:** Verdana
* **Style:** Regular
* **Font Size:** 36 pt
* **Leading:** Auto
* **Vertical Scale:** 140%
* **Horizontal Scale:** 100%
* **Color:** White
* **Normal**
* **Anti-aliasing method:** Smooth

18 Type **QUIET KNOB** in a new layer.

19 Select individual letters and change the size and thickness so that the letters alternate from large to small to thick and so on. You may even change the font from Verdana to something like Arial Black to get an even thicker font.

20 Rasterize the type layer. Select the Eraser tool and choose a spattered brush from the default set. Ensure that the opacity for the brush is set to 100%, and increase the size of the brush to 50 pixels or so.

21 Make spot-erasures around the type as shown in the example provided.

22 Select the Smudge tool. Select a speckled brush again. Set the brush size to 15-20 pixels and the strength of the smudge to 30%. Create vertical and horizontal smudge distortions on the type, as shown in the example provided.

(23) Many times the studios create the advertisements for their movies without credits. Instead, they simply provide a Website address.

A short recap

I don't know about you, but this end photo gives me the chills — which in this case is the desired effect. The technique of creating the goth-child is very similar to the hero, but with a much darker edge. The text is broken and cracked, reflecting the feel of the piece. That is all for this chapter. I enjoyed our trip to the movies, and we will have to do it again sometime soon!

potpourri – fx
without a home

Most of this book has been comprised of type effects and how they relate to the images that contain them. Other techniques have focused on creating the images in which you place the type. This last chapter shows you eight quick effects that really do not have an application already in mind, but are just fun to play with. Enjoy!

Those Things Will Kill Ya

I smoked cigarettes for a lot of years, and I can appreciate how difficult it is to quit. I do still smoke a pipe occasionally, but that will soon be going by the wayside as well. This tutorial shows you one way to generate text out of smoke, or smoke out of text if you prefer. Remember, the easiest way to quit smoking is to not start in the first place!

THE PLAN

- Add a text message to a photo
- Turn the text into a smokey version of itself
- Distort the text to finalize the effect

1 Open the image ashtray.jpg.

2 Select the Type tool and open the Character palette. Enter the following font settings:

- ✱ **Font:** Futura (if it is not installed, then Verdana or Arial will work as a substitute)
- ✱ **Style:** Light
- ✱ **Font Size:** 80 pt
- ✱ **Leading:** Auto
- ✱ **Vertical Scale:** 60%
- ✱ **Horizontal Scale:** 115%
- ✱ **Color:** White
- ✱ **Anti-aliasing method:** Smooth

3 Type **QUIT IT** above the ashtray. Position the text so that the smoke from the cigarette meets the 'T' in 'IT.'

4 Set the foreground color to white. Select the Brush tool and choose a round, feathered brush. Open the Brushes palette and select Brush Tip Shape. Set the size of the brush to 45 pixels, the angle to 180 degrees, and the roundness to 80%.

- ✱ **Size Jitter:** 95%
- ✱ **Minimum Diameter:** 15%
- ✱ **Angle Jitter:** 15%
- ✱ **Roundness Jitter:** 50%
- ✱ **Minimum Roundness:** 25%

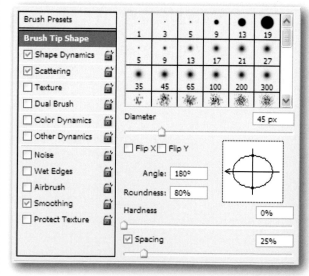

5 Turn Scattering on and adjust the settings as follows:

* **Scatter:** 70%
* **Both Axes:** checked
* **Control:** Off
* **Count:** 1
* **Count Jitter:** 50%
* **Fade:** 25

6 Select the 'Other Dynamics' option and enter the following settings:

* **Opacity Jitter:** 50%
* **Control:** Rotation
* **Flow Jitter:** 40%
* **Fade:** 25

7 Select the Smoothing option. Create a new layer above the type layer. Paint over the letters with the brush.

8 Follow the line of smoke from the text down to the cigarette. Once you have painted the entire message, turn the type layer off.

9 Select the smoke layer. Choose Edit⇨Transform⇨ Distort. Narrow the area closest to the cigarette, but widen that portion of the text that is farthest away.

10 To add a bit more smoke, duplicate the smoke layer. Choose Filter⇨Blur⇨Motion Blur. Set the angle to -80 and the distance to 160. Click OK.

A short recap

Quick and to the point! Try widening the brush or using a variety of Scattering settings to create other types of smoke.

Skywriter

Now that you have mastered smoke, this section will show you another smoke technique. Have you ever seen the contrails from a jet on a clear day? Of course you have. Now imagine those trails drifted together in such a way as to convey a message to those below. This tutorial offshoots the smoke theme and places the vapory dialog in the sky.

THE PLAN

- Open an image
- Set up the Paintbrush tool for wispy paint application
- Paint your message in the sky

(1) Open the image bluesky.jpg.

(2) Set white as the foreground color and select the Paintbrush tool. In the Options bar, select a feathered, round brush, 100 pixels in size. Set the opacity to 60%, and then open the Brush Presets dialog box. Select Shape Dynamics and set up the brush as follows:

- **Size Jitter:** 100%
- **Minimum Diameter:** 0%
- **Angle Jitter:** 0%
- **Roundness Jitter:** 0%
- **Minimum Roundness:** 25%

(3) Select the Other Dynamics option and enter the following settings:

- **Opacity Jitter:** 50%
- **Control:** Rotation
- **Flow Jitter:** 50%
- **Fade:** 25

(4) Select the Smoothing option. Create a new layer. Using your mouse, paint a message in the clouds. This guy needs to be knocked down a peg, and so the message that I am going to convey is "Loser."

(5) Choose Edit⇨Transform⇨Distort. Expand the area closest to the top of the screen, and narrow it where it would recede into the distance.

A short recap

This is the shortest tutorial in the book, but it goes hand in hand with the previous one. Practice with the opacity of the brush, and again with the shape dynamics and scattering, for fluffier clouds or tighter messages.

In Orbit

We've looked into the air and saw some wisdom hanging there, so for this project let's expand our senses a bit further and venture beyond our limiting atmosphere. What if the message in the sky were seen from the vantage point of, say, a satellite or spacecraft? Early in this book, a few projects deal with circular type, or rather type that runs around a circular shape. This project is a variation of that theme, placing text in orbit around a sphere. I don't use a planet, but you'll see how easy it is to replace the globe I'm using with a celestial body of your choosing. Without further ado, let's get this party started.

THE PLAN

- Create a path around a globe
- Type on the path
- Transform the path
- Mask some of the text to make it appear to go behind the object

1 Open the image bugball.jpg.

2 Use the Magic Wand tool to select the black area around the sphere. Choose the Paths palette and click the Path from the Selection icon.

3 Set the foreground color to white. Select the Type tool. The font really does not matter, but set the size to 60 points.

4 Move the cursor over the edge of the path on either the top or the bottom of the sphere. When the cursor changes, click on the path and type a line of text that runs around the entire circle.

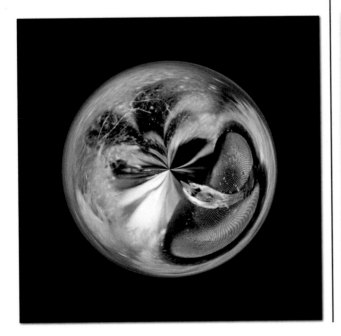

5 To distort the path, choose Edit⇨Transform Path⇨ Scale. Squish the path into a wide oval. The text follows the path once you accept the transformation.

6 Choose Edit⇨Transform Path⇨Rotate and rotate the path at about a 30-degree angle. Accept the transformation.

7 Create a mask for the type layer. Set the foreground color to black and select the Paintbrush tool. With a hard-edged, round brush, paint over the text in the mask where the text would pass behind the sphere.

A short recap

This quick tutorial demonstrates the transformation of a path, which can create many design possibilities. Try working with other types of shapes, and always remember that perspective is key to achieve an effective end result.

Blades and Blood

I've demonstrated several variations of metal effects in this book, but I've yet to tackle one of my favorite variations: combining sharp edged metal with a splash of color — in this case, faux blood. Words have been used as weapons for as long as there have been lawyers and marriages, so let's take that thought a bit further and actually create cutting-edged text (pun intended). Here's a variation on metal that is easy to achieve and also looks great, especially on a dark background. Just be careful not to slice or dice yourself — this tutorial creates some sharp edges.

THE PLAN

- Create text using a sharp font
- Turn the text into metal with sharp edges
- Apply color to act as blood

1 Create a new image with the following attributes:

- **Name:** Blades
- **Preset:** Custom
- **Width:** 9 inches
- **Height:** 5 inches
- **Resolution:** 300 pixels/inch
- **Color Mode:** RGB, 8 bit
- **Background Contents:** White

2 Fill the image with black. Select the Type tool and open the Character palette. Enter the following font settings:

- **Font:** Gothic Love Letters (any font with sharp edges will work as a substitute)
- **Style:** Regular
- **Font Size:** 120 pt
- **Leading:** Auto
- **Vertical Scale:** 80%
- **Horizontal Scale:** 100%
- **Color:** White
- **Anti-aliasing method:** Smooth

3 Type your text in a new layer. I am using *Deth*, and yes, I know it is misspelled.

4 Change the foreground color to R = 196, G = 196, and B = 196. Change the background color to R = 85, G = 85, and B = 85.

5 Command/Ctrl-click the type layer to generate a selection. Create a new layer. Select the Gradient tool, and choose the default foreground-to-background gradient. Click on the Radial icon in the Options bar and ensure that the opacity is set to 100%.

6 Draw the gradient through the selection, beginning in the upper-left corner and proceeding to the lower-right corner.

7 Open the Layer Styles for the gradient layer and select Bevel and Emboss. Enter the following settings:

* **Style:** Inner Bevel
* **Technique:** Smooth
* **Depth:** 1000%
* **Direction:** Up
* **Size:** 13 px
* **Soften:** 0 px
* **Angle:** 120 degrees
* **Use Global Light:** unchecked
* **Altitude:** 25 degrees
* **Gloss Contour:** Ring - Double
* **Anti-aliased:** checked
* **Highlight Mode:** Screen
  * **Color:** White
  * **Opacity:** 100%
* **Shadow Mode:** Multiply
  * Color: R = 91, G = 2, and B = 2
  * Opacity: 100%

8 Open the Contour settings. Select the Ring - Double contour. Save the Layer Style and click OK.

9 Create a new layer above the text and set the Blend mode to Overlay. Change the foreground color to R = 91, G = 2, and B = 2.

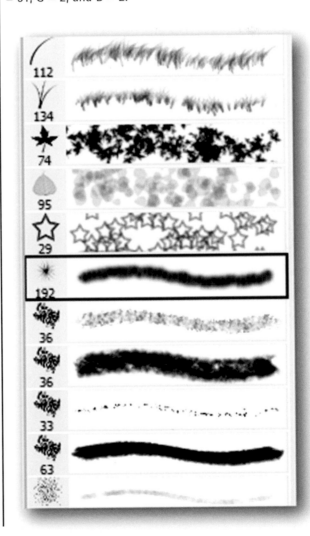

10 Using a round, semi-hard-edged brush, paint over the lower portions of the text, especially where any sharp edges occur. Switch to a spatter brush; you should find a suitable brush in the default brush set, below the star. Paint spots of blood so that they appear to have been sprayed on the blades in the heat of battle.

A short recap

The trick to making this effect work is in the contour that you apply, the grays that you use, and the distinct edges of the fonts. The black background definitely helps as well, as the metal really shines and the blood looks more realistic. You can also try dodging and burning the metal for a more dramatic effect.

Age Got It

In my neck of the woods, people actually buy old boards torn off of ancient buildings (barns in particular) to fashion rustic furnishings or artwork for their homes. Some think it nostagic, and I have to admit I love the atmosphere such pieces or decorations create. I have been known to do it myself, as it simply makes the house seem more comfortable. Here in the Northwest there are entire companies whose sole function is to create these types of objects, whether barnwood picture frames or wrought iron door fixtures. The real antiquities are actually cheaper in many cases than the fabrications. This tutorial creates wooden text, but applies some age to it by creating the appearance of several peeling layers of paint.

THE PLAN

- Create three-layered text
- Apply bevels to each layer
- Alter the top layer to generate the aged, peeling paint effect

1 Open the image woodtexture.jpg.

2 Select the Type Mask tool and open the Character palette. Enter the following font settings:

* **Font:** Goudy Stout (any thick font will work as a substitute)
* **Style:** Regular
* **Font Size:** 400 pt
* **Leading:** Auto
* **Vertical Scale:** 80%
* **Horizontal Scale:** 100%
* **Anti-aliasing method:** Smooth

3 Type **BUGS** or a similar word in the center of the texture.

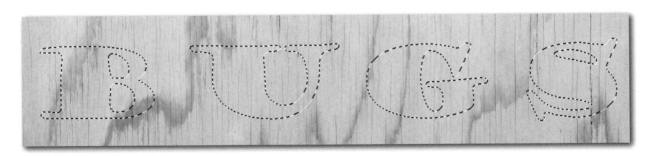

4 With the type selection active, choose Layer⇨New⇨ Layer via Copy. Open the Layer Styles for the new wooden type layer, select Bevel and Emboss, and enter the following settings:

* **Style:** Inner Bevel
* **Technique:** Smooth
* **Depth:** 60%
* **Direction:** Up
* **Size:** 20 px
* **Soften:** 0 px
* **Angle:** 120 degrees
* **Use Global Light:** unchecked
* **Altitude:** 30 degrees
* **Gloss Contour:** Linear (default)
* **Anti-aliased:** checked
* **Highlight Mode:** Screen
* **Color:** White
* **Opacity:** 75%
* **Shadow Mode:** Multiply
* **Color:** Black
* **Opacity:** 75%

5 Duplicate the type layer. Choose Image⇨ Adjustments⇨Curves and create a multipoint, alternating curve as shown in the example. Click OK.

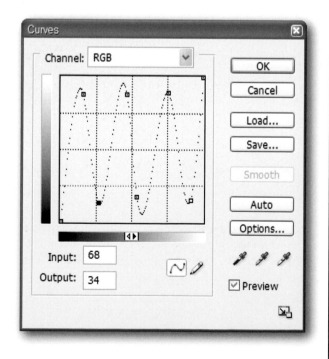

6 Open the Layer Styles and enter the following Bevel and Emboss settings:

* **Style:** Inner Bevel
* **Technique:** Smooth
* **Depth:** 300%
* **Direction:** Up
* **Size:** 5 px
* **Soften:** 0 px
* **Angle:** 30 degrees
* **Use Global Light:** unchecked
* **Altitude:** 30 degrees
* **Gloss Contour:** Linear (default)
* **Anti-aliased:** checked
* **Highlight Mode:** Screen
  * **Color:** White
  * **Opacity:** 75%
* **Shadow Mode:** Multiply
  * **Color:** Black
  * **Opacity:** 75%

7 Change the Blend mode for the top layer to Linear Burn, and the opacity to 50%. You can now see the paint smeared all over the wooden text.

8 Command/Ctrl-click the original type layer, and then choose Select⇨Modify⇨Contract. Contract the selection by 20 pixels and click OK. With the original type layer selected, choose Layer⇨New⇨Layer via Copy.

9 Open the Layer Styles and enter the following Bevel and Emboss settings:

* **Style:** Inner Bevel
* **Technique:** Smooth
* **Depth:** 1000%
* **Direction:** Up
* **Size:** 5 px
* **Soften:** 0 px
* **Angle:** 120 degrees
* **Use Global Light:** unchecked
* **Altitude:** 30 degrees
* **Gloss Contour:** Linear (default)
* **Anti-aliased:** checked
* **Highlight Mode:** Screen
  * **Color:** White
  * **Opacity:** 75%

* **Shadow Mode:** Multiply
  * **Color:** Black
  * **Opacity:** 75%

10 Open Drop Shadow and enter the following settings:

* **Blend Mode:** Multiply
* **Color:** Black
* **Opacity:** 60%
* **Angle:** 120 degrees
* **Use Global Light:** unchecked
* **Distance:** 10 px

* **Spread:** 0%
* **Size:** 5 px
* **Contour:** Linear (default)
* **Anti-aliased:** checked
* **Noise:** 0%

11 Hold down the Command/Ctrl key and click on all three type layers. You can now use the Move tool to reposition the text on other parts of the image to alter the location of the wood grain, so that the text does not appear to be made from the same piece of wood as the background.

A short recap

There you have it — five effects that are short, sweet, and directly to the point. If you enjoy type effects and would like to add more to your Photoshop arsenal, then please visit me at ActionFx.com. As of this writing, there are over 50,000 Photoshop presets available for you to download, with more being added all the time. I create and host Photoshop training videos as well. I look forward to seeing you there!

Hot Online

Website designs come in all varieties. Some are basic white with links, some are extreme with advanced metallic interfaces that are animated with Flash, while the majority fall somewhere in between these two extremes. In conjunction with ImageReady, Photoshop CS2 is one of the few programs that allow you to not only design a Web page graphically in the image editor, but also allow for the image to be sliced and diced into a Web page. I still recommend using a program such as Dreamweaver, but you can also create a page with just Photoshop and ImageReady.

This project doesn't demonstrate the ImageReady half of the equation, but it does show how you can collage multiple images into a Web-page layout.

THE PLAN

- Use multiple images to create a themed Web-page layout
- Collage the images together
- Add Web-style text and links

1 Open the image funky.jpg.

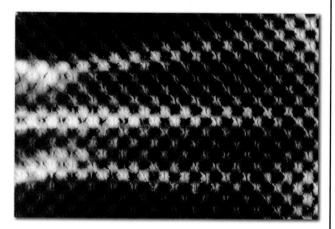

2 The background texture doesn't matter much, as you will be distorting it beyond recognition. Choose Filter⇨Blur⇨Gaussian Blur. Set the Radius setting to 40 px.

3 Click OK. Choose Image⇨Adjustments⇨ Hue/Saturation and enter the following to change the overall hue to blue:

- **Hue:** -130
- **Saturation:** 0
- **Lightness:** 0
- **Colorize:** unchecked

4 Most collage images are done by cleverly adjusting blending modes and opacities, but this tutorial takes another route: Apply Image. Open the images sun-bathe.jpg and tech-01.jpg.

5 Change the image sizes to match that of the original blurred photo.

* **Width:** 2400 pixels
* **Height:** 1600 pixels

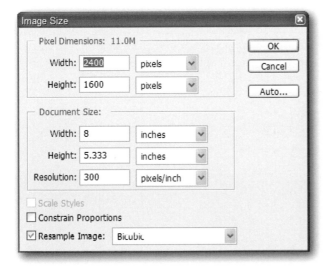

NOTE

In order for the Apply Image feature to work, the photos that you are blending must have the same horizontal and vertical pixel dimensions.

6 Return to the first document and choose Image⇨Apply Image. Enter the following settings:

* **Source:** sunbathe.jpg
* **Layer:** Background
* **Channel:** RGB
* **Invert:** unchecked
* **Blending:** Soft Light
* **Opacity:** 100%
* **Preserve Transparency:** unchecked
* **Mask:** checked
* **Image:** funky.jpg (or the name of your original photo)
* **Layer:** Background
* **Channel:** Gray
* **Invert:** unchecked

Click OK. The background has been merged (albeit faintly) with the image of the woman.

7 You can add elements of the technical background in the same way. Staying with the original background photo, choose Image⇨Apply Image again and enter the following:

* **Source:** tech-01.jpg
* **Layer:** Background
* **Channel:** RGB
* **Invert:** unchecked
* **Blending:** Darken
* **Opacity:** 100%
* **Preserve Transparency:** unchecked
* **Mask:** checked

* **Image:** tech-01.jpg (or the name of your original photo)
* **Layer:** Merged
* **Channel:** Gray
* **Invert:** unchecked

Click OK. If the image is a bit dark, you can brighten it by choosing Image⇨Adjustments⇨Brightness/Contrast and adjusting it to taste. In this example, I'm using the following settings:

* **Brightness:** +25
* **Contrast:** +40

Click OK when you are done with the adjustment.

8 My thought for a theme is that of a crime-tracking Web site, and so the splash screen/Web page should reflect that theme. I'm a fan of film noir, with the genre's unkempt gumshoes and less-than-savory damsels in distress. What font style best reflects those dark movies of the 1940s and 1950s? I'm thinking of a choppy, type-writer-style font, and so that is what I'll use. The font for this particular tutorial is called Last Words, and you can download it from the Simply The Best Fonts Website at http://simplythebest.net.

TIP

When you download and install new fonts on your system, you must close Photoshop CS2 and reopen the program before the fonts will appear in the font list. If you use the Last Words font, save your project as a PSD file on your hard drive and close Photoshop. Install the font, reopen Photoshop, and then open the PSD file once again.

9 Select the Type tool. Open the Character palette and set up the font as follows:

* **Font:** Last Words
* **Style:** Thin
* **Font Size:** 80 pt
* **Leading:** Auto

* **Tracking:** 0
* **Vertically Scale:** 60%
* **Horizontally Scale:** 115%
* **Baseline Shift:** 0 pt
* **Color:** White
* **Normal**
* **Anti-aliasing method:** Smooth

Type out **Trag dy**, complete with the space where the *e* should be. To give this an old typewriter feel, you can set the *e* at an angle on its own layer. Position the type layer in the lower-right corner of the page.

10 Next, create a new type layer and type **e** with the same settings. Position the *e* between the *g* and the *d* in the text. Choose Edit⇨Transform⇨Rotate and turn the *e* a bit. Click OK.

11 Change the Blending mode for both type layers to Soft Light.

(12) Open the Image crimetape.jpg. Choose Select⇨Color Range and select the white area. Click OK. Next, choose Select⇨Inverse and press Command/Ctrl+C to copy the selection. Return to the original document and press Command/Ctrl+V. Move the newly pasted layer to the upper region of the image.

(13) Command/Ctrl-click on the crime tape layer icon in the Layers palette to generate a selection around it, and then create a layer mask. Choose Select⇨Reselect and click on the Gradient tool. Using a gradual black-to-white gradient, fill the selection with the gradient from left to right to mask a portion of the tape.

(14) Select the Type tool again. Use the same character settings as before, but change the font size to 12 pt in the Options bar. Set the layout to Left Justify, and then open the Paragraph palette. Indent the type by 4 points.

Create a paragraph box on the left side of the screen, about twice as high as it is wide. Type in a series of links. Use the example provided as a guide.

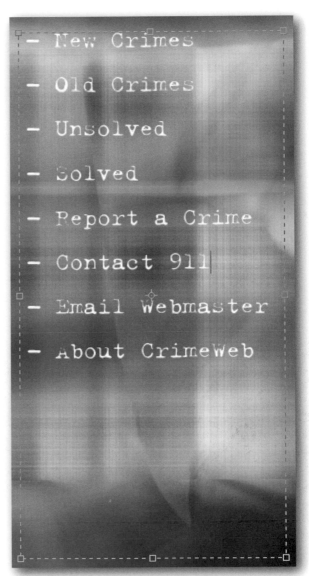

(15) For a final touch, select the Paintbrush tool. Load the brush set named BrushSplats found on the CD. Select one of the brushes that appears as a smear with spots. Change the foreground color to R = 225, G = 9, and B = 9.

16 Create a new layer and set the brush settings to Normal at 100% opacity. Click once with the brush in the lower-left corner of the image.

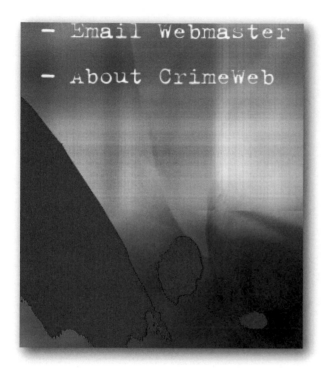

17 I'll add one final embellishment to the image, to contrast the blood with the imprint of a rose. Open the image rose.jpg. Copy the image and paste it into the background document at the top of the layer stack, and then position it so that the rose appears in the lower-right corner. Use the transform tools to resize the rose to taste.

18 Open the Layer Styles for the rose layer and select the Blending options. In the Blend If area, move the sliders to the following positions:

* Blend If: Gray
* This Layer:
  * Black Stops: 0 (both)
  * White Stops: 8 / 115
* Underlying Layer:
  * Black Stops: 0 / 105
  * White Stops: 255 (both)

19 Change the Blend If to red, and enter the following:

* Blend If: Red
* This Layer:
  * Black Stops: 0 (both)
  * Red Stops: 170 / 255
* Underlying Layer:
  * Black Stops: 0 (both)
  * Red Stops: 255 (both)

Click OK.

TIP

You may also use a faint rectangular shape beneath the links to emphasize help them stand out a bit from the background.

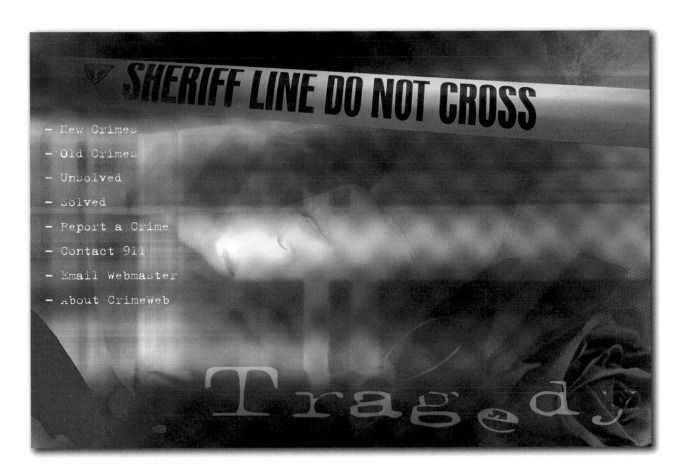

A short recap

Where blending images is concerned, Apply Image has been, and remains, one of my favorite features. Granted, you don't have the control that you would if each photo were in its own layer, but the effects you can create using Apply Image can create some fairly stunning blends.

Experiment with the blending settings when practicing on your own, and use a variety of images. Just remember that all of the images have to be open in Photoshop *and have the exact same pixel dimensions,* or the feature does not work.

Game Over

Remember Pong? Space Invaders? PacMan? If you can, then you can appreciate how far video games have come over the past three decades. (Has it been three decades already?) My dad was quick to shut down our Pong tournaments once he began seeing white lines burned into the television screen.

The video games created these days are stunning in both scope and graphics. This project uses blending similar to that of the previous project, but applies it toward a computer game splash screen.

To follow this tutorial completely, you should first go to the Website http://simplythebest.net/fonts/ and download the Unreal Tournament font. Install this font on your computer, then open Photoshop, and proceed with this section.

THE PLAN

- Merge images to create a background
- Add metallic type
- Insert additional firepower images
- Add the game's logo

(1) Open the images rusty.jpg, manhole.jpg, and manhole_01.jpg.

(2) Select the image rusty.jpg and choose Image⇨Apply Image. Enter the following settings:

- **Source:** manhole_01.jpg
- **Layer:** Background
- **Channel:** RGB

- ✳ **Invert:** unchecked
- ✳ **Blending:** Hard Light
- ✳ **Opacity:** 100%
- ✳ **Preserve Transparency:** unchecked
- ✳ **Mask:** unchecked
- ✳ **Invert:** unchecked

Click OK.

(3) Choose Image⇨Apply Image again, this time with the following settings:

- ✳ **Source:** manhole.jpg
- ✳ **Layer:** Background
- ✳ **Channel:** RGB
- ✳ **Invert:** unchecked
- ✳ **Blending:** Pin Light
- ✳ **Opacity:** 80%
- ✳ **Preserve Transparency:** unchecked
- ✳ **Mask:** unchecked

Click OK. The resulting image is a blend of all three images, with the rusty photo still being predominant.

④ Select the Type tool and open the Character palette. Set up the font as follows:

* **Font:** Unreal Tournament (if installed; substitute with your own selection if not installed)
* **Style:** Regular
* **Font Size:** 80 pt
* **Leading:** Auto
* **Tracking:** 0
* **Vertically Scale:** 90%
* **Horizontally Scale:** 100%
* **Baseline Shift:** 0 pt
* **Color:** R = 99, G = 98, B = 98
* Normal
* **Anti-aliasing method:** Smooth

Type the name of your game at the top of the screen. For this example, I'm naming the game *Unearthly*.

⑤ Open the Layer Styles for the type layer, and select the Bevel and Emboss settings. Enter the following:

* **Style:** Pillow Emboss
* **Technique:** Chisel Hard
* **Depth:** 400%
* **Direction:** Up
* **Size:** 27 px
* **Soften:** 0 px
* **Angle:** 120 degrees
* **Use Global Light:** unchecked
* **Altitude:** 25 degrees
* **Gloss Contour:** Linear (default)
* **Anti-aliased:** checked
* **Highlight Mode:** Screen
  * **Color:** White
  * **Opacity:** 100%
* **Shadow Mode:** Multiply
  * **Color:** Black
  * **Opacity:** 85%

⑥ Open the Blending options and adjust the Blend If sliders as follows:

* **Blend If:** Gray
* **This Layer:** Default Settings
* **Underlying Layer:**
  * **Black Stops:** 0 / 172
  * **Red White Stops:** 255 (Both)

Change Blend If to the Red channel and enter the following:

* **Blend If:** Red
* **This Layer:** Default Settings
* **Underlying Layer:**
  * **Black Stops:** 0 / 45
  * **Red Stops:** 93 / 255

⑦ Save the style if you would like to apply it to something later, and click OK. These settings allowed you to raise the type from the surface, and also allowed for some of the background to be seen through it.

⑧ Change the foreground color to R = 133, G = 9, and B = 6. Change the background color to R = 235, G = 197, B = 82. You will also need these colors for a gradient shortly.

⑨ Duplicate the type layer. This step will fill the raised text with reflective, stained metal. Open the Layer Styles for the type layer, and select the Bevel and Emboss settings. Open the Layer Style Bevel and Emboss settings for the new type layer and adjust the settings as follows:

* **Style:** Inner Bevel
* **Technique:** Smooth
* **Depth:** 1000%
* **Direction:** Down
* **Size:** 9 px
* **Soften:** 0 px
* **Angle:** 120 degrees
* **Use Global Light:** unchecked
* **Altitude:** 25 degrees

* **Gloss Contour:** MetalContour (found in the Chapter 5 Additional Presets folder on the CD)
* **Anti-aliased:** checked
* **Highlight Mode:** Screen
    * **Color:** White
    * **Opacity:** 100%
* **Shadow Mode:** Multiply
    * **Color:** Black
    * **Opacity:** 84%

(10) Go to the Gradient Overlay settings and enter the following:

* **Blend Mode:** Soft Light
* **Opacity:** 100%
* **Gradient:** Foreground to Background – Gradual (default)
* **Reverse:** unchecked
* **Style:** Linear
* **Align with Layer:** checked
* **Angle:** 90 degrees
* **Scale:** 100%

A few chapters ago, when creating the public awareness ad about fire, you saved a pattern that was composed of the photo that you used in the poster. You can also overlay this pattern on the text in this technique to add stains to the metal. If you have that pattern loaded, go to the Pattern Overlay settings and enter the following:

* **Blend Mode:** Normal
* **Opacity:** 100%
* **Pattern:** Fire image pattern
* **Scale:** 35%
* **Link with Layer:** checked

Save the Layer Style and click OK.

(11) Open the image pistols.jpg. Copy the entire image and paste it into the splash screen document on a new layer. Position the layer so that the pistols are beneath the text. If you need to resize the layer, do so with the Transform tools so that the guns cover the majority of the image, but do not overlay the text.

12 To blend the guns into the background, Blend If is again the tool of choice. Open the Layer Styles for the pistols layer and select the Blending options. In the Blend If area, move the sliders as follows:

* **Blend If:** Gray
* **This Layer:**
  * Black Stops: 0
  * White Stops: 30 / 86
* **Underlying Layer:**
  * Black Stops: 0
  * White Stops: 113 / 255

Click OK.

13 Select the Type tool and open the Character palette. Enter the following font settings:

* **Font:** Unreal Tournament
* **Style:** Regular
* **Font Size:** 36 pt
* **Auto**
* **Vertical Scale:** 100%
* **Horizontal Scale:** 100%
* **Color:** R = 98, G = 98, and B = 98
* **Normal**
* **Anti-aliasing method:** Smooth

14 Create a catch phrase for the game. In this example, I'm using, "Dying is just the beginning." Position the text at the bottom of the image, and open the Layer Styles for the type layer. Open the Bevel and Emboss settings and enter the following:

* **Style:** Pillow Emboss
* **Technique:** Chisel Hard

* **Depth:** 400%
* **Direction:** Down
* **Size:** 30 px
* **Soften:** 0 px
* **Angle:** 120 degrees
* **Use Global Light:** unchecked
* **Altitude:** 25 degrees
* **Gloss Contour:** Linear (default)
* **Anti-aliased:** checked
* **Highlight Mode:** Screen
  * Color: White
  * Opacity: 60%
* **Shadow Mode:** Multiply
  * Color: Black
  * Opacity: 85%

15 Save the layer style. Duplicate the new type layer and open the Layer Styles again. Open the Bevel and Emboss settings and change them as follows:

* **Style:** Inner Bevel
* **Technique:** Smooth
* **Depth:** 100%
* **Direction:** Up
* **Size:** 21 px
* **Soften:** 0 px
* **Angle:** 120 degrees
* **Use Global Light:** checked
* **Altitude:** 70 degrees
* **Gloss Contour:** Linear (default)
* **Anti-aliased:** checked
* **Highlight Mode:** Screen
  * Color: White
  * Opacity: 90%
* **Shadow Mode:** Multiply
  * Color: R = 127, G = 6, and B = 6
  * Opacity: 75%

16 To aid the transparency of the type, open the Inner Shadow settings:

* **Blend Mode:** Multiply
* **Opacity:** 60%
* **Angle:** 120 degrees
* **Use Global Light:** unchecked
* **Distance:** 9 px

- **Choke:** 0%
- **Size:** 8 px
- **Contour:** Default
- **Anti-aliased:** unchecked
- **Noise:** 0%

Save the layer style and click OK.

(17) A final embellishment could be a logo of some sort burned into or painted on the background. Select the Custom Shape tool. In the Options bar, load the shape set Nature, and select the shape called Sun 1 from the loaded shapes. Click the Fill Pixels button on the left side of the Options bar, third from the left.

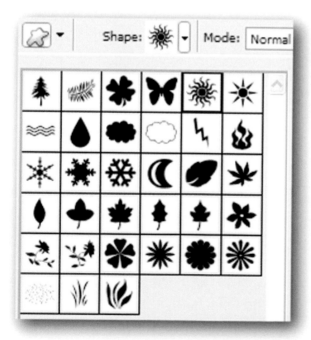

(18) Create a new layer and draw the shape in the new layer. Open the Layer Styles for the shape layer and select Color Overlay. Enter the following settings:

- **Blend Mode:** Multiply
- **Color:** R = 255, G = 0, and B = 0
- **Opacity:** 100%

(19) Next, choose the Stroke settings and enter the following:

- **Size:** 25 px
- **Position:** Outside
- **Blend Mode:** Normal
- **Opacity:** 100%
- **Fill Type:** Gradient – Black to White. Set the Black color stop at the 40 position, and the White to 60.
- **Reverse:** unchecked
- **Style:** L Shape Burst
- **Align with Layer:** checked
- **Angle:** 90 degrees
- **Scale:** 100%

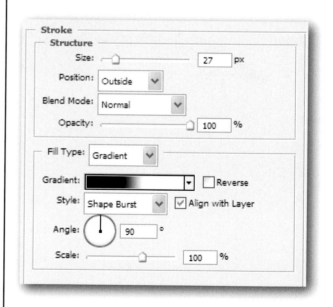

Click OK.

20 To blend the logo into the background, create a new layer just beneath it. Select the logo layer again and choose Layer⇨Merge Down. Change the opacity of the layer to Overlay and reduce the opacity to 50%.

A short recap

By now, I imagine that a few of you have thought, "Hey, Al, haven't we done variations on these techniques in other parts of the book already?" To which I answer, "Of course." What I hope that you are taking away from techniques like this are ideas in which the techniques that you have learned may be applied in other ways or in combination with each other. This is an area where I believe that other type effects books have fallen short. The examples that I give here are simply my concoctions. I encourage you, as always, to experiment on your own with the techniques that you learn here, with other image types or collage combinations.

It's All in the Game

What kind of title is that? What can I say — I'm a fan of music that was popular before I was born. As for what it has to do with this technique, you will be creating a CD cover that is specific to the game that you worked on in the previous tutorial. This project goes still further than the CD cover that you created for the rock group created earlier in this book, as you will create an actual jewel case for storing the CD.

To follow this tutorial completely, you should first go to the Website `http://simplythebest.net/fonts/` and download the Unreal Tournament font. Install this font on your computer, then open Photoshop, and proceed with this section. If you already did this, then you may skip this step, open Photoshop, and begin.

THE PLAN

- Create an image to attract violent gamers to your product
- Add text and a logo to the image
- Create a jewel case for the game, complete with reflections
- Add metallic type
- Insert additional firepower images
- Add the game's logo

1 Open the image redhead.jpg.

2 You will first add the shaped emblem that you used in the previous tutorial for continuity and product-recognition purposes. Create a new layer and select the Custom Shape tool. Open the shapes, and load the Nature set that shipped with Photoshop. Select the shape Sun 1 and draw it over the right eye of the man. The size of the shape should be large enough so that the man's eye, if it were visible, could be seen in its entirety if the center circle of the shape were transparent, as it is about to be.

3 In the previous project, you should have saved the style that you applied to the shape in the last step. Open the Layer Styles and apply this style to the shape layer.

X-REF

See the section "Game Over" to create this layer style.

4 Create a mask for the shape layer. With a hard-edged round brush set to 300 pixels in size, paint with black over the center circle in the shape, revealing the man's eye beneath.

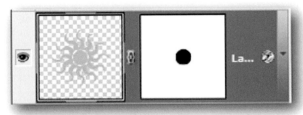

5 Create a new layer just above the shape layer. Press the D key to set black as the foreground color, and select the Pencil tool. Change the brush size to 3 pixels. Click at the top-center of the circle. Hold down the Shift key and draw a straight line down through the center of the transparent area. Create a crosshair by repeating the process from left to right through the center of the circle. Name the layer **crosshairs**.

6 Create a new layer. Set the foreground color to R = 193, G = 241, and B = 16.

7 Change the Blend mode of the new layer to Color. Select the Paintbrush tool and choose a round, feathered brush from the default brush set. Set the size to about 300 pixels or so and paint over the crosshair area, changing the 'lens' to a greenish yellow but allowing the eye to be seen beneath. Rename the new layer 'lens'.

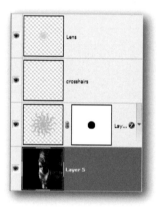

8 Select the Type tool and open the Character palette. Enter the following font settings:

* **Font:** Unreal Tournament
* **Style:** Regular
* **Font Size:** 100 pt
* **Leading:** 60 pt
* **Vertical Scale:** 90%
* **Horizontal Scale:** 100%
* **Color:** R = 99, G = 98, and B = 98
* **Normal**
* **Anti-aliasing method:** Smooth

9 Type **Unearthly** across the face of the image. Open the Type Warp dialog box from the Options bar and enter the following settings.

* **Style:** Arc
* **Horizontal**
* **Bend:** -30%
* **Horizontal Distortion:** 0%
* **Vertical Distortion:** 0%

10 Click OK. Apply the same layer style to the text as you did the shape.

Choose Edit⇨Transform⇨Rotate and rotate the text slightly, as shown in the example below. Once you have an angle that you are happy with, accept the transformation.

⑪ Select the Rounded Rectangle shape tool. Set the radius of the shape's corners to 100 pixels in the Options bar. Create a new layer and draw a rectangular shape at the top of the image in which to place the catch-phrase. The shape doesn't need to be very high, but it should run almost the width of the image. Apply the layer style that you applied to the text, to the new shape layer.

⑫ Select the Type tool and open the Character palette. Enter the following font settings:

* **Font:** Unreal Tournament
* **Style:** Regular
* **Font Size:** 36 pt
* **Leading:** 60 pt
* **Vertical Scale:** 90%
* **Horizontal Scale:** 100%
* **Color:** White
* **Normal**
* **Anti-aliasing method:** Smooth

⑬ Type the slogan **Death is only the beginning** over the shaped box.

⑭ Click in the lower-right corner of the image with the Type tool and open the Character palette again. Enter the following settings:

* **Font:** Typewriter (any typewriter-style font will do)
* **Style:** Regular
* **Font Size:** 36 pt
* **Leading:** 60 pt
* **Tracking:** 0
* **Vertically Scale:** 90%
* **Horizontally Scale:** 100%
* **Baseline Shift:** 0 pt
* **Color:** White
* **Normal**
* **Anti-aliasing method:** Smooth

⑮ Type a rating for the game. In this example, I'm rating the game for age 17 and older.

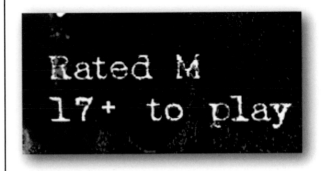

⑯ Let's add some ballistics. Open the image bullets01.jpg.

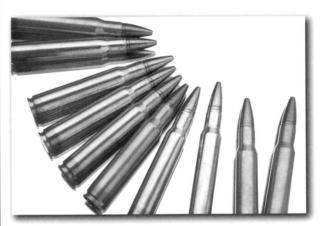

⑰ Press Command/Ctrl+A to select the entire image, and then press Command/Ctrl+C to copy it. Paste it into a new layer in the game cover image. Choose Select➪Color Range, and select the white area, and then press Delete.

⑱ Create a mask for the bullets layer. Select a rough, speckled brush from the default brush set and set the size to 1000 pixels. Select the mask and set black as the foreground color. Paint around the shell casings to fade them a bit. Change the Blend mode of the bullets layer to Difference, and then reduce the opacity to 80-85%. With the Move tool, position the shells so that they point toward the center of the image. Ensure that the bullets layer is beneath the rating layer. If it is over the shape layer, that is okay.

(19) The cover is basically done at this point — at least, the graphic is. Now it is time to move on to the jewel case.

Duplicate the image. Merge all layers together (Layer⇨Flatten Image), and then double-click the Background layer. Rename it **CD_Cover**.

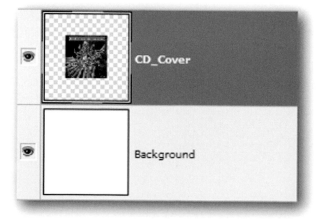

(20) Create a new layer and move it beneath the CD_Cover layer. Choose Image⇨Canvas Size and increase both the height and width to 200%. Fill the Background layer with white.

(21) Select the CD_Cover layer and choose Edit⇨Transform⇨Perspective. Move the top-right corner toward the center slightly to alter the perspective view of the image. Use the image here as a guide. When you are done, accept the transformation.

(22) Create a new layer. Select the Polygonal Lasso tool and ensure that the Feather is set to 0. Make a selection along the left side of the box in the shape of a plastic edge with the perspective to match the CD case. Include extensions at the top and bottom of the CD cover edges that follow the cover a short distance, as shown in the example provided.

(26) Create another layer for reflections. Using the Polygonal Lasso tool, make a selection similar to that in the example provided here.

Fill the selection with white. Reduce the opacity of the layer to 15–20%. You may also fill the selection with a white-to-transparent gradient, going from top to bottom or from upper left to lower right.

(27) Create a new layer and select the Paintbrush tool. Using the brush that you used to mask the bullets, set the brush size to 300-400 pixels. Hold down the Shift key and paint three or four angled strips of white across the face of the CD, going from upper right to lower left. Don't go overboard — ensure that the angle looks natural on the face of the CD.

(23) Fill the selection with black. Name the new layer **Case Edge**.

(24) Create another layer and, with the Polygonal Lasso tool once again, create a new selection that is the same shape as the CD cover, but slightly larger. Leave the edge of the plastic area unselected, but include the tabs at the top and bottom in the selection.

(25) Fill the selection with white, and then change the Blend mode to Screen and the opacity to 25%. Rename the layer **Clear Cover**.

28 With the Streak layer selected, choose Filter⇨Blur⇨Gaussian Blur. Enter a radius of 40 pixels and click OK.

29 Select the Case Edge layer and open the Layer Styles. Select Gradient Overlay. Create a gradient using alternating blacks and the color R = 77, G = 77, B = 77. Use the image here as a guide to creating the gradient.

30 Position the gradient so that the corner has a distinct light and dark edge. Click OK.

31 Select the Clear Cover layer and open the Layer Styles. Select Color Overlay and set the overlay color to R = 100, G = 78, B = 78.

32 Click OK. Change the Blend mode of the layer to Soft Light, and the opacity of the layer to 50%. This reduces the transparency of the plastic, bringing it into the real world.

A short recap

With the game now in the case, we can venture into the realm of other media. There you have it! If you enjoy type effects and would like to add more to your Photoshop arsenal, then please visit me at ActionFx.com. As of this writing, there are over 70,000 Photoshop presets available for you to download, with more being added all the time. I create and host Photoshop training videos as well. I look forward to seeing you there!

appendix

online resources

We all start our path to knowledge somewhere, and mine began online many years ago with tutorials and information that were authored by some distinctive talents. Today, there are many great resources available as you continue your quest to become the next hot digital artist. Here are a few Websites that I think are particualrly helpful — I encourage you to visit them.

Action Fx Photoshop Resources

www.actionfx.com

This is the Website that I call home. I created Action Fx in 1998 to showcase my favorite Photoshop feature: actions. Action FX has come a long way since those humble beginnings, and now boasts over 50,000 custom presets that I have created for Photoshop and Photoshop Elements. It offers actions, custom shapes, brushes, layer styles, and more, as well as written and video tutorials to get you started.

Photoshop Café

www.photoshopcafe.com

My good friend Colin Smith, a fantastic author and trainer in his own right, created the Photoshop Café a number of years ago, and it is going stronger than ever today. Colin offers some of the most advanced Photoshop tutorials that are available online. Stop by the forum and say hello, as I am usually lurking there somewhere.

Photoshop User: The Official Website of NAPP (National Association of Photoshop Professionals)

www.photoshopuser.com

This is the site of the biggest and best organization in the world that is devoted to you, the Photoshop user. This is where my career began thanks to Scott Kelby, the face of NAPP and renowned author and Editor-in-Chief for Photoshop User Magazine. If you are serious about learning all aspects of Photoshop (including photography, digital art, and Web design), then seriously consider joining NAPP and give your digital career a jumpstart.

Planet Photoshop

www.planetphotoshop.com

Planet Photoshop is NAPP's free online resource for people new to Photoshop, and is a great starting point. I've written for "Planet" for years, and you will find a veritable potpourri of tutorials to get you going. There are also opportunities for training, a community forum, and many for interesting and helpful features.

Adobe's Tutorial Section

http://studio.adobe.com/

The Adobe Exchange is the place to go to download Photoshop presets created by other users. You may also share your own presets with the masses, and all for free. Actions, Layer Styles, Custom Shapes, Brushes, and more are available, as well as presets for other Adobe products. A free registration is required, but access is definitely worth much more than the price of admission.

Phong

www.phong.com

What can I say? This site is simply incredible. Phong has been around for a while, and age has only made this remarkable site better. The visuals of the page itself are stunning, and the tutorials are top-notch. Beginners may want to test their chops elsewhere first, as the tutorials offered are a bit advanced for new users. Once you have the nuts-and-bolts down, Phong is the place to be.

Photoshop Tutorials 100

www.photoshoptutorials100.com

A bare-bones, no-nonsense beginners' tutorial website, Photoshop Tutorials 100 is a great place to learn the basics. Many of the tutorials are for older versions of Photoshop, but they are easy to read and follow, and new users can see results in their work right away.

Graphics.com

www.graphics.com

This website is operated by the folks who brought you Photos.com and Clipart.com. I've contributed to this site in the past, and they offer excellent tutorials and articles from a variety of authors. You can also download free plug-ins for your software.

PanosFX

www.panosfx.com

Though limited in content at this writing, PanosFx offers free tutorials and Photoshop downloads that you may find beneficial. There is even something for Adobe Photoshop Elements users, so stop by and give them a try.

Photoshop 101

www.photoshop101.com

Tutorials, tutorials, and still more tutorials! Photoshop 101 is a resource that not only allows the reader access to some great free training, but tutorial writers also can submit their own for the masses. The site also offers a rating system where visitors can vote for the best-of-the-best.

Tutorial Kit

www.tutorialkit.com

Still more free tutorials! A site similar to Photoshop 101, Tutorial Kit allows you to peruse their content for free and submit your own gems of knowledge for mass consumption. Most tutorials focus on web graphics, but are excellent at getting the reader to think about Photoshop processes in new and interesting ways.

There you have it! If you enjoy type effects and would like to add more to your Photoshop arsenal, then please visit me at ActionFx.com. As of this writing, there are over 70,000 Photoshop presets available for you to download, with more being added all the time. I create and host Photoshop training videos as well. I look forward to seeing you there!

index

Numbers

3D text, creating, 137–138

A

A Balanced Breakfast tutorial
    Character palette, 10
    duplicating the background layer in the, 11–12
    Flag tool, 11
    Horizontal Type tool, 10
    merging the logo with the box in the, 13
    resetting the foreground/background colors in the, 10, 12
    resizing the backdrop in the, 12
    saving the, 12
    Warp tools, 11
A Spot o' Tea tutorial
    Burn tool, 28
    Character palette, 27
    Custom Shape tool, 25
    entering type in the, 26–27
    Horizontal Type tool, 27
    opacity, 26, 28
    placing the logo on a curved, transparent surface in the, 28
    resizing the logo in the, 28
    Warp tool, 27–28
Action Fx Photoshop Resources, website, 279
Actions palette, No News Is Bad News tutorial, 97
Add Noise dialog box, 91
Add Noise filter, using the, 91, 188
Adobe's Tutorial Section, website, 279
advertisement, creating an, 32–39
Age Got It tutorial
    aging painted text in the, 256–257
    Bevel and Emboss layer style, 256
    Character palette, 255
    creating three-layered text in the, 255
    Drop Shadow, 257
    Move tool, 257
    opacity, 256
    Type Mask tool, 255
Alien League font, downloading the, 186
Alien Skin's Eye Candy, preset filter package, 119
Alphabet Soup tutorial
    adding a drop shadow in the, 18
    Burn tool, 23
    changing character settings in the, 17–18
    Character palette, 17, 20
    Cleanup tool, 19
    creating a border around the logo in the, 18
    Dodge tool, 23

    Edge Touchup tool, 19
    Horizontal Type tool, 17, 20
    inserting an image in the, 18–19
    Magic Marker tool, 18
    opacity, 24
    Rectangular Marquee tool, 16, 18, 21
    resizing in the, 21
    Type tool, 20
anger.jpg, Signs of the Times tutorial, 120
Apply Image feature, using the, 259–260, 264
ASCII characters
    adding the copyright symbol, 17–18
    adding the trademark symbol, 34
    searching for, 18
ashtray.jpg, Those Things Will Kill Ya tutorial, 244
Ask.com, website, 4
At the Beach tutorial
    Bevel and Emboss layer style, 157–158
    Character palette, 156
    entering text in the, 156
    manipulating text in the, 156–158
    Type tool, 156

B

Back in a Minute tutorial
    Character palette, 214
    entering text in the, 214–215
    manipulating text in the, 215–216
    Move tool, 215
    opacity, 216
    Paintbrush tool, 216
    Type tool, 214
backdrop
    lighting in the Rockin' Out tutorial, 75
    resizing in the A Balanced Breakfast tutorial, 12
background layer
    A Balanced Breakfast tutorial, 11–12
    I Need Coffee...STAT! tutorial, 5
band logo, creating a, 129–132
Bareback.jpg, Under Your Skin tutorial, 179
bark.jpg, Carved in the Tree tutorial, 175
bath.jpg, In a Lather tutorial, 47–48
beach-01.jpg, At the Beach tutorial, 156
Bevel and Emboss layer style. *See specific tutorials*
Bif! Pow! tutorial
    adding a UPC code in the, 70
    Bevel and Emboss layer style, 68
    Character palette, 66
    creating a logo in the, 66–71
    Diffuse filter, 67

continued

C

index

index

continued

index